DO (NOT) FEED THE BEARS

DO (NOT)

Feed the Bears

The Fitful History of Wildlife and Tourists in Yellowstone

Alice Wondrak Biel

UNIVERSITY PRESS OF KANSAS

© 2006 by the University Press of Kansas
All rights reserved
Published by the University Press of Kansas (Lawrence, Kansas
66045), which was organized
by the Kansas Board of Regents and is operated and funded by
Emporia State University,
Fort Hays State University, Kansas State University, Pittsburg State
University,
the University of Kansas, and Wichita State University

Library of Congress Cataloging-in-Publication Data
Wondrak Biel, Alice.
  Do (not) feed the bears : the fitful history of wildlife and tourists
in Yellowstone / Alice Wondrak Biel.
     p.   cm.
  Includes bibliographical references (p.   ) and index.
  ISBN 0-7006-1432-x (cloth : alk. paper)
  1. Bears—Feeding and feeds—Yellowstone National Park—
History. 2. Bears—Effect of human beings on—Yellowstone
National Park—History. 3. Captive wild animals—Feeding and
feeds—Yellowstone National Park—History. I. Title.
  QL737.C27W65 2006
  639.909794'47—dc22   2005026972

British Library Cataloguing-in-Publication Data is available.

Printed in the United States of America

10 9 8 7 6 5 4 3 2

The paper used in this publication meets the minimum
requirements of the American
National Standard for Permanence of Paper for Printed Library
Materials Z39.48-1984.

For my mother and my father,

who brought me to the park and

never let me leave,

and for Mark.

CONTENTS

A photograph section appears following page 76.

ACKNOWLEDGMENTS

As is true of all authors, I am deeply indebted to many people without whom this work would not have been possible. Paul Schullery has done more than anyone else to inspire me, share his thoughts and time, provide me with information, and keep me on the right track. He also read this manuscript and offered his comments—twice. Kerry Gunther shared his knowledge and experience and, along with Mark Biel, let me paw through files in his office for many hours. Thanks also to Lee Whittlesey, who read parts of this manuscript, and to Harold Housley, Kathryn Kirby, Tara Cross, Barb Zafft, and Alissa Cherry for hauling box after box out of the Yellowstone National Park Archives (and places beyond) for me. Thanks also to Steve Tustanowski-Marsh and Colleen Curry for helping me acquire the photos to illustrate this book. Kerrie McCartney provided friendship and advice along the way. And anyone who loves Yellowstone history owes much to the late Aubrey L. Haines, without whose work none of us would know anything at all.

At the University of Colorado, my advisers, Tim Oakes and Don Mitchell, gave me ceaseless support and helped shape the thinking and theory that produced this book. Bill Travis, Erika Doss, and James Huff offered diverse and valuable perspectives, teaching, and help.

I am grateful for the financial support provided by the indescribably generous Canon National Parks Science Scholars Program, without which this book would never have been more than an interesting thought I had one day. The University of Colorado's Dean's Small Grant program also supported this project.

I have also been the lucky recipient of Clark Whitehorn's professional support and wise advice; he, along with Molly Holz, made parts of this manuscript far better. Thanks also go to Glenda Bradshaw. James Pritchard kindly read the manuscript; provided copious, careful comments; and sent me moral support and organic coffee—all of which were much appreciated. John Freemuth also read the manuscript and provided valuable suggestions.

Jim and Edna Caslick, Faye Black, Frank Smith, Norman Miller, Frank Markley, and many others shared their remembrances with me, and 150 Yellowstone visitors answered survey questions for me as they waited for Old Faithful to erupt. This manuscript is richer for their thoughts and ideas. Helen Heaton graciously allowed me to reproduce a set of song lyrics she wrote in 1968. Paul Shea of the Yellowstone Historic Center encouraged me to see the project through, Giles Toll provided me with information about his uncle Roger, and Richard West Sellars offered advice as well. Many thanks to Nancy Scott Jackson for her guidance, enthusiasm, and skill.

I could not have wished for more loving, supportive, and extraordinary parents; this book is dedicated to them, and to my husband, Mark, who makes my dreams come true.

I have been an employee of the National Park Service for the past five years, but it must be made clear that in this book I do not represent the National Park Service either formally or informally; nor does the National Park Service endorse this book in any way. The research and writing of this book took place entirely on my own time, on my own computer, to fulfill the requirements of a Ph.D. program begun before I was in the employ of the federal government. The content of this book was not derived in any way from my work with the National Park Service, and my research involved no information not available to any other writer. My sources are shown in the notes.

DO (NOT) FEED THE BEARS

In the summer of 1920, a small black bear sat down in front of a big yellow touring car, and things in Yellowstone changed forever. The bear leaned back on his haunches, his front legs folded up, looking a lot like a begging dog. Women cooed, men chuckled, and a few tossed the bear bits of food they had brought with them on the trip to West Thumb that day.

"Jesse James," as the bear aptly came to be known for his ability to "hold up" vehicles in this manner, was the celebrated prototype for Yellowstone's famous roadside begging bears, which were fed by park visitors both before 1920 and for the better part of the next five decades. As other bears learned to imitate his behavior and gain the same rewards, feeding the bears of Yellowstone became the capstone tourist experience in a park whose appeal has always been based on nature's performances. Whereas the attractions of other national parks are typically described in passive terms—"The scenery of Yosemite is spectacular"; "The Grand Canyon was sublime"—Yellowstone has always been active. Geysers spout, hot springs bubble, fumaroles spew foul air. The earth, simply, vibrates with movement and change.

Though Yellowstone's wildlife had long been an important component of the active landscape and bear feeding was not new in the park, it was the particular combination of people, nature, and modernity that set humans and bears off on an odyssey that has yet to end. In Yellowstone (and elsewhere), roadside feeding introduced a new spirit of interaction, proximity, and structure to national park visitation that transformed passive spectators into active participants and shapers of bears' lives and behavior. On some level, the tourists were changed by the experience as well. The easy familiarity that developed between people and the park's most famous wild animals was addictive to visitors, and people fed the bears for many, many years. They fed them at garbage dumps, through car windows, and at campsites (purposely or not). They threw marshmallows. They offered cookies from the hand, sometimes coming away with a scar or two for their trouble. People fed the bears in spite of the fact that it was against the rules; they did it because it was "fun." Because it got the bears to come close to them. Because it was the thing you did when you made the trip to Yellowstone. And they did it for the stories. Just about everyone who visited the park before about 1971 has a tale about their own close encounter with the bears of Yellowstone. "My father strung hot dogs on the clothesline so bears would come to our campsite at night." "And then that bear, he stuck his whole head into the car and the lady started screaming so loud you'd have thought he was taking her arm off!" "A bear sat on my dad."

Talk to people who have visited in the years since then, and you're far less likely to hear about the time a bear cub tried to climb into the car on top of Mom after she decided he had had enough potato chips and it was time to keep driving. Ask the telephoto- and tripod-toting folks who line the road-sides today if they'd like to send their little daughter out to have her picture taken feeding a bear, and you're more likely to get an incredulous stare than a hearty "You betcha!" There are still some who try to engage in the old-time ways of seeing bears, like the man who was bluff-charged by a sow grizzly a few years ago after he wandered up to pet her cub. Perhaps recalling the pet-ting zoo–like atmosphere of past decades, or laboring under the common misapprehension that wild animals somehow become "tame" when they venture into human landscapes, he explained that he thought the bears by the roadside were "exempt" from the rules requiring visitors to remain one hundred yards away from any park bear.

But those stories are far fewer these days. The Yellowstone bears of today are no longer circus performers, coaxed and conditioned to lean back and wave hello for goodies. Just what they are instead is more open to interpreta-tion than in the past. Wildlife photographers depict them as majestic lords of the wilderness. To environmentalists and biologists, they are indicators of total ecosystem health. For visitors, who have largely embraced the bears' wholesale image change, they remain an exciting, sought-after sight, still ca-pable of generating "bear jams" that can back up traffic for miles.

The central question that drives this book is, how did we get from there to here? What in the world were people thinking for all those years that made them decide it was okay to plop down on a log right next to a bear, feed one from the hand, or pose their children with a few at the roadside? Where did they get those ideas? It was always against the rules for park visitors to feed the bears—why didn't they listen? And what makes today so different—or is it? In addition, one might wonder, how did the National Park Service fit into all of this, and of course, what were the effects on the bears themselves?

The search for answers winds a path through ramshackle zoos, finely ap-pointed garbage dumps, car-clogged roadsides, 1960s television and the Na-tional Park Service (NPS) reaction to it, some very significant changes in the way the NPS conceived of itself, and American thought about the nature of Nature. It also traverses piles of archival evidence left behind by the park's managers, interpreters, and decision-makers. The archive is a source of both historical information and cultural process. At its best it reveals not only the kinds of decisions that were made about bears and people in the park but also something about the thought processes that drove those decisions and, ultimately, the kinds of messages that park managers communicated to Yellowstone's visitors about its bears. Interjected, self-selectively, are snippets that suggest how visitors responded to the messages and meanings generated by what was essentially the development of bear management in Yellowstone. Taken together, what emerges is a series of NPS "narratives" of the bears of Yellowstone; in other words, a collection of discourses—*stories*—that have defined the essence of the Yellowstone bear in changing fashion over time.

Those narratives have been myriad, and the ones discussed here have often either reflected or conflicted with the needs of the park's managers during different periods of management philosophy and policy; the Yellowstone bear has proven highly malleable. As one of Yellowstone's most beloved and enduring symbols, the bear has served as a flash point for controversies related to the park's evolving wildlife policies and ideologies. Always a powerful stimulator of the human imagination, the Yellowstone bear has also been both a catalyst and a bellwether for the relationships between park policies and their public reception, and sometimes for situating the development of those relationships within the broader contexts of American cultural history and change. As the NPS's goals, philosophies, and policies have changed, so has the image and context of the Yellowstone bear.

A seminal example: when Yellowstone's first NPS superintendent, Horace Albright, arrived in the park in 1919, he faced two major tasks: managing the park and establishing precedents regarding what a national park should be and do. Congress had mandated that he manage the park for both preservation and recreational use. Albright, a devotee of what has been called "aesthetic conservation," was determined to maximize both elements.[1] He was also aware that in order for his fledgling agency to have a future, it had to be both clearly understood—differentiated, for instance, from its rival, the U.S. Forest Service—and beloved by the American citizenry. Accordingly, Albright set out to create a park landscape that was full of easily accessible visual appeal and unique experience. With an aim toward achieving that goal, he supervised the establishment of several wildlife viewing areas where visitors could easily see examples of the park's charismatic megafauna.

In addition to a buffalo corral, these areas included a short-lived zoo and the elaborate development of Yellowstone's famed "bear feeding grounds," a series of dumps located close to the park's major hotels, where visitors had been gathering to watch grizzlies feed since the nineteenth century. Under Albright's direction, NPS rangers began to formalize and interpret the spectacle. The dumps were equipped with seating, and the entire happening became a bona fide show, complete with ursine actors who entered and exited as if from the wings each night. The shows were wildly popular with visitors and were also conducted at several other national parks, with the blessing of the park service. Bears were described and seen as wild, yet tame. Above all, they were entertaining.

After the automobile arrived in the park, the NPS tacitly encouraged visitors to feed bears themselves along the roadsides; the cover of the park's 1922 "Rules and Regulations" pamphlet featured a photograph of this activity. Visitors who read the pamphlet might have been surprised to learn that it was actually against the rules for them to feed bears.[2] Bear narratives perpetuated by the NPS—baffling or not—have almost always been rooted in the bear-visitor relationship, and often bears existed in the narratives to teach a lesson—about fun in the national parks, environmental stewardship, wilderness, science, or proper visitor behavior. In the old days, contradiction was a constant, often leaving visitors unsure of what kind of behavior was expected of them, and what to think of the park's bears. In those earliest days, when the park managers' primary goal was making people happy, Yellowstone's bears were depicted as performers and as surrogate pets for vacationing visitors, the rules be damned. A narrative of friendship between people and bears was established and perpetuated.

Of course, there was more to this story than just the *story*. That convenient early narrative of friendship encouraged patterns of behavior with palpable consequences. A steady stream of injury reports and property damage claims led managers in later years to bemoan the park's "bear problem" as one of their most vexing dilemmas. In response, at least 1,119 bears were removed from the Yellowstone ecosystem, either by live-shipping to zoos or, more frequently, by lethal action, from 1931 to 2004. Ninety-eight percent of those "management removals" occurred prior to the mid-1970s, when roadside feeding was effectively ended.[3]

Once established, curious habits proved hard to break. Visitors continued to illegally feed Yellowstone's bears despite major changes in NPS thought and policy. Beginning in earnest in the 1940s, and with its efforts growing stronger between the 1960s and today, the NPS has worked to transform the image of the Yellowstone bear from circus performer to wild animal and, more recently, core of a unique ecosystem. Success required changes in visitor behavior and, literally, people's ways of seeing bears. Park managers accomplished these changes not only by altering the physical act of seeing bears—through closure of the zoos and feeding grounds and enforcement of laws prohibiting feeding at the park's roadsides—but also by embarking on the much more complex project of altering the way visitors perceived bears and their role in Yellowstone.

As park managers tried to convince visitors to stay away from bears and, later, to understand their needs, the bear as circus performer disappeared. Instead, images of dangerous "horror" bears clawed from pamphlets. Famous funny bears ironically tried to cajole visitors to leave them alone. Wilderness bears sought solitude in the backcountry, and imperiled bears were more vulnerable to manipulation than most. Today, ecosystem bears need scientific understanding, natural foods, and habitat protection. What quickly becomes apparent in a reading of all these different incarnations is that it's not so much the bears that have changed in Yellowstone—it's their image that has been made and remade, in concert with a set of attitudes that encompassed more than changing policies and regulations.

The process of restoring the sense of wariness between people and bears in the park has been a long one, requiring monumental shifts in attitudes, habits, and perceptions that began at home. Before they could change the behavior of the park's visitors, determined managers first had to convince their own staff that a more "natural" Yellowstone bear was a more desirable Yellowstone bear. For decades, many NPS employees, including Horace Albright, were reluctant to believe that Yellowstone's visitors and its bears *should* be separated, let alone that they *could* be. When the park superintendent announced the closure of the last remaining formal bear feeding grounds in 1942, Albright's public opposition made the episode a key turning point in Yellowstone's conservation history and signified a transition in NPS management philosophies at the highest levels.

On a broader scale, many park narratives have showed strong connections to the cultural waves of modern American life. When the first Model T Fords rolled off the assembly line in 1908, they signaled a sea change not only in the lives and habits of most Americans, but also in the lives and habits of Yellowstone's bears and the visitors who encountered them. When, during its early years, the NPS struggled to gain legitimacy and support in Washington, Yellowstone's bears were called upon to do their part. One might not expect that the Great Depression had much effect on the day-to-day lives of bears in Yellowstone National Park—but it did. The Japanese bombing of Pearl Harbor opened the door for tremendous change in what Yellowstone's bears communicated to people about the purpose and meaning of the national parks. And the modern environmental movement and postwar dominance of science as a national narrative of authority resulted in profound effects on both NPS policies and the lives and stories of bears in Yellowstone.

This story is not always pretty. As Paul Schullery pointed out, it is easy to look into the past and see many management decisions as "mistakes," giving those who made them too little credit for having lived and worked within a certain cultural and political context: "They did not do these things because they were stupid . . . they did them because their view of nature, and of their relationship with it, was substantially different from our own. . . . They did not have our values, but that does not mean they were without values."[4] Schullery correctly observed that it would be foolish to believe that all of the mistakes have been made and that we now "know better," or, as he put it, "have arrived at some finished form of the national park"; that our decisions today are based strictly on science (a narrative in its own right) rather than social events and politics.

Yellowstone's bears have been many things to many people over the years. This book is not a nostalgic account of the days when bears lined Yellowstone's roadsides, hanging off the sides of cars and scarfing up garbage at the feeding grounds. Bears and people suffered too horribly during those years for any responsible person to be able to look back on that time with unadulterated fondness. Rather, it is an investigation of the intersection of nature and culture as it is played out in the national park landscape, an exploration of the cultural value of a natural resource. What is gained in the end is a more complete picture of how the NPS has communicated its philosophies and policies to its constituencies through its imagery and treatment of the Yellowstone bear, as well as how others have challenged those official representations. It is also a chronicle of the agency's internal struggles to change itself, and of what has succeeded and what has not as the park has worked to establish, change, and redefine the relationship between visitors and bears in Yellowstone. This is the story of the story of the Yellowstone bear.

Zoos, Feeding Grounds, and Roadsides

The Wild Yet Tame Bear

During Yellowstone National Park's formative years, no model existed for how wildlife should be treated in a national park. Today, we take for granted that national parks are places where wildlife "roams free"; captive animals are the purview of zoos. However, Yellowstone's early managers tended to treat wild animals much as they were treated elsewhere—the exception, of course, was that hunting was not permitted after 1883. Predators, except those that people liked, such as bears, were viewed as vermin and killed. Other animals were sometimes held captive for purposes of entertainment, profit, or education. In 1874, Yellowstone residents Harry Horr, Jack Baronett, and Frank Grounds made plans to exhibit live elk, black-tailed deer, antelope, mountain sheep, and other animals as part of an 1876 celebration of the U.S. centennial. Yellowstone's first civilian superintendent, Philetus Norris, once proposed that a zoological garden be developed in conjunction with steamboat service on Yellowstone Lake. In 1895, Acting Superintendent George Anderson kept more than one bear chained to the side of his house, where his maid could sometimes be seen feeding them. In 1903, Theodore Roosevelt noted that concessions employees occasionally kept bears as pets.[1]

Superintendent Norris's idea eventually came to fruition, but probably not in a manner of which he would have approved. Yellowstone's first permanent zoo was located on Yellowstone Lake's tiny Dot Island. It was operated by E. C. Waters, owner of the Yellowstone Lake Boat Company. Waters was a businessman from Fond du Lac, Wisconsin, who began his Yellowstone career as a general manager with the Yellowstone Park Association (the park's hotel concessioner) in the 1880s. Later he ran a store on the shores of Yellowstone Lake and conducted boat tours for visitors. From the start his excursions generated a steady stream of complaints. Not only were his vessels barely seaworthy, but Waters also tended toward nefarious business practices. Notable but far from exceptional was the case of visitor Mrs. P. K. Sturgis, who in 1907 paid Waters the lofty sum of $25 for a birding excursion to one of the lake's islands. Though Waters had claimed the island was a mere six miles from the dock, the Sturgis party steamed for two and a half hours without seeming to near their destination. When Mrs. Sturgis finally concluded that Waters actually had no idea where they were going and requested that the boat be turned around, she and her companion were deposited in a rowboat with one of Waters's employees, who rowed them fifteen miles back to shore. Waters declined to refund his fee.[2]

This and countless other escapades, as well as a notoriously unpredictable personality, earned Waters a reputation for being an unscrupulous malcontent who was equally corrupt in his dealings with the public, his fellow concessioners, and the park, which was administered by the U.S. Army from 1886 to 1918. According to Waters, this ill repute was ill deserved; it was the result of a general conspiracy against him. In 1904, photographer and concessioner F. J. Haynes wrote that Waters had a "diseased imagination" that produced a "hallucination that everyone in the Park is trying to rob him." Years of visitor complaints and intractability in the face of park regulations led Lieutenant General S. B. M. Young, Yellowstone's superintendent from 1907 to 1908, to describe Waters as "a disgrace to the Park and . . . a dangerous bad man" after their acquaintance had ended.[3]

Although most complaints against Waters focused on his boat concession, several others centered on his treatment of the animals in his Dot Island menagerie. In 1894, Captain Anderson had granted Waters permission to open the zoo as an incentive to convince tourists to patronize his boat tours. The zoo animals, which included bison, elk, and bighorn sheep, were purchased outside the park and wintered on a tract of land near the Lake Hotel. In a bit of traditional imperialist oddity, Waters also obtained permission, in 1899, to exhibit an assemblage of Crow Indians in his zoo, with the provision that they would be in the park only seasonally and of their own volition. There is no evidence, however, that Waters took advantage of this opportunity.[4]

By 1907, tourists had begun to express their displeasure regarding the dismal state of the zoo and its emaciated animals to Superintendent Young. In the spring of that year, the menagerie was housed in corrals located about 150 yards from the Lake Hotel until late June, when they were moved out to the island for the summer. In early June, Young received complaints from visitors and fellow concessioners that Waters's animals were scraggly and their pens deep with mud and manure, leaving the creatures nowhere to lie save in their own excrement and providing shelter from neither sun nor inclement weather.[5]

Particularly troublesome to visitor F. W. Vowinckel was the sight of this animal squalor in such close proximity to the grandeur of the Lake Hotel. Upon seeing Waters's reeking, ramshackle corrals, Vowinckel was "surprised and shocked to find conditions in the immediate neighborhood of this splendid hostelry which might be highly offensive to all visitors, and especially to guests occupying the eastern part of the Hotel."[6]

After receiving letters from Vowinckel and others, Superintendent Young dispatched Captain M. O. Bigelow to the scene. Bigelow confirmed the decrepit state of the corrals and also noted that Waters's considerable collection of livestock (in 1906, these had included 1 cart horse, 1 driving team, 1 four-horse team, 2 cows, 21 sheep, 20 chickens, 2 guinea hens, 2 geese, 1 hog, 20 Belgian hares, 30 pigeons, and 1 cat) were faring little better than his game. He concluded, "In our opinion, this collection of tumbledown huts is . . . a public nuisance and should be abated. As to the animals, it seems nothing less than inhuman to confine them in surroundings so utterly filthy and unwholesome." In response, Young obtained permission from the office of the Secretary of the Interior to release the wildlife if the living conditions were not improved. Waters, in typically irascible fashion, responded with a curt note stating that his "animals would have been removed to [Dot] island long ago and yards cleaned had not government detained our work."[7]

By late June, Waters had finally removed his animals to the less publicly visible confines of Dot Island, accessible to visitors via a trip on his steamer *Zillah*. At his follow-up inspection, Captain Bigelow noted that the corrals were clean, but skeptically added that they had been occupied for only a few days. What disturbed Bigelow in addition to the conditions under which Waters's elk and buffalo were likely destined to live was the fact that captive animals existed at all within the boundaries of a national park. Bigelow wrote, "It seems utterly at variance with the entire spirit of the Park to keep wild animals in such captivity. I recommend that they be set free."[8]

This pronouncement is worth noting primarily because neither visitors nor other park personnel seem to have shared Bigelow's concern over whether a zoo in a national park was inappropriate. On the contrary, all the surviving letters of complaint from tourists focused specifically on the deplorable conditions under which the animals were forced to live and the idea that the sight of them was offensive. The more philosophical question of whether their captivity in that particular space was in concert with a "spirit of the Park" did not arise. Acting Superintendent Anderson, with his own chained bear, had approved Waters's proposal to exhibit game. And if such questions had occurred to Waters, he certainly wasn't saying so.

Young concurred, however, and with the support of Acting Secretary of the Interior Jesse E. Wilson borrowed from Bigelow's prose when he officially notified Waters that "keeping . . . wild animals in captivity is at variance with the spirit of having this greatest of all national parks maintain with fidelity the original conditions of Nature as far as possible." Young told Waters to remove the animals from the park no later than October 1907.[9] Whether because he shared Bigelow's vision of what the park was for or because by that point he was keen on diminishing Waters's privileges, Yellowstone's superintendent had gone on the record with the notion that zoos were inconsistent with the spirit of the national park.

In the meantime, visitors to Dot Island were being treated to even more horrifying sights than had been on display at the Lake Hotel corrals. In August 1907, Superintendent Young received missives regarding the diets of Waters's captive ungulates from three prominent members of national conservation organizations that were meeting in the park. T. Gilbert Pearson, secretary of the National Association of Audubon Societies for Bird and Game Preservation, wrote that to see elk being fed largely upon garbage "was a disgusting sight to any one who in the least understands what is the proper food of these valuable animals." T. S. Palmer, a game preservation official for the U.S. Department of Agriculture, agreed: "Soon after [we] landed several large tubs of garbage were brought ashore and dumped in troughs in the elk enclosure. The hungry animals eagerly picked out potato peelings, pieces of vegetables, and even bits of meats. The filthy corrals, the noisome odors and the sight of elk fed like hogs on stale garbage disgusted several of the passengers and caused unfavorable comment."[10]

Perhaps most compelling was the tale told by W. F. Scott, president of the five-year-old National Association of Game and Fish Wardens and Commissioners, who wrote:

> When we landed at Dot Island for the purpose of seeing the elk and buffalo confined there . . . my attention was attracted by a nauseating and sour smell. Upon looking around I saw a deck hand following me, carrying two buckets of the vilest smelling slop or swill. Upon being asked what the same was used for he replied that it was the feed for the

elk. When we reached the corral this repugnant mess was poured out into a trough where these poor emaciated creatures, driven to desperation by hunger, fought for an opportunity to eat at the trough, where, for the first time in my life, I saw elk eat flesh. I saw one cow elk plunge her nose into the trough, seize a huge chunk of some kind of meat, trot across the corral and there devour it like a dog. . . . When I reflect upon the repulsive conditions that were witnessed . . . and the further fact that this inhuman sight is witnessed daily by hundreds of tourists from all over the world, I am impelled to make this protest in the name of humanity.[11]

Superintendent Young continued to demand that Waters remove his animals. After a brief dispute in which Waters attempted to argue that maintaining the exhibit was within his rights (despite an expired permit), and then offered to sell the haggard animals to the park for $6,000, they were released on October 15, 1907.[12] Yellowstone's first zoo was history.

By 1924, however, another zoo was operating in the park, though not under a concessioner. Yellowstone's second menagerie was established by the National Park Service and enthusiastically embraced by Yellowstone's first NPS superintendent, Horace M. Albright. Albright, born in California's Owens Valley on January 6, 1890, was only twenty-nine years old when he became superintendent of the world's first national park in 1919. Tapped by Secretary of the Interior Franklin Lane in 1914 to steer the national parks' new chief administrator, Stephen Mather, "through the red tape" of federal bureaucracy and "keep him out of trouble," Albright, along with Mather, became perhaps the seminal figure in the development and evolution of the NPS, exerting influence over its policies and practices until his death in 1987. According to historian Robert Utley, Albright played a "pivotal role" in the 1916 passage of the act creating the NPS, in formulating the principles and policies governing the parks, in defending park resources from exploitation during World War I, and in other issues critical to the success of the new agency.[13]

In part, the zoo was the product of the NPS's need to build a strong fan base. Albright realized that as long as their destiny rested in the hands of a political entity (Congress), the national parks would have to build a public constituency that was strong enough to ensure their continued funding and protection and ward off the efforts of the more powerful U.S. Forest Service to take over NPS lands. As Albright would later recall, "We knew the Congress would count tourist visitation to decide how much money our bureau would get to operate the park system. Dollars would be doled out according to the number of visitors." Mather and Albright wanted their infant agency to grow, and so the two embarked on a campaign of boosterism and people-pleasing.[14]

They took as their primary task the maximization of tourist visits and satisfaction with the national parks and accomplished it by constantly improving accessibility, accommodations, and visitor entertainment. While Mather worked on improving park accessibility and accommodations on the national scale, Albright set about trying to create in Yellowstone a park landscape of easily accessible visual appeal and unique experience. Naturally, Yellowstone already had plenty of such attractions, with its bubbling hot springs, spouting geysers, and magnificent Grand Canyon of the Yellowstone River. However, Albright recognized that the park's wildlife was another of its chief attractions, and that not all visitors had the opportunity to see as much of it as they wanted to during their visits. To remedy this problem, Albright, beginning in the early 1920s, established several wildlife viewing areas where visitors could easily see examples of the park's charismatic megafauna. In their various forms, these viewing areas included a "buffalo show corral," the menagerie, and a series of "bear feeding grounds" located near the park's hotels. Albright also continued the army's predator control policy, designed to reduce the numbers of many of the animals that preyed upon the more popular park fauna.

In addition, Albright believed that the NPS had a "duty to present wildlife as a spectacle" for public enjoyment; upon its opening in June 1924, Albright explained that the zoo was needed so that tourists could closely inspect and photograph examples of the park's wildlife. "The tourist [often] sees animals at a distance and tries without success for a close view. His time in the park is usually limited and, unless he can see the animal in captivity, his interest in a close acquaintance may go unrewarded," he wrote.[15] The zoo made wildlife watching more efficient.

Albright's belief that it was important for visitors to see examples of the wildlife being protected in the park reflected his devotion to "aesthetic conservation," a philosophy that adhered to basic principles of sustainability and efficiency but departed from traditional utilitarian conservation by advocating nonextractive forms of resource use, such as recreation and sightseeing. Utilitarian and aesthetic conservation shared a common goal: that resources not be wasted, and a common guiding principle: the greatest good for the greatest number for the longest time. However, where utilitarian conservation met that goal by scientifically regulating extractive practices, aesthetic conservation strove to ensure that the nation's resources produced pleasure in the people for whom they were conserved.

Although he did not employ the term, Horace Albright described aesthetic conservation thus: "Our group and followers were conservationists and preservationists. No use of resources, no change in the general state of national park areas. But roads to enjoy the outstanding, easy-to-visit features of a park while leaving most areas in wilderness, accommodations for the people of all incomes in a wide price range, conveniences for health and safety."[16] This conservation philosophy is clearly present in the language of the NPS Organic Act, which literally directs the agency not to "preserve" but to "conserve the scenery and the natural and historic objects and the wild life therein and to provide for the enjoyment of the same in such manner and by such means as will leave them unimpaired for the enjoyment of future generations."

According to Albright, he and others "understood [it] to be the standing policy" that the NPS's mandate required preservation and use. In order to ensure that both halves of the mandate were fulfilled, the geographic space of the national parks in the early era was typically divided on a broad scale according to its purpose. Albright advocated that only the areas around a park's truly outstanding features be considered for development: "the remainder, usually seventy-five percent or more of the total, were to be reserved as wilderness areas."[17]

Aesthetic conservation elevated the human spirit instead of human industry. Utilitarian conservationists of the early twentieth century, believing that the purpose of natural resources was to provide for the material needs of an industrializing society, sometimes expressed frustration at the management of the national parks, where they perceived that managers had wastefully "locked up" resources, having "locked out" the possibility of extractive development.[18]

Although they were averse to the idea of extractive development (such as mining or logging) in the parks, early park managers still worried that the parks' features, that is, resources, could be wasted. Instead of denoting a lack of material production, however, "waste" in this case indicated the lack of pleasure production that resulted when the park's visitors failed to adequately see and experience its resources. Captive wildlife (oxymoron or not), available for viewing appreciation, proved an attractive solution.

This was why the problem with E. C. Waters's zoo, for many people, was not that the animals were captive but rather that their living conditions were deplorable—Waters was a poor steward, rendering his animals incapable of representing nature's grandeur, and so the resource was being wasted (in addition to being treated inhumanely). Thus, although several NPS scientists were advocating the preservation of primitive conditions (i.e., habitat) in the 1920s, Yellowstone's administration sought to conserve specific, well-liked species such as elk and bison, and part of that project meant making them available for people to see. Because they were very effective in fulfilling this role, zoos and other forms of organized wildlife spectacle were considered important components of wildlife conservation during Albright's tenure in Yellowstone.[19]

Zoos also provided a "close-up view," allowing a person the opportunity to "look an animal in the eye." When conservation giant and New York Zoological Society president William Hornaday made a list of elements that should be included in an ideal bear enclosure in 1922, the last item on his list, italicized, was *"close-up views of all bears for all visitors."* In accordance with this priority, early NPS documents reveal a belief that wild animals became more desirable when they were "tamed" and made available for close inspection by tourists. In his annual report for 1917, Rocky Mountain National Park superintendent L. Claude Way wrote that the park's mountain sheep "have become surprisingly tame. . . . The writer this summer approached to within 50 feet of 2 rams without [their] becoming frightened. The fact that sheep can be approached in automobiles seen in this way most everyday adds to their value in the Park."[20]

In 1918, Superintendent Way revealed a deeper motive for the production of tame animals—the desire to awaken the American public to the benefits of wildlife conservation: "One band of 56 [mountain sheep] . . . was almost surrounded by automobiles, and 20 persons were counted on foot, with kodaks. The frolicking lambs are especially interesting to travelers, and convince the great majority of them that the kodak furnishes more real and lasting pleasure than the gun." During his tenure in Yellowstone, Horace Albright also embraced close interaction between visitors and animals as a way to get people to see that wildlife had value beyond hunting. Countless photos of Albright feeding bears, sometimes in the company of U.S. presidents, promoted the idea that bears had entertainment value that would be lost if they were shot instead of fed. In fact, Hornaday, Way, and Albright, all advocates of the close-up view, also shared a common contempt for market hunting; in the early twentieth century Hornaday had led the fight to get the first federal hunting laws passed.[21]

Yellowstone's second zoo was established as a companion to the park's Buffalo Jones museum and "buffalo show corral" at Mammoth Hot Springs, where approximately fifteen bull bison had already been displayed for several seasons. Each summer, park rangers drove the most attractive specimens of the park's "tame" buffalo herd to Mammoth Hot Springs from the park's

Buffalo Ranch in the Lamar Valley so that visitors could easily see these animals that had themselves been rescued from the brink of extinction through joint efforts by Hornaday and the park. The show corral proved so popular that the zoo was added to it. The new zoo, located roughly in the area of today's horse corrals at Mammoth, included two black-tailed deer fawns, an elk calf, and two young badgers, all captured within a mile of Mammoth Hot Springs. Most were given names; one of the badgers was called Socrates. Park naturalist E. J. Sawyer, who was in charge of the zoo, also constructed a "flying cage" for avian specimens, but was crushed one morning to discover that its inhabitants had escaped when a bear had apparently broken in.[22]

Park staff devoted a tremendous amount of time and energy to the zoo's construction and maintenance and to the collection and care of its animals. In March 1925, Albright expressed the high priority of the "zoo and pets" to his chief ranger, Sam Woodring, and by the week of June 20, Sawyer was complaining that the "naturalists [are] so busy with [the] zoo that none can stray far from Mammoth between 7:30AM and 8:30PM daily."[23] Sawyer's weekly and monthly reports showed that his primary springtime activities consisted of locating and capturing suitable zoo specimens.

As Albright's memo to Woodring—along with a story titled "Mammoth Pets" in *Yellowstone Nature Notes,* a park newsletter—indicated, some of the zoo's inhabitants were, in fact, treated like domestic pets. Although the coyote was generally vilified at the time as a malicious predator of "more desirable" animals and was a target of predator control efforts in Yellowstone, the NPS's zoo included a coyote that Sawyer had obtained from a man in Livingston, Montana, and named Gyp—likely after the dog in the recently published *Doctor Dolittle.* In his reports, Sawyer expressed some initial trepidation over whether a member of such a despised species would be accepted as a zoo inhabitant. However, in his subsequent contributions to *Yellowstone Nature Notes,* Sawyer depicted Gyp as man's best friend, which seemed to help assuage any potentially negative feelings toward him. In the March 1925 issue, Sawyer wrote of the coyote's "peculiarly doggy habits"; not only did Gyp "submit with every appearance of enjoyment to having his head rubbed and petted," but he also played with a ball and later in the year was taken for a daily walk to Mammoth's museum, information center, and hotel.[24]

By June 1925, Gyp was heralded as the most photographed, petted, and admired animal at Mammoth, if not in the entire park. In fact, by early July he was such a popular subject for tourist photography (the zoo was receiving approximately five hundred visitors each day) that rangers had to alter his environs. Because tourists wanted pictures of him unimpeded by the wires of his cage, park staff were having to lead him out of the cage several times each day, which proved time-consuming. Their solution was to construct an enclosure resembling a dog run, in which Gyp was attached by a chain to a wire running overhead, allowing for a clear view of the animal and his activities.[25] Gyp did his job well, serving as an excellent ambassador of aesthetic conservation by seeming to bridge the gap between wild and tame and helping visitors to feel more at home in nature while at the same time giving them a taste of the "wild."

In July 1925, Gyp was joined by Juno and Pard, two three-and-a-half-year-old black bears that had been raised from cubs by Mrs. Reta Hamilton of Weippe, Idaho. Mrs. Hamilton's donation came with two stipulations: Juno and Pard must be provided with a spacious den with running water and never be separated from one another. In accordance with these wishes, park employees erected an eight-foot wooden fence around an eighteen-by-sixty-foot area; a seven-by-eight-foot swimming pool was planned for one end. Visitors were to be provided "an unobstructed view from behind the outer wall of the pool."[26]

Juno and Pard received a care package from Mrs. Hamilton each Christmastide, and over the next two years Juno became fat from candy thrown to him by tourists. The bears were a constant presence in the *Yellowstone Nature Notes,* which told of their frequent escapes from what was apparently an inadequate enclosure, wintertime rambles (like many of the zoo's other animals, they were set free for the winter), and springtime attempts to evade their keepers. Although Mrs. Hamilton had given Juno and Pard to the park because she had wanted them to be "liberated," park officials found that Mrs. Hamilton had been "too successful in taming them. They did not want to be wild bears again. They were just like dogs," according to Albright.[27]

In addition to visitor pleasure, the zoo provided E. J. Sawyer with a laboratory for scientific inquiry. It was the job of the park naturalist in those days to double as the park's scientist, and the captive setting allowed easy observation. On occasion, Sawyer also used the zoo animals to conduct field observations. In December 1924, he noted that a buffalo carcass in the show corral was attracting a good deal of attention from local scavengers. About fifty feet from the carcass Sawyer erected a tent-blind, from which he could watch the scavengers without being seen by them. He then temporarily freed the zoo's coyote near the carcass and made notes, sketches, and moving pictures of its behavior—effectively creating his own wildlife tableau for behavioral study.[28]

Sawyer's successor, Dorr Yeager, collected fewer scientific observations of the zoo animals but left quite a colorful literary trail detailing his experiences with them. Following the zoo's closure (which was not noted in park records but seems to have occurred just a couple of years after its inception), Yeager adopted a black bear cub, named him Barney, and moved him into his own home. The *Nature Notes* were subsequently filled with tales of Barney's escapades ("I never realized how rapidly a bear grows until I tried to keep one in the kitchen"). Barney also reportedly talked on the telephone, sucked on a pacifier, and enjoyed listening to the opera. The experience provided fodder for children's books about Barney written by Anne Wolfson and Esse Forrester O'Brien and for a chapter in Yeager's own semiautobiographical book, *Bob Flame—Ranger.*[29] If any Yellowstone animal ever epitomized the conflation of wild and tame, it was surely Barney.

After the zoo became defunct, the NPS found other ways to concentrate wildlife so people could easily see it. Concurrent with the development of the zoo, the NPS established the park's famous bear feeding shows as a staple of any Yellowstone visit. Although Congress set aside Yellowstone National Park in 1872 primarily to protect its geothermal wonders, it wasn't long before bears emerged as one of the park's most compelling attractions. According to geographer Judith Meyer, there was a sharp rise of interest in bears among visitors from 1890 to 1900. Meyer found that in the park's first two decades bears had proved far less interesting to tourists than the park's "wilderness qualities." By the 1890s, however, the number of comments visitors made about bears had doubled and in fact surpassed the number of comments about wilderness.[30]

Unfortunately, we do not know the nature of those comments. Bears were a bothersome presence in the park's tent camps by 1891; the rise in comments may have indicated a rise in annoyance rather than pleasure associated with bears. Nevertheless, by the 1890s the bears of Yellowstone were clearly a growing source of interest to park visitors. A 1902 article in *Rocky Mountain Magazine* declared that "the bears [were] becoming one of the features of the Park" but averred that the park's geysers still elicited the greatest degree of "uncontrolled excitement" from visitors.[31]

Whether positive or negative, the rise of interest in Yellowstone's bears coincided with the spectacle-ization of their eating habits at the Fountain Hotel's garbage dump. The Northern Pacific Railroad financed the construction of the Fountain Hotel in 1891 in order to provide its wealthy passengers with the sort of accommodations to which they were accustomed, which were otherwise sorely lacking in the Old Faithful area, where the hotel was located. Built at a cost of $100,000, the Fountain Hotel accommodated 350 visitors and, with its steam heat, electricity, and baths of geyser water supplied by the nearby Leather Pool, provided an oasis of civilization in the midst of the park's wilderness.[32] It was located on a low ridge overlooking an area known as Fountain Flat, selected because it was at the greatest distance from Mammoth Hot Springs that a stagecoach's horse team could travel in a single day. With Old Faithful just a few miles to the south and with the bubbling mud of the Fountain Paint Pots, the symmetrical terraces of the Great Fountain Geyser (at the time a favorite wading pool), and the sublime watercolors of the Grand Prismatic Spring and Excelsior Geyser all nearby, the main attractions for visitors to the Fountain Hotel were initially thermal rather than mammal. All that would change with the advent of the hotel's bear feeding shows.

Refuse produced in Yellowstone today is hauled to sites outside park boundaries. Until the early 1970s, however, the park's remote location meant that earlier concessioners and administrators found it far easier to dump their garbage at sites within the park than to transport it elsewhere. Bears, attracted by the garbage, had fed at hotel dumps since the 1880s, but it took the operators of the Fountain Hotel to simultaneously dispose of waste and provide visitor entertainment by dumping their refuse at a site within walking distance—about one hundred yards—from the hotel. Each evening the loads of dinner scraps and cooking remnants drew crowds of ten to sixteen hungry grizzlies and dozens of curious people who watched them feed, and occasionally fed them from their own hands.[33]

Visitors may have been feeding Yellowstone's bears informally almost since the park's inception; in her diary *Camping Out in the Yellowstone, 1882,* Mary Bradshaw Richards wrote that it was common practice for guided parties to simply leave their evening's trash next to their campfires for the bears who "gain[ed their] summer livelihood by appropriating all eatables left."[34] However, the practice was institutionalized with the advent of these first "bear shows," in which concessioner staff fed the bears while groups of tourists watched. The bear shows grew into a self-perpetuating tourist sight and Yellowstone tradition lasting almost five decades.

The Fountain Hotel closed in 1917, but its bear shows had proved so popular that they were later instituted at three of the park's other large hotels: Lake, Old Faithful, and Canyon. The shows were promoted by the NPS, which delighted in the high level of visitor pleasure they generated. According to Esse Forrester O'Brien's *Clowns of the Forest,* the bear shows were designed to serve four practical and philosophical purposes: (1) to feed the bears, (2) to dispose of the garbage, (3) to provide a "safe" place for people to watch bears and learn more about them, and (4) to discourage the bears from hunting and fishing (i.e., to help "conserve" ungulates and sport fish). Horace Albright also claimed that providing the bears with garbage at the bear pits kept them from scavenging in the campgrounds, because "Mr. Bear knows he can eat a lot more in an eight-hour day if he eats 'combination salad' at the bear pits than he can if he nibbles at tidbits stolen from campers." Albright argued that as scavengers, bears found garbage to be an entirely acceptable dietary supplement.[35] Thus, at the time, feeding refuse to bears was understood to be in keeping with the park's duty to preserve natural conditions while providing visitor enjoyment.

At their most primitive, the park's bear feeding grounds consisted of a thin wire strung around three sides of a trash pile, with the open side facing a wood. In 1909, visitor F. Dumont Smith explained that at the Lake Hotel, one had to "go around the back of the hotel, past the meat house . . . follow a little road through thick woods and strike an open glade where the bears come to eat." In the evening, a garbage cart appeared on the road and entered the dump area, whereupon hotel employees shoveled the trash off the cart for consumption by the waiting bears, the vast majority of which were always grizzlies. As they crowded around with their cameras, Smith and his fellow visitors were continually warned by armed soldiers to stand back from the bears. Sometimes, though, selected tourists got to ride in with the garbage, allowing those lucky souls to take their photos from within ten feet of the animals. Smith considered this privileged treatment an unspeakable outrage, and castigated both the U.S. Army and the "kitchen scullion" who "could be bought" for perpetuating this experiential inequity.[36]

Aesthetic conservation was built into the Yellowstone landscape when NPS employees transformed its trash heaps into amphitheaters at the Old Faithful and Canyon locations. At Old Faithful, the feeding station was located on the current site of the parking lot behind the new Snow Lodge. Log benches were assembled in a semicircle around what came to be known as the "Lunch Counter," a wooden feeding platform, bearing its own marquee, erected so that the bears would be slightly elevated for easier viewing. The feeding platform was about 125 feet from the crowd and 50 feet from the adjoining woods. In later years, according to O'Brien, a four-sided wire fence was erected around the spectators for protection, effectively caging them instead of the bears: "Then the bears began looking upon the people as the show." Little evidence exists, however, to show that this comment was anything but wishful anthropomorphizing. Typical accounts of the bear shows indicated that the bears frequently fought with one another over the choicest scraps but rarely took any interest in the people watching them. For many visitors, these tussles were a highlight of the show. In 1929, the park's chief ranger estimated that 90 percent of the park's visitors saw the bear show at Old Faithful.[37]

The feeding ground for the Canyon area was built at Otter Creek in 1931 and was the most elaborate by far. There, park employees built an eighteen-by-forty-foot feeding platform made of reinforced concrete to serve as a stage for the bears. The platform was equipped with running water for cleaning, made possible through the construction of a small concrete dam built on a spring about 450 feet away. Solid log benches with seating for 250 rose high up the side of a hill overlooking the dump, but the bear shows were often standing-room-only affairs, as more than six hundred cars crowded the specially built parking lot and up to 1,500 people squeezed into the amphitheater space. By the mid-1930s, the Otter Creek feeding ground was attracting between fifty and seventy grizzly bears each evening.[38]

Although Horace Albright firmly believed that people came to the national parks for recreation rather than education, he also understood that visitors came to Yellowstone partially out of curiosity, and that if the parks expected to succeed in promoting both conservation and themselves, then visitors would require some environmental education. Then as now, education and interpretation in the parks served a dual purpose of providing information and offering a perspective that would "make each an enthusiastic protector of natural things and of things worth while in life." In keeping with these purposes, the NPS augmented the bear shows with nightly educational lectures about bears, delivered by a park ranger. Ranger Philip Martindale's evening programs at Old Faithful may have been the most memorable, as he delivered them while mounted upon a horse that he would back up to within thirty feet of the feeding grizzlies. Martindale was a spectacle in and of himself, and up to two thousand people at once attended his lectures, where they learned that the bears they saw eating garbage in front of them, snout to snout and fighting over the choicest scraps, were majestic wild animals that the park was proud to be charged with protecting.[39]

If considering a human-fed, garbage-eating animal to be "wild" seems incongruous, it was not so to many who witnessed the spectacle. In his *Book of a Hundred Bears*, F. Dumont Smith wrote, "Your first sight of a real wild bear gives you just a little thrill. It is not like a caged or menagerie bear. You realize that there are possibilities of danger when, just at dusk, they came galloping down the hill."[40] On the other hand, it was frequently commented that the park's bears seemed "half-tame," and the physical arrangement of the feeding grounds reinforced this notion. The dumps were typically located adjacent to a wood, out of which the bears emerged each evening and into which they returned after the show. This arrangement created a sort of theater space in which the bears emerged as if from the wings at the appointed time each evening in order to perform their own Shakesbeare in the Park for the assembled audience. At the feeding grounds, Yellowstone's bears became performers as well as wild creatures—a reputation that they would retain for decades.

The half-human, half-wilderness arrangement of the stations, coupled with the sight of the bears crossing the line from wilderness to human landscape and back, likely blurred the line between the human and natural landscapes and gave the impression that the animals' "natural" lives were only briefly interrupted each day when they entered the human landscape for the pleasure of visitors. The possibility that the bears were eating the leftovers of the very people watching them likely encouraged the sense of closeness and paternalism the tourists felt for the animals, which seemed to be desired by both the park's visitors and its administration. The bear feeding shows helped cement the bear–human relationship so solidly in people's minds that it was later doubted whether Yellowstone's bears could survive in the absence of human refuse.

As bear feeding spread to the park's roadsides in later years, the public, ensemble performances of the feeding grounds were replaced by a kind of private table dances. This situation was made possible by the arrival in Yellowstone of the private automobile, which was both a democratizing and an individualizing force. No longer was travel to the park primarily restricted to those who could afford passage by train and stagecoach, accompanied by several nights' stay at a park hotel and meals in its restaurant, or to those able to pay a private guide. In their own automobiles, increasing numbers of individual families could decide exactly where they wanted to go in the park and when, and could also eat and camp out of their cars. Although the park's hotels were by no means emptied by the decline in railroad traffic, the automobile era brought an increase in the number of car camps (and thus places for bears to find human food) around the park, offering visitors the opportunity to feed and lodge themselves and eschew, if they so chose, the more group-oriented experiences of the recent past.

Roadside feeding of bears was reported as early as 1910, but did not become widely popular until after the introduction of automobiles to the park.[41] After the first automobiles were allowed into the park in 1915, it proved to be a short leap from tourists' watching bears being fed at the hotel dumps to tourists' habitually feeding bears themselves. More and more bears were seen begging along the roadsides and rooting around the campgrounds. By 1920, a bear that park employees named Jesse James had become a fixture at the roadside near West Thumb, at the park's southern end. When a car approached, Jesse James would step into its path and rear up on his hind legs to beg in that all-too-familiar pose that has become a trope of Yellowstone imagery, forcing the vehicle to a halt and thereby staging "hold-ups" of countless private automobiles and touring cars passing through the area. Other bears soon followed suit and came to be known as "Jesse James bears."

Although the practice of feeding bears had already begun to result in numerous injuries to visitors, Horace Albright was reluctant to put a stop to Jesse James's activities in light of his popularity and in spite of the staff's feelings that the bear was more of a headache than an attraction. In his monthly report for July 1921, Chief Ranger James McBride reported, "A two-year old black bear, commonly known as the 'Hold-up Bear,' has made it a habit of meeting all yellow cars as they cross the Continental Divide on their way to the Lake on each afternoon. Contrary to rules and regulations tourists in yellow cars and private cars fed this bear and while doing so have tied up traffic and many persons feeding this animal have received minor injuries as a result of either teasing him or allowing him to scratch them with his paws. . . . It is recommended that this bear be captured and shipped [away]." (It was not uncommon, during these years and up to today, for "problem" bears to be donated to zoos when such institutions had space for them.) In his own report for that month, Albright summarized McBride's comments but left out the parts about visitor injuries as well as his ranger's recommendation that the bear be removed: "The small black bear known as the 'Hold Up Bear' is still in evidence along the road between Thumb and Lake Outlet and is seen and fed daily by travelers."[42]

In fact, in Albright's report for the same month of the previous year, he had noted that a congressional party had been "held up" at the same spot, "much to the delight of the distinguished visitors." Jesse James's "performances" (Albright's term) were also noted in a memo to the press in June 1923, and when President Warren G. Harding visited later that month, Secret Service agents and park rangers held other travelers at bay until the presidential party had passed so that the president might see more wildlife. At Lake, Harding fed two bears that had been treed by rangers, making for an excellent photo opportunity.[43]

Unlike the bear shows, roadside feeding was not institutionalized through formalization of the visible landscape. Rather, it was subtly encouraged by

decades of visual imagery and lax enforcement by the NPS; visitors ultimately came away with the notion that feeding the bears should be a primary experiential goal of every visitor to Yellowstone. Back in 1913, the
Shaw & Powell Camping Company, which operated a series of tent camps
around the park, had published a brochure featuring a photograph of a
woman feeding a bear among its depictions of Yellowstone's sights and activities. Concessioner advertising had to be submitted to the park administration for approval, and although they did not always strictly enforce the
park's prohibitions against bear feeding, Yellowstone's army administrators
took a dim view of the brochure's imagery, which was inconsistent with
park regulations stating that bear feeding would be permitted only "at the
regular garbage dumps at hotels and camps." The army's acting superintendent requested that "some other picture be substituted for this one in your
next edition of the circular."[44]

When faced with the same issue during the next decade, the NPS, as it
had on the question of zoos, differed from the army in its interpretation
and enforcement of park policy regarding visitors and wildlife. In a short
brochure published during the 1920s, the Union Pacific Railroad (UP) included two photos depicting people feeding bears: one of visitors feeding
bears by the roadside and one of Jesse James. During the same period, the
UP also published a series of forty-page, cardboard-bound booklets describing the park and the sorts of activities visitors might expect to engage
in there. The 1926 version included two photos of visitors feeding wildlife.
In the first photo, situated in the "What to Do" section, a fashionably
dressed woman held a treat over the head of a bear standing on its hind
legs. The caption read, "Yellowstone bears have a well developed taste for
dainty morsels."[45] In the second photo, a deer was shown eating from a
woman's hand.

This imagery was clearly a reiteration of what had gotten the Shaw & Powell Camping Company into trouble, yet there is no evidence that the UP was
censured by the park's NPS administration. This was likely because the NPS
during the 1920s was strongly invested in promoting whatever made visitors
happy, and in spite of the injuries that resulted from bear bites, Yellowstone's
visitors were happy feeding the bears. In fact, Superintendent Albright himself was photographed many times posing with and feeding Yellowstone's
bears, and the cover of the park's own 1922 broadside (an informational
booklet or folder printed annually and distributed to visitors at the park's entrances) featured a F. J. Haynes photo of a man leaning out of an open-
topped touring car to feed a "hold-up bear."[46] If a picture is indeed worth a

isand words, then Yellowstone's visitors could hardly have been expected
bey the official rules against bear feeding. Albright was apparently com-
able with that contradiction.

Albright maintained that tourists were bear-crazy in part because the
bears seemed more than a little like themselves: "Bears are no longer wild animals to us," he wrote in *Oh Ranger! A Book About the National Parks,* first
published in 1928. "They have become personified. They are like people, and
the visitors to the parks want to treat them as such. That probably explains
some of the foolish things people try to do with the national park bears."[47]
Those "foolish things" included the hand-feeding of bears. Albright's writings repeatedly demonstrated a belief that there was a right way and a wrong
way to feed bears, and that as long as people behaved accordingly and didn't
run into bad bears, the visitor happiness that feeding generated far out-
weighed its negative aspects.

Feeding a bear the "right way" meant throwing food to it rather than
hand-feeding, and never teasing the bear by pretending to have food when
you didn't. Though feeding was technically against the rules, the park's 1926
broadside featured a section titled "The Bears: Good Friends Provided You
Treat Them Fairly" that sympathized with visitors' desire to feed and offered
advice on how to do it properly. "The bears of the Park are very interesting,
and we are not surprised that you want to feed and photograph them," cooed
the brochure. "But you must remember that they are wild animals, and are
TREACHEROUS and DANGEROUS. Do not tease the bears by pretending you
have food for them when you have none. You may get bitten."[48]

Whether or not he truly believed it, creating the mythology that all bear-
related injuries resulted because individual humans or bears had broken the
rules of "proper feeding" provided Albright with the justification he needed
to continue to allow bears and people to interact closely. As long as the park
maintained that bears were dangerous, rather than that the act of feeding
them was dangerous, problems could be explained away as stemming from
individual mischief, and the way people interacted with bears would not
have to be changed.

As might be expected, the bear–human relationship was an unequal one.
Humans who misbehaved came away with bites; bears who raided camps
and habitually bit people who were behaving "properly" were characterized
as "criminals" and paid with their lives. In a 1927 memo, Albright wrote
about a bear at West Thumb who had bitten several people, "apparently for
the mere love of biting and as soon as we saw the way his mind was working, we killed him."[49] How many other bears were killed for similar offenses

during Albright's administration is not really known, because bear-related injuries and the numbers of bears killed as a result were not systematically recorded until 1931, after Albright had left Yellowstone to become director of the NPS. In that year, visitors reported 78 bear-related injuries and 209 incidents of property damage.

Albright outlined his ideas about the structure of fair play between visitors and bears in various official correspondence as well as in *Oh, Ranger!*, cowritten with the freelance writer Frank Taylor: "A Dude, with no candy or food, held out his hand as though there were candy in it. That made Mrs. Murphy [a roadside bear] angry and she nipped the man on the toe . . . fully two score people fed Mrs. Murphy and her cub that day in the proper way, by throwing candy to her, and were entertained for hours by the bears with no incidents nor accidents." Later, Albright responded to injury reports by criticizing tourists for carelessness and for treating bears like domestic dogs: "We have reports of several people being bitten while feeding bears . . . it has been observed that each incident of this kind has been due to extreme carelessness on the part of the tourist. It is apparent that the greater number of visitors regard the bear in the same light as a dog . . . and are as careless in their manner towards the bear as they might be to a dog."[50]

Ironically, Albright had previously encouraged visitors to think of bears as surrogate pets while they visited the park. Fearing that they would disturb or kill birds and other wildlife, he had strictly prohibited dogs and other domestic pets from entering the park, and actually argued that it was this exclusion of domestic dogs from the parks that had prompted the current "era of friendship between mankind and bears." Hence, while vacationing in Yellowstone, the black bear replaced the family pet; Albright wrote elsewhere that bears were "like dogs," and rangers often described the noises that they made as "woof, woof!"[51] Also like pets, the bears acquired names, especially those that were frequently associated with specific park locations and facilities, having grown used to being fed from the back doors of restaurant kitchens. In *Clowns of the Forest,* Esse Forrester O'Brien wrote of Mrs. Murphy, Saturday Night, Maria, Old Pat, and One Eye, among countless others.

In *Oh, Ranger!,* not only did humans accept bears as surrogate pets, bears accepted humans as surrogate parents. In his description of the family structure of bears, Albright chided the males for "abandoning" their families, and expressed regret at what he described as the mother's desire to "be rid of" her cubs after a year. Interpreting these practices from within the scheme of human social mores instead of treating them as evidence of the natural patterns of bear life, Albright called it "strange indeed that the bears should prosper and increase in numbers under these harsh conditions of youth," and proclaimed it "no wonder they turn to the [tourists] for kindness and candy!"[52] Weary of their nasty, brutish, and short existence in the state of nature, knowing that people were their stewards, and in the convenient absence of the domestic dog, according to *Oh, Ranger!,* bears became man's best friend, and vice versa, in the idyllic setting of Yellowstone.

As geographer Yi-Fu Tuan has written, "the dream that ferocious animals, on the approach of man, would kneel in docility and thus be a fit companion in a perfect world may be among the most vainglorious of human aspirations."[53] Yet in Yellowstone this was exactly the kind of relationship that was purported and promoted by park management—what could more closely resemble Tuan's Edenic "perfect world" than a sublime natural playground whose primary human inhabitants (tourists) were free from labor and whose animal inhabitants wanted nothing more than to please? Indeed, it is hard to deny that in much of the park's early imagery, that "most vainglorious of human aspirations" appeared to have been fulfilled in Yellowstone, where, according to the park's top administrator, bears had proven so easily and fully adaptable to the human presence that any transgression could be attributed either to human misconduct or individual personality defects in the bear. In real life, this mythology manifested itself in the form of an enduring, unfortunate belief that the best way to improve human–bear relations was to identify and eliminate "problem" bears rather than to alter the relationship.

Albright was forever steadfast in arguing that while he was superintendent there were no significant bear problems—just a few bad apples of both the ursine and the human variety who refused to conform to the economy of interaction he described. However, in the summer of 1925, for instance, the West Thumb Ranger Station *alone* reported 88 bear bites or scratches, 43 of which required medical attention, and in 1930, Superintendent Roger Toll, who succeeded Albright, estimated that 100–300 tourists each year received bear bites. Yet in 1972, Albright wrote, "In my time [1919–1929], the bears presented no serious problem . . . sometimes a finger was bitten when held up without food while posing for a picture." When someone got seriously injured, Albright often soothed the hurt by telling an amusing tale of someone else who had fed the bears with unexpected results. One of his favorites concerned a woman who had been holding food over a bear's head in order to get it to stand, and whose dress was torn off as the bear dropped down to all fours, in front of the flashbulbs of about five hundred visitors. He was also proud to have accompanied so many famous people and dignitaries on their bear feeding adventures, as was the custom of the time in Yellowstone, and was apparently adept at convincing people that the scars they acquired from feeding bears would prove, by far, to be their most interesting and lasting souvenirs of Yellowstone.[54]

By the time Superintendent Horace Albright left Yellowstone to become NPS director in 1929, patterns of closeness had been established between the park's visitors and its wildlife, especially its bears, that included emotional as well as physical proximity. If the park's zoo animals were held captive by rangers, then bears at feeding grounds and roadsides had been captivated by visitors and their food—and visitors captivated by bears. These patterns would remain entrenched in the coming decades and spawned a host of attitudes and habits that it would take the NPS and its visitors decades to break.

2

Admitting You Have a Problem
Making the Dangerous Bear

By the beginning of the 1930s, Yellowstone's bears and visitors had developed a complex, close relationship that was encouraged by park administrators. As NPS director Horace Albright would put it, Yellowstone was and would always be known as the "bear park," and not even scourges of bear bites would (or should) change that fact.[1] The narrative of friendship between humans and bears was perpetuated most prominently by Albright himself, who during his time as the park's superintendent had not only recognized but also stimulated the desire of visitors to have "up-close and personal" experiences with the bears of Yellowstone. As long as people and bears followed the "rules" of feeding, Albright maintained that it was a generally unproblematic practice.

Albright was replaced as Yellowstone's superintendent by Roger Toll: author, naturalist, mountaineer, and former superintendent of Rocky Mountain National Park. Where Albright had not recognized a problem, Toll quickly identified one, and in the summer of 1929, biologist Joseph Dixon of the NPS's new Wildlife Division (created for the purpose of surveying wildlife and identifying wildlife problems in the parks, and led and initially funded by George M. Wright) was in the park for the purpose of observing and making recommendations for improving what came to be known as "the bear situation."[2]

Although Dixon found that bear–human relations had indeed become problematic, his findings echoed two of Albright's firm beliefs: first, that most of the damage and injuries were caused by "relatively few individuals," and second, that although it would be preferable for visitors to refrain from feeding the bears, to get them to actually obey the regulations would be utterly impossible. Therefore, the NPS should simply warn visitors that any hand-feeding would be conducted at the visitor's "own risk" and leave it at that, rather than attempt to enforce the regulation. The admonition would be given primarily to exempt the NPS from legal liability in potential court cases resulting from feeding-related injuries; claims were on the rise.[3]

In order to warn the public that feeding the bears was risky, Dixon recommended that "numerous placards of fair size and with print sufficiently large to be read easily could be displayed at the points where bears are most frequently encountered, explaining that *all persons feeding bears do so at their own risk and peril.*" Dixon also recommended that the park move the feeding grounds farther away from areas occupied by people, try to give some grizzly cubs away to zoos, and avoid excessive duplication of bear feeding grounds and shows. He believed that too much emphasis was placed upon visitors' seeing bears in the park, and that if visitors had to work harder to see them, they might appreciate them more.[4]

Admitting the need to warn the public about the dangers of bears was tantamount to admitting that close bear–human interactions were risky, which was a very different position than that of the Albright administration. Not surprisingly, the NPS director's office took an active interest in what sort of warning message the park might plan to convey, in what form, and to what degree. Early attempts were in keeping with Dixon's contention that enforcement should not be a priority; stories appearing in the *Yellowstone Nature Notes* in the summer of 1930 included the following ambivalent attempts to discourage feeding:

Yellowstone Park is famed for its "tame" animals, and the National Park Service courts that fame—but as everyone knows, Fame is a fickle lover, and on occasion we have most unexpected experiences with our friends of the forests. . . . Of course, there are really very few tame animals in this great National Playground. . . . They have . . . in most cases become used to, and trustful of the presence of humans, but it is never safe to become too friendly with any of the larger animals.[5]

The bears of Yellowstone . . . should be treated as protected wild animals but not as pets. Their vicious side is aroused when teased by lack of food or by too close contact with humans, and it is therefore dangerous to feed even an apparently tame bear out of one's hand or to ever get between a mother and her cubs. . . . The bears are not to be feared if they are not teased or treated as pets, and as the situation stands at present they are one of the greatest attractions in Yellowstone Park.[6]

An NPS release dated July 21, 1931, informed the public that "all National Park bears are *wild animals*. Persons feeding bears do so at their own risk. Teasing, molesting, or touching bears is prohibited by Park Regulations." Notably absent from all of these admonitions was a general ban on feeding. Even after the summer of 1931, when one in every 2,800 visitors reported a bear-related injury and one in every 1,000 reported property damage, Director Albright remained hesitant to admit that any action should be taken, stating that "a very careful analysis . . . fails to convince me . . . that the situation is very much worse than it has always been," which according to Albright was never bad at all. In 1932, 34 bear-related injuries and 451 incidents of property damage would be recorded; it is important to note that injuries were likely underreported, as they were largely the result of bear-feeding, technically an illegal activity in the park.[7]

Another proposed solution to the bear situation was that the park should bring its bear population into line with its visitor population, which had not only decreased since the start of the Great Depression, but whose demographics were changing as well. In a 1931 letter to Director Albright, the park's acting superintendent, Guy Edwards (probably acting on Toll's behalf during a temporary absence), indicated that because the number of rail visitors had decreased "considerably more than 100% [*sic*]" in recent years, "the proportional amount of food for bears is only about a fourth of what it was in 1923 or 1925," and thus the bears, whose numbers had increased during that same period, had reached a point of "overpopulation." An undated report from the early 1930s reiterated that "there is hardly any doubt but that the increase in the bear population, together with the decrease in the number of visitors to the hotels and lodges, where most of the edible garbage for use in feeding the bears was procured, has been the greatest cause for the large increase in the number of bear depredations." Also, in October 1930 the Department of the Interior had issued a press release explaining that "while the bears of Wall Street got fat, their Yellowstone brethren have lacked their usual roly-poly appearance this summer" because of the scarcity of human garbage, which the bears "preferred" to the foods that made up their natural diets. Edwards concluded that Yellowstone's bear population should be regulated to correlate proportionally with the number of rail visitors to the park.[8]

In its way, the Great Depression was affecting the bear situation, and over the next couple of years the park received letters of complaint from visitors that reflected the class differences—and underlying conflict—that were a sign of the times. Specifically, campers who had been bothered by ursine night marauders accused the NPS of favoritism toward the wealthy. In 1933, one visitor wrote that because he could afford only to camp during his trip, rather than stay at one of the park's hotels, he had been awake all night long shooing bears away from his campsite. This statement bespoke the reality that despite Horace Albright's assertions to the contrary, the bear shows most assuredly had not decreased bears' presence in the auto camps to any noticeable degree. Quite the opposite, in fact; the 451 total reported incidents of property damage that year represented a 116 percent increase over the previous year's total. In 1932, one in every 319 visiting parties had property damaged by bears, a good percentage of whom were likely auto campers. The angry writer informed the park's administration that "this fact should be clear: the bears are not wild animals, nor are they tame. They are semi-wild animals who have been transformed by hotel and cabin guests into hungry pests." In a similar letter to Secretary of the Interior Harold Ickes, another unhappy visitor castigated the park for not protecting its campers, and reminded Ickes that the park's Roosevelt Arch didn't proclaim the park to be "'for the benefit of the people who can afford to stay at the Old Faithful Inn.'"[9]

Yellowstone's administration agreed that class differences were contributing to the park's bear problem, but placed the blame on newcomers like those who had written the aforementioned complaint letters rather than on the park's traditional wealthier class of visitors. In a letter to the director dated November 8, 1930, the park's administration had "stated that the bear problem had been accentuated somewhat by the changing class of park visitors. That is, more people are in private cars and more use the campgrounds and housekeeping cabins than in past years, so come into greater contact with the bears."[10]

Roger Toll continued to be reluctant to prevent visitors from feeding bears. In February 1932, he told Joseph Dixon that although it was clear that everyone agreed about some aspects of the bear situation and how to fix it, what was paramount in Yellowstone was not increased visitor safety but continued visitor viewing opportunity:

It seems desirable to have as many bears along the roads as possible. In order to accomplish this result I do not believe we can prohibit feeding along roads. If there is absolutely no feeding along roads the bears will leave the roads and visitors will see few bears, except at feeding grounds. Visitors are not hurt feeding the bears from automobiles, but they do get bitten when they get out of the cars to either feed or photograph the bears. . . . It may be difficult to educate the public to take proper precautions, but I think the main trouble is not through the feeding of the bears, but usually through taking chances in order to secure a good photograph.[11]

Later that year, Chief Ranger George Baggley devised a program for bear control during the upcoming summer. Park managers had recently solicited and received information from officials at other national parks about how they handled their bear problems, including Sequoia, Glacier, Mt. Rainier, and Crater Lake. Crater Lake, they were told, equipped a night watchman with a flamethrower to keep bears away from a campground. Other parks prohibited feeding by employees, shot bears that went where they weren't supposed to, and deployed tear gas at them.[12]

Only a couple of these ideas appealed to Baggley, whose plans did not end up including any use of a flamethrower. Instead, Baggley strongly advocated visitor education. His recommendation that "the use of more prohibitive signs would not seem desirable" seems to indicate that placards of the type that Joseph Dixon had recommended had been erected at various places throughout the park; what exactly they said is not known. Baggley suggested that the park's checking stations could pass out small cards bearing a printed warning or verbally warn every visitor entering the park not to feed the bears, and that visitors spotted near bears should receive further warnings from rangers. He also recommended that all educational lectures include an antifeeding message. "In other words," Baggley wrote, "'Do not feed the bears—they are dangerous' might easily become the watchword of all park people."[13]

In addition to his public education recommendations, Baggley suggested that the park reorganize its system of garbage collection; feed the bears as late in the day as possible; uniformly punish employees who broke the no-feeding rules; kill bears that were destructive, dangerous, or had been crippled by humans (because drugs and "shocking plates" were sometimes used to prevent bears from eating the park's fish stock, maimed bears were apparently not an uncommon sight in the park at the time); and increase efforts to place surplus bears in zoos. In addition, he recommended the use of ammonia-filled pyrene guns; smoke bombs; and, in a couple of cases, dogs for aversive conditioning. Baggley advocated that dangerous and destructive bears be killed only when absolutely necessary, that authority to dispose of them must come from the park superintendent or chief ranger, and that such actions should occur far out of the public eye.[14]

Baggley began his report by admitting his hesitation "about expressing my opinion, especially so when my ideas are not in perfect accord with men who are older and far more experienced with bears than I"; indeed, his ideas were met with palpable administrative resistance and defensiveness. In a May 24 memo, Guy Edwards, again the park's acting superintendent, squelched Baggley's recommendation that the bears be fed as late in the evening as possible (in order to discourage them from raiding campgrounds at night) on the grounds that the park's concessioner had already complained that the bear shows and lectures were held "too late." He also vetoed Baggley's idea of passing out cards, as "the Sanitary Department will be busy picking them up." Instead he suggested stamping *"DO NOT FEED BEARS"* onto the park's broadsides.[15]

Edwards's comments indicate a general reluctance to change anything at all. Rather than having an important message conveyed by a ranger and on a card devoted exclusively to that purpose, visitors would simply read a message stamped onto something else. The problem was that stamping a message onto the broadsides wasn't that different from what was already being done. At a higher level of review, Senior Assistant Director Arthur Demaray echoed Edwards's concern about inconveniencing the park's concessioner and worried about the costs of implementing Baggley's ideas.[16]

Director Albright, in response to Baggley's report, turned the discussion from the practical to the theoretical. Although the park's 1926 broadside had already warned people that bears were dangerous, Albright had apparently decided that the park's message should now be different: "Constantly warn[ing] tourists . . . 'Do not feed the bears—they are dangerous' will tend to frighten people and interfere with their enjoyment of the park. . . . It would be better just to say, 'Do not feed the bears' or 'Feeding of bears is prohibited.' . . . Then when there is an opportunity to explain why feeding the bears is dangerous the word 'dangerous' could be used. We have got to be careful that we do not give the public generally the feeling that it is dangerous to travel in Yellowstone Park."[17]

Albright's reluctance to fully inform the public of the dangers of handfeeding may have reflected a lasting fear that a decline in the number of visitors would lead to the parks' demise. Though visits to Yellowstone would begin to climb again following the election of Franklin Roosevelt, they had dropped almost 30 percent from 1931 to 1932. In a 1937 letter to the Wildlife Division's Victor Cahalane, William Finley, a vice president of the General Wildlife Federation who carried on an extensive correspondence with the NPS's Wildlife Division in regard to bear depredations and controls, claimed that "years ago . . . Albright told me that when a person was injured by a bear he kept the matter as quiet as possible . . . if people knew of these things it was liable to discourage them from coming into the park." Many years later Cahalane himself wrote to then park biologist Mary Meagher that in the past Yellowstone's superintendent's office had ordered park staff to "never tell any visitor that the bears are dangerous. We do not want our guests to be disturbed."[18]

Whether or not he believed that bear feeding was problematic, there is further evidence that Albright was clearly aware that feeding and its consequences had become a serious public relations dilemma. In December 1930, the director circulated a memo among his superintendents ordering them to destroy all visual evidence in their possession that people fed bears in the national parks (ironically, of course, many of these were photos of Albright himself feeding the bears). Many such images survived, but subsequent correspondence from various park officials does show a general administrative purging of photographs, negatives, lantern slides, and motion-picture film, which not only had the effect of diluting the historical record but also frustrated the desires of magazine reporters and other culture-makers who wished to illustrate their projects. The purging was purported to be necessary because "the feeding of the park bears by visitors is strictly against the regulations and we must back our printed instructions by putting out of circulation pictures giving the idea that it is safe to feed these animals."[19] One might think the director would also have instructed park managers to start backing those printed instructions in practice. In the absence of any such directive, however, the destruction of images fitted the established pattern of appearing to address the problem without really doing it.

In September 1932, Superintendent Toll proposed a "general program" for managing bears during the 1933 season to George Wright (founder and chief of the Wildlife Division). Toll's program had two primary goals: to ensure that grizzly bears did not outcompete black bears at the park's feeding grounds, and to reduce the amount of annoyance that bears caused to humans while continuing to ensure visitors' entertainment. Concerned that the reduced supply of garbage at the park's dumps was insufficient even to feed grizzly bears, let alone black bears, Toll suggested that the park should "dispose of" one-third of its grizzlies by shipping them to zoos or museums. The black bear population should be reduced by disposing of destructive bears—that is, "the criminal element." He also proposed that any considerable bear population in the vicinity of Fishing Bridge, Lake, Thumb, or Mammoth was unnecessary because no bear feeding would be performed at those points, and eliminating bears from those areas would minimize annoyance to campers. In essence, Toll seemed to feel that the presence of bears in the absence of spectators was superfluous, and that the "surplus" bears at those locations should therefore be removed.

Toll concluded that his program would fulfill the NPS's desired goal of maintaining a bear population that was "approximately normal for the area under natural conditions." His program for 1933 focused on teaching bears, rather than people, how to behave. Toll worried that there was still an "urgent need of finding some way to impress upon the bear population the fact that they are not wanted in the public camp grounds. . . . If you [Wright] have any ideas on this subject, I should be glad to receive them."[20]

Although Dixon had suggested that Yellowstone had a "surplus" of bears whose population should probably be reduced, it does not appear that Wright went along with Toll's ideas for systematic reduction of the bear population. Instead, he urged the park to try to change the behavior of people rather than bears. In the summer of 1934, Wright, who acknowledged the value of the bear shows as educational tools and pleasure providers, recommended that the standing regulation, which specifically prohibited "feeding directly from the hand, touching, teasing or molesting of bears," be changed to simply prohibit any "feeding, touching, teasing, or molesting" of bears. In a July letter to new NPS director Arno Cammerer (Albright departed in 1933 to join the United States Potash Company), Superintendent Toll expressed his belief that visitors who simply stayed in their cars and fed the bears were in no danger, as well as his fear that if the bears were not fed at the roadsides, then visitors would be unable to see them. Accordingly, Toll suggested that the regulation be changed to read, "'Feeding of bears in campgrounds and populated areas is prohibited; feeding directly from the hand, touching, teasing or molesting of bears is prohibited.'" In September, he reiterated this suggestion and claimed that "the only change suggested in the Rules and Regulations . . . is one . . . suggested by the Wildlife Division. It is proposed to change the regulations . . . so as to read somewhat as follows: 'Feeding from the hand, touching, teasing, or molesting bears is prohibited: any feeding of bears in campgrounds and populated areas is prohibited.'"[21]

Whether due to misinterpretation or misrepresentation, Toll's version of the new regulation bore little resemblance to Wright's, and its clear ambivalence in regard to the act of feeding led Cammerer to wonder, in a note typed onto the bottom of Toll's missive, why the NPS should allow feeding of bears at all: "Wouldn't it be better to word this something like this: 'Feeding, touching, teasing or molesting bears is dangerous and therefore strictly prohibited.' This would give the necessary general prohibition, and at the same time call attention to the purpose of the order which is because the bears are dangerous under those conditions."[22]

All of this epistolary wrangling over exactly which sorts of behaviors should and should not be allowed represented more than semantic disagreement. It indicated a growing power struggle between two forms of national park preservation—the old-style aesthetic conservation established by Albright and Mather and carried out by Toll and the new, science-based ideas about "natural conditions" espoused by Cammerer and the Wildlife Division. Although Horace Albright had supported the creation of the Wildlife Division, he did not always prove to be an advocate for its recommendations, which sometimes conflicted with his ideas about how and to what ends the parks should be managed.[23] After his 1933 retirement, Albright remained an influential fixture in the agency until the end of his life, and over the years he displayed vituperative reactions to any policy changes that had the effect of reducing visitor opportunity to see and interact with wildlife.

By the end of Roger Toll's superintendency, the park's broadside demonstrated either a curious compromise or an unintentional ambivalence about bear feeding. Printed on the first page of the 1936 version was Toll's wording of the no-feeding regulation: "Bears: It is unlawful and extremely dangerous to molest, tease, or touch bears. Feeding of bears in camp grounds and populated areas is prohibited. If you feed or photograph them, you do so at your own risk and peril."[24] Inside, the guide warned visitors specifically against the dangers of grizzly (dump) bears and prohibited their feeding entirely, but left the legality of feeding black (roadside) bears ambiguous.

Despite the Wildlife Division's continued suggestions that Yellowstone help solve the bear problem by changing visitor behavior and garbage disposal procedures, park managers continued to focus on trying to teach bears to play by the "rules." When the number of bear-related injuries among visitors, which had dropped from 78 to 22 in 1931–1933, rose to 36 by the end of the 1935 season, George Wright noted the increase in a letter to Toll. In response, Toll expressed his desire to find a way to encourage the bears to visit the roadsides and the feeding grounds but to prevent them from entering the park's "city limits," that is, campgrounds and residence areas. Toll proposed that the NPS simply kill all bears that entered developed areas or other forbidden zones. Wright responded with what by that point may have been a studied degree of caution, asking for greater detail and expressing concern that the NPS would run the danger of "too great a reduction in the bear population" if Toll's plan were enacted.[25]

Tragically, and probably to the detriment of efforts to improve Yellowstone's bear situation, Roger Toll and George Wright were killed in an auto accident near Deming, New Mexico, in February 1936, leaving both the park and the Wildlife Division without leadership. The bear problem aside, Toll had been a strong, innovative advocate of resource preservation in Yellowstone; had he lived, historian Aubrey Haines felt that Toll likely would have been director of the NPS one day.[26]

The summer of 1937 brought a 270 percent increase in the number of reported bear-related injuries over the previous season: there were 115 reported injuries that year, a new record. The signage campaign seemed to be ineffective, and in October of that year the Wildlife Division was still recommending that the park's informational circulars "cut out entirely the reference to feeding from the hand," indicating that the park's administration still had not adopted that suggestion.[27]

Meanwhile, the NPS was receiving letters pointing out the inconsistency in the park's own actions regarding bear feeding. Specifically, if it was wrong for visitors to feed black bears along the roadsides, then why was the NPS still feeding grizzlies at the feeding grounds? Perhaps wanting to know the answer himself, new Wildlife Division chief Victor Cahalane forwarded this inquiry to NPS assistant director H. C. Bryant. Bryant was forced to explain that the practice did, indeed, infringe upon the NPS's general wildlife policy and had just sort of "grown up."[28] The park's policies were resulting in stagnation rather than improvement of the situation, and tension rose between old and new ideas about conservation and even about what constituted the park's natural conditions. Change was necessary, and it was coming, if incrementally.

Edmund Rogers succeeded Roger Toll from 1936 to 1956. Although his twenty-one years at the park's helm still make him Yellowstone's longest-tenured superintendent, the dates of Rogers's superintendency doomed him to relative obscurity. With visitation reaching a nadir of 64,144 in 1943, and the NPS in general stripped down to bare-bones staffing, historians have sometimes tended to assume that little of consequence happened in the parks during the war years. As a result, vital management decisions have occasionally been overlooked. The low profile of the NPS during that era opened the door for some extraordinary philosophical and managerial changes, especially when it came to bears and people in Yellowstone. Edmund Rogers was at the forefront of those changes.

Rogers inherited the issue of whether and how to police bear feeders. He personally believed that feeding should be prohibited in all instances except at the park-sponsored feeding grounds, but opposed enforcement due to its expense. In December 1937, Rogers told NPS director Cammerer that in the midst of the Depression, the park was having trouble enough dealing with the arrests it had to make for other reasons. He also explained that enforcing the bear feeding regulation would be emotionally problematic because feeders felt they were doing bears an act of kindness in such troubled times. Finally, Rogers pointed out that crowds assembled at "bear jams" tended to "get caustic" with rangers who tried to get the lanes moving, and concluded that enforcement would be unpopular because in Yellowstone everyone from regular citizens to presidential parties wanted to feed a bear sooner or later.[29]

In March 1938, however, Rogers received a letter from Director Cammerer indicating that Secretary of the Interior Harold L. Ickes had approved a systemwide regulation forbidding the public to feed bears in any manner.[30] Declaring, "It is now up to the Service to do its part in acquainting park visitors with this prohibition," Cammerer outlined his plans for succeeding in the difficult task ahead: convincing the public to reconceive its notions of what to expect from the bears of Yellowstone.

The first task was to get visitors to change their behavior. Cammerer proposed to accomplish this objective by "initiating a publicity campaign stressing the desirability and necessity of treating the wild animals in the parks as such." He recognized that getting people to abandon feeding would mean getting them to change their perceptions and attitudes about bears, and ambitiously proposed that the NPS reteach visitors how, literally and conceptually, to see them: "There is a need for a gradual education of the public away from the idea of a staged show and toward a better appreciation of animals observed in natural conditions. . . . It has been suggested that an appeal to a photographer's sporting instincts would be useful here; that is, point out how much more pride he would have in a photograph attained with difficulty in natural surroundings as against a photograph taken of a bear eating candy which could just as well be duplicated in any city zoo."[31] In essence, Cammerer advocated two things: an attempt to influence the imagery disseminated outside the national parks, and the promotion of a new visual aesthetic encouraging visitors and photographers to appreciate animals in their natural surroundings and embrace the fruits of hard-won efforts *because* they were hard-won.

Although Cammerer's ideas would undoubtedly prove challenging to implement, they made sense to Rogers. By that summer, a vigorous education campaign was in place to teach visitors to stay away from bears. Of course, the results were not immediate. On July 20, 1938, the park announced that a record thirty-four people had thus far reported receiving injuries from bears, four of which occurred when people got too close while trying to photograph the bears. Even to publicize bear injuries was a departure from past practices, but Rogers went further, promising to enforce the park's no-feeding regulations. That week all entrance permits and accompanying literature were stamped, "FEEDING BEARS IS PROHIBITED."[32] However, little evidence exists to show that the rules were actually enforced in any meaningful fashion.

Although the NPS's Wildlife Division was short-lived (its biologists were transferred to the Bureau of Biological Survey in 1940), its influence, in conjunction with progressive changes in the NPS's Office of the Director relative to conservation, was great. Historian James A. Pritchard wrote that the Wildlife Division made four main contributions to attitude changes and ecological understanding in the NPS: (1) its assessment of wildlife problems in the parks, (2) its creation of the first clearly stated policies and rationale for wildlife management in the parks, (3) its introduction of elements of ecological thinking into that rationale and recognition of a role for natural processes in park management, and (4) its statements about the purpose of the parks and the relationships between wildlife and park visitors.[33] The division's influence was clearly apparent when, in November 1939, Director Cammerer, along with Ira Gabrielson, chief of the Bureau of Biological Survey, sent to Secretary Ickes a memorandum outlining a set of policy principles for NPS wildlife management that, if embraced, would set the stage for big changes throughout the agency. Several of those points seemed to specifically address the bear situation in Yellowstone; Yellowstone's bears, which in the recent past had been accused of being "on the dole," were soon to be weaned off it:

- No management measure or other interference with biotic relationships shall be undertaken prior to a properly conducted investigation.
- Every species shall be left to carry on its struggle for existence unaided, as being to its greatest ultimate good, unless there is real cause to believe that it will perish if unassisted.
- Where artificial feeding, control of natural enemies, or other protective measures, are necessary to save a species that is unable to cope with civilization's influence, every effort shall be made to place that species on

a self-sustaining basis once more; whence these artificial aids, which themselves have unfortunate consequences, will no longer be needed.

- Presentation of the animal life of the parks to the public shall be a wholly natural one.
- No animal shall be encouraged to become dependent upon man for its support.
- Problems of injury to the persons of visitors or to their property or to the special interests of man in the park, shall be solved by methods other than those involving the killing of the animals or interfering with their normal relationships, where this is at all practicable.[34]

In August of the following year, Cammerer resigned as NPS director due to illness. He was succeeded by Newton Drury, a former executive secretary of the preservationist Save-the-Redwoods League who would devote much of his energy as director to preventing national park resources from being commandeered for the war effort. Influenced by the growing wilderness movement and building upon the ideas proposed by Cammerer and the Wildlife Division, Drury and Edmund Rogers started to rethink the NPS's purpose regarding wildlife and visitors. Where Albright had felt that the NPS had a duty to present wildlife as a spectacle, Drury interpreted his duty to preserve "natural conditions" differently, and a bit more literally. One of the first orders of business under his administration was to close Yellowstone's last remaining bear feeding ground, Otter Creek.

With its concrete feeding stage and log seating for 250 spectators, the Otter Creek feeding facility was a monument to Horace Albright's guiding philosophy of aesthetic conservation in Yellowstone. But NPS officials had wanted to close Otter Creek since the late 1930s, and by the summer of 1940, managers in other national parks were complaining that the continued operations at Otter Creek were generating complaints from visitors to parks that had already eliminated their bear shows.[35] The problem was that the Otter Creek shows were still wildly popular with the park's visitors and its main concessioner, which transported visitors to and from the shows.

After the end of the 1941 summer season, neither the NPS nor its visitors knew for certain that Yellowstone had staged its final formal bear show. The December 7 Japanese attack on Pearl Harbor, however, changed everything in the United States. In Yellowstone, its results included a personnel shortage, closure of some of the park's visitor facilities, and an expectation of slight visitation in the summer of 1942.[36] It was the perfect time to end the feeding shows for good.

The park's announcement in the spring of 1942 that it would not reopen Otter Creek for feeding shows was immediately opposed by park concessioner William Nichols, who had counted the shows among the Canyon area's chief attractions. With a push from the NPS's Washington office, however, Nichols's spirit of patriotism ultimately prevailed over his quest for profit. At a meeting between Nichols, NPS officials, and the director of the Office of Defense Transportation, it was agreed that all sightseeing trips in the national parks, including Nichols's trips to the feeding grounds, would be eliminated that summer because of gasoline rationing. With Nichols on board, the closure became a reality. Garbage that would previously have been deposited at Otter Creek was either incinerated or dumped at several areas out of public view.[37]

Park officials were not so naïve as to believe that the grizzlies who frequented Otter Creek would simply understand that they were no longer wanted there and go away. Experience had taught that bears became habituated to human foods very quickly and easily, and that once habituation occurred it was exceedingly difficult, if not impossible, to undo. It was anticipated that bears might seek food from alternative human sources located nearby and increase their presence in the campgrounds and other developed areas. Drury asked Rogers to keep him apprised of such incidents and to monitor the bears' dispersal as well as any adverse effects that the sudden cessation of feeding might have on their population. He also counted on the superintendent to "use ingenuity whenever possible to avoid shooting troublesome bears." In the preceding eleven years, 354 Yellowstone bears had been removed from the park in "control actions," a euphemism for "killed by rangers" that the NPS had started using in 1939 "to avoid the appearance of slaughter."[38]

As expected, visitation in the summer of 1942 (191,830) decreased 68 percent from what it had been in 1941. The number of bear-related injuries (29) showed a proportionate drop. Perhaps in response to the dump closure, however, the number of incidents of property damage *increased* from 102 in 1941 to 118 in 1942, representing an increase of 72 percent when placed in the context of the 68 percent drop in visitation. Per Drury's instructions, Rogers submitted a preliminary report of bear incidents for the 1942 season on August 20. By that time, the park had responded with a 242 percent increase in the number of bears killed in control actions compared to the previous year, perhaps giving rise to the question of how much ingenuity the rangers were using regarding Drury's request for restraint. Rangers had killed 63 bears by August 20, compared to the previous year's *total* of 26. Rogers specified that

21 of those killed were grizzlies, 6 of which were shot at Canyon (near Otter Creek), but offered no explanation for his rangers' having killed more bears in a single season than had been killed since 1935.[39]

On August 23, three days after Rogers submitted his preliminary report to Drury, visitor Martha Hansen, a forty-five-year-old nurse from Twin Falls, Idaho, left her cabin at Old Faithful about 1:45 A.M. to make a trip to the lavatory. According to varying reports, Hansen was either attacked from in front or from behind, by a black bear or by a grizzly. The results were the same: She died five days later from the severe mauling.[40]

Soon after the incident, Ellen Hansen, Martha's sister, sought reimbursement from the NPS for the expenses her family had incurred in caring for her dying sister. Visitors had been filing reimbursement claims for bear-related medical costs and property damage for decades—always unsuccessfully—and so Lawrence Merriam, NPS director for Region 2 (which included Yellowstone), responded to Ellen Hansen with what sounded like a fairly standard letter explaining that although he was sorry about her sister, all funds appropriated by Congress were designated for specific purposes, and those purposes did not include paying legal claims. Merriam's lesson in federal budgetry failed to convince Ellen Hansen, and she eventually succeeded in obtaining recompense in 1944, when President Roosevelt signed a bill whose rider granted her family $1,894.95 in damages for the death of Martha Hansen.[41]

On the list of problems created for the NPS by Martha Hansen's death, Ellen Hansen's $1,895 was very near the bottom, although the notion that the NPS could be held financially liable for costs incurred as the result of bear misbehavior almost certainly alarmed park managers. The death itself was a public relations and political nightmare and, based on the events that followed, raised the "bear problem" to an unprecedented level of urgency. The gruesome death of a woman answering nature's midnight call couldn't be explained away as the result of her own foolish desire to get too close to a bear, or as one of the simply unavoidable by-products of the park's normally commendable goal of providing visitors with the opportunity to see wild bears (though Merriam tried this latter tack with Ellen Hansen). It blew a hole through the fiction that bears and people could peaceably coexist on common ground while on a common diet if both would only behave themselves, and it was traumatic enough to require action. Twenty bears were killed between August 20, when Rogers had submitted his preliminary report, and the end of the 1942 tourist season one month later, for a seasonal total of 83, the highest in park history to that date. Fifty-five black bears and 28 grizzlies were killed that summer.[42]

Martha Hansen's death also served as the catalyst for a series of reevaluations of the park's bear management policies, though there was little consensus about what exactly should be done. In a confidential memo to Superintendent Rogers, Regional Director Merriam dismissed out of hand several "less drastic" measures such as electric fences, improved visitor education, and relocation of offending bears, and instead zeroed in on "controlling"—that is, killing—bears, arguing that as visitation continued to fall, as expected during the war, rangers would have more time to devote to bear control operations. Merriam's idea was that making the older generation of bears suffer for their offenses would deter the younger generation from following in their footsteps. He was aware, however, that such wanton killing would be unpopular with the public, and so advocated secrecy: "In the spring of the year . . . before the general public arrives, a 'scare campaign' . . . should be initiated in an endeavor to cause bears to fear human beings. Torture methods are not advocated but anything short of that should be tried. The incurables should then be trapped and disposed of as quietly as possible, the object being to instill a fear of human beings . . . as well as reduce the bear population which is probably the major contributing factor to the current bear problem."[43]

Merriam's recommendations demonstrated adherence to long-established policies that identified the bears themselves as being the primary problem to be attacked, rather than the set of human behaviors and institutions that had grown up around them and influenced their behavior. His focus on overpopulation as the root of the problem was also shaky, as bears are notoriously difficult to count due to their sleep patterns and preference for edge habitats. Getting an accurate number was particularly difficult in the days before aerial population monitoring, when rangers had to rely on ground sightings to provide approximate bear numbers and trust their own ability to recognize pelage and other identifying marks in order to avoid counting the same bear multiple times.

In a response to Merriam, Director Drury acknowledged that the situation was critical but also cautioned that although the possibility that the park had excessive numbers of bears should be investigated further, "the wildlife technicians" examining the issue doubted that overpopulation was the reason why bear-related injuries continued to persist. The problem was more likely systemic. Drury also made it clear that he desired to study the situation carefully rather than embark on a hasty campaign of pain and slaughter, and asked Merriam for a complete report and evaluation of the measures that had been taken thus far to protect visitors from bears, including reductions in artificial feeding, removal of bears from areas of human concentration, visitor education, warning signs, ranger patrols, and elimination of problem bears.[44]

One nonlethal suggestion that started to gain popularity was a plan to erect fences around the park's campgrounds. Campers had been suggesting the fence idea since at least 1931; in 1932, Roger Toll had received a petition signed by eighty-seven campers at the Fishing Bridge campground asking him to either dispose of the bears raiding the campground, "reserving a few for exhibition purposes," or fence the campground. The idea had been consistently rejected on the grounds that such an enclosure would be expensive, unsightly, unnatural, confining, and frightening by implication to visitors who might think they were unsafe when outside it. Just as the administration had been hesitant to warn people that feeding the bears was dangerous, so was it reluctant to establish the appearance of safe and unsafe zones within the park. The Wildlife Division was opposed to the idea in principle but periodically acknowledged the fence as a possible solution to campground problems.[45]

Despite this apparent lack of enthusiasm, the National Archives include a map of the Fishing Bridge area, dated January 1, 1939, upon which the outline of a proposed fence was drawn in red pencil by an employee of the NPS's Branch of Plans and Design. The proposed enclosure would have surrounded not just the campground but the entire developed area at Fishing Bridge. With Pelican Creek forming a natural border on the south, the fence would extend approximately one thousand feet north to surround the area's incinerator and one thousand feet to the east of the developed area. The design included four road gates and three hand gates that could be opened to provide human passage in and out of the fence's confines.[46] In theory, these gates could be used as outlets for errant bears that might somehow breach the barrier and find themselves stuck on the inside. However, the specter of a panicked, enraged grizzly bear charging up and down the chain-link, searching frantically for a way out, ultimately proved to be another major argument against the enclosure's construction.

Martha Hansen's death gave prolonged life to the fence idea. Though Merriam initially rejected it in favor of his "scare campaign," Superintendent Rogers included fencing for long-term consideration in his bear management action plan for the 1943 season. By the spring of 1945, project construction proposal M-44, for a fence around the campground at Fishing Bridge, went out for comment from NPS staff.[47]

Some still disapproved of the idea. Drawing on recent horrors on the world scale, one employee stated that fencing a campground would be tantamount to confining visitors in "concentration camp stockades." Ironically, given the context of his allusion, he suggested that the NPS try new, more torturous forms of deterrence. Bears could be "stabbed with a goad, lashed with a bull whip, sprayed in the eyes with ammonia, turpentined you-know-where, or given a whiff of some chemical which made breathing difficult, or produced sneezing" each time they came in contact with a ranger, in order to instill a fear of people in them over the course of two or so generations. Rather than acquiesce to repeated suggestions that bears be taught to associate the sight of humans with intense physical pain, Victor Cahalane, who collected the comments and was a reluctant supporter of the fence, recommended that the fence plan be approved by the director and "given detailed study by the Park Superintendent."[48]

When asked to comment on project M-44, the NPS's landscape architects and engineers developed creative design alternatives to make the idea more palatable. One such design called for a fence rigged with a series of trap doors. When a bear approached the fence, a spring would be tripped and the animal would drop into a pit, where it would remain until rangers could come and relocate it (just how the bear would be extracted from the pit was unclear). Acting Chief Engineer A. W. Burney, cognizant of the aesthetic objections to fencing, submitted four drawings of a "dry moat" scheme that could be made attractive and inconspicuous through landscaping.[49]

On October 9, Regional Director Merriam requested a more complete analysis of the conditions that had led up to the fence plan. In a detailed report, Rogers recounted that in order to curb the park's bear problems, the Civilian Conservation Corps had installed experimental bearproof food lockers and garbage cans in one of the campgrounds. The number of garbage collections had been increased to several times daily. Rangers patrolled campgrounds to chase out bears and chased "beggar bears" from roadsides. Visitors had been strongly warned, and a few arrests had been made for especially egregious bear feeding violations. Tear gas and other repellents had been deployed against bears in developed areas, and all NPS feeding of bears had been discontinued. In the end, though, all of those efforts had proven problematic or largely ineffective: Martha Hansen had been killed, and visitors were asking for fenced areas for their own protection.

Rogers proposed the Fishing Bridge area for the fence because it was heavily visited and its physical situation and topography would lend themselves well to the plan. The type of fence suggested was "Cyclone Non-Climbable, using No. 6 gauge wire and 2-inch mesh," six feet high and topped with a foot of barbed wire extending at a 45-degree angle. Where the fence met Yellowstone Lake, removable panels would extend 100–150 feet into the lake, to be removed each winter and reinstalled the following spring. With U.S. Steel providing the materials and building the fence, the project's grand total construction cost was estimated to be $38,863, with annual maintenance costs projected at an additional $3,908.[50]

Although it continued to be discussed over the next few years, the fence project never found enough support to make it viable. In fact, NPS officials were never even able to agree on where it should be built. In 1948, Merriam told Drury that West Thumb would be a better place than Fishing Bridge for the experiment, but those involved were still unable to concur on whether fencing would be anything but an extravagantly expensive short-term solution that would be too geographically specific to make any overall difference. In September 1949, the project was tabled indefinitely in favor of directing the funds it would have required into areas of more urgent need, such as the construction of overnight accommodations. The fence idea never quite went away, and was held in the background as an option even into the 1990s.[51]

As the fence proposal sorted its way through evaluation committees, Superintendent Rogers continued to pursue the innovative, ambitious idea of changing visitor attitudes toward the park's bears. In a 1942 report, Rogers described moderate progress in some areas, but indicated that his biggest problems stemmed from misconceptions about bears that had been planted in the minds of visitors both by their own past experience of watching bears at the feeding grounds and by visual and textual media they encountered outside the park, such as schoolbooks, magazines, newspapers, and children's bear stories. Rogers argued that the combination of these influences inculcated the typical visitor with "erroneous ideas [about the bear], which they do not have concerning other animals," and made it difficult to convince him or her that feeding bears could be dangerous. He suggested that perhaps the park should attempt to introduce its own message into externally produced and disseminated travel literature and try to correct the misinformation that was out there.[52]

Rogers knew, too, that the park needed to revise its own primary message about bears. He felt that for the past decade or so, the park had mistakenly overemphasized the idea that the *act of feeding* bears was dangerous, rather than that *bears* themselves were dangerous.[53] He sought to eliminate the bears' ambivalent image by emphasizing their wild and unpredictable side, thereby eliminating the potential for confusion and changing the sight of people feeding bears into a source of shock rather than appeal. If the NPS could unravel the complex tangle of emotional connections that people had developed with the bear by convincing them that bears were not the "tame," "friendly" creatures visitors had come to believe they were, then the bears' confusing historical duality as both wild and tame should disappear, opposition to enforcement should end, and bear feeding should cease to be a problem as people became disinclined to feed and interact with bears. In theory.

Director Drury seemed to understand that unless the old ambivalence was obliterated, Rogers's ideas wouldn't work. He ordered that signs and literature be revised to acquaint the public "in the plainest terms with the necessity for treating the bears as wild animals," that any public material not conforming to that principle should be discarded, and that his office review all material before its public dissemination. In time for the 1943 season, all park literature provided to the public bore this rubber-stamped message in bold print and red ink:

WARNING

BEARS ARE DANGEROUS WILD ANIMALS.

YOUR SAFETY AND PARK REGULATIONS

PROHIBIT FEEDING, MOLESTING, OR

APPROACHING BEARS.

KEEP A SAFE DISTANCE FROM BEARS[54]

Regional Director Merriam described this warning as brief, to the point, and almost certain to be read by visitors. More important, it was an unequivocal statement, a departure even from assertions that "bears at distance are safe bears; bears fed or fooled are dangerous," as the 1940 broadside had claimed. Now the park's message was that all bears were dangerous, regardless of how humans behaved around them. Visitors also received informational sheets titled "Bears Are Wild Animals" in 1943.[55]

Regardless of these attempts to remake the bears' image and educate visitors, rather than just kill bears, the events of the previous summer had not escaped notice in the larger scientific community. In May 1943, Chief Naturalist C. P. Russell reported that a group of scientists at a conference he had attended had castigated the park for its apparent policy of killing every bear that caused problems, with no knowledge about the bear itself or whether such killing was really an effective deterrent to injury and damage. In response or by coincidence, wildlife biologist Olaus Murie began the first true study of the "life history" of Yellowstone's bears in July of that year.

Murie and his brother Adolph, also a wildlife biologist, were born and raised in turn-of-the-century Moorhead, Minnesota. By the 1920s, both were established scientists who often worked jointly on wildlife studies in national parks under the auspices of both the NPS's Wildlife Division and the Bureau of Biological Survey. Adolph Murie served in the Wildlife Division from 1934 to 1939, and during that time conducted a groundbreaking study of the ecology of the coyote in Yellowstone. He found that coyote predation had only minor effects on ungulate populations, a conclusion that proved influential in the fight to end predator control in the national parks.[56]

The main focus of Olaus Murie's study of Yellowstone's bears was their food habits. He determined, contrary to previous beliefs, that garbage made up but a small percentage of their intake; that even bears that made a habit of raiding campground garbage cans gained only 10 percent of their sustenance through those efforts and acquired the rest of their caloric intake from natural foods. In another contradiction to entrenched belief, Murie found that punishing individual bears for their misdeeds was ineffective, or at least offered no "permanent help." Finally, Murie stressed that in order to understand the life history of the bear, it was necessary not only to observe the habits and mental characteristics of bears but also to understand the habits and characteristics of tourists. Like Rogers, Murie identified part of the bear problem as being that "over a period of years the bears of the Yellowstone have been publicized, not as a wild animal in a wilderness setting, but as a picturesque 'highwayman' begging from automobiles. . . . It seems to me this is conducive to a viewpoint that the bear of the Yellowstone is almost a domestic animal, not to be feared. The bear becomes more or less associated with the humanized Three Bears of nursery days, safe within the covers of a book."[57]

Murie, Rogers, and Drury thought it was time to dispense with the bedtime stories and rid the NPS of the Albrightian assumption that one of its primary duties was "to present wildlife as a spectacle" once and for all. In 1944, Drury requested Victor Cahalane to ask Olaus Murie to ruminate on "the inalienable right assured in some quarters to see at least one bear." In an eloquent missive, Murie averred that "it is a question of whether we are justified in sacrificing some of the main purpose of a park, and endangering lives and property, in order to maintain a special display, furnish cute bear antics, however stimulating this may be to the public." Murie wrote that he had observed visitors who seemed to have become bored with the omnipresent bears, and concluded, "I think the quality of a national park experience can be improved if we do not try to hand the visitor his recreation on a platter, but let him make at least a little exertion to find it . . . and the resulting deeper satisfaction that comes from some form of personal achievement."[58]

If Murie's thoughts evoke Edward Abbey's contention that "a man on foot, on horseback, or on a bicycle will see more, feel more, enjoy more in one mile than the motorized tourists can in a hundred miles," it may be because Murie and Abbey were not all that far apart when it came to their beliefs about recreation and wilderness (if not in the tactics they believed necessary to preserve it). Olaus Murie's relatively purist views about wilderness were a matter of public record by 1944. He had been a key figure in the Wilderness Society since its founding, and was known for his disavowal of "democratic wilderness"; in the late 1930s, he had written, "Wilderness is for those who appreciate," and if "the multitudes" were brought into the backcountry without really understanding its "subtle values," "there would be an insistent and effective demand for more and more facilities, and we would find ourselves losing our wilderness and having these areas reduced to the commonplace"—much as he posited that the bear had been reduced to the commonplace by tourists' overexposure to it.[59]

Drury likely knew, then, what Murie would produce in response to his request: a treatise that supported the park service's recent policy changes and dismissed any obligation to guarantee the public an animal sideshow. Murie accomplished this goal and also echoed Arno Cammerer's suggestions that the NPS try to convince the public that a bear encounter that required some effort was more valuable than one supplied on demand. The success of the new message would necessitate a reformulation of people's ideas about nature—a shift from human-oriented conservation to a "nature-oriented" preservation. Acceptance of the idea that wildlife had the right to live apart from human desires represented a pivotal moment in NPS history—a philosophical and narrative shift from making nature accessible to the people to encouraging visitors to expend some effort to enjoy nature "on its own terms."

Horace Albright came out from retirement with literary guns blazing to oppose the closure of the bear feeding grounds and new efforts to curb roadside feeding. In a public protest published in the April 1945 issue of *The Backlog,* the journal of the Campfire Club, a conservation organization to which Albright, Stephen Mather, and other notable conservationists of the era belonged, he wrote that the new policies would mean "the ultimate total deprivation of the public from a sight of the best loved park animal."[60]

Albright had already told Newton Drury that what irked him about Olaus Murie and his ideas was that Murie seemed not to worry about the desires of "the public who like the bears . . . much more than the geysers." "Murie knows mighty little about the traveling public," Albright wrote, "and apparently is not particularly concerned about whether the public enjoys the parks or not."

In spite of Murie's scientific findings and all the reasons NPS management had identified as just cause for major policy changes, Albright argued, "I cannot see why the public cannot have access to one or two big feeding grounds where they can see both black bears and grizzlies, photograph them, and enjoy their funny antics and be safe." He also pointed out that during his superintendency, an average of two hundred people annually had been bitten by bears to no significant negative effect. Albright objected to wildlife policies that encouraged animals to return to their "natural" states, and warned that the park would suffer severe public relations problems with visitors and its surrounding state governments if it did not reinstate feeding.[61]

Without mentioning any names, Albright used his *Backlog* article to take careful aim at NPS administrators who he felt were listening too closely to the advice of wilderness advocates such as Murie when they made management decisions. In "New Orders for Bears," he pleaded for a democratic approach to conservation in the face of what he saw as an exclusionary turn in NPS thinking. While Murie contended that a visitor's experience with an animal would be more meaningful if he or she expended some effort to have a look at it, Albright adamantly felt that the national parks were no place to be experimenting with the wilderness ethic as a guiding managerial strategy: "Not all park visitors can see bears along the roads. This does not disturb the scientific group. They think that if a person wants to see a bear he should go out into the wilds and find one, and then he would see a bear as a child of Nature and be vastly more thrilled and inspired by such a spectacle than to observe one near a highway. . . . The traveling public . . . has every right to see [bears] . . . and if those rights are denied them the reaction against the National Park Service will be seriously detrimental."[62] Albright also retold the story of "the lady who lost her dress," reiterated his claim that people were proud of their bear-inflicted scars, and downplayed the number of bears to be seen at park roadsides.

It should be noted, of course, that Albright was not opposed to wilderness—Donald Swain even titled his biography of Albright *Wilderness Defender*. What bothered Albright was the idea of the national parks being reserved and managed for such a purpose. In his view, the needs and desires of the public should not be sacrificed for the sake of what the ecologists defined as a "purer" nature: "The special group of naturalists who apparently have gained a position of leadership in policy-making are mainly ecologists at heart if not by training. They are chiefly interested in the relationships of animals to their environment and the maintenance of what they regard as purely natural conditions, regardless of what interests the national park visitor."[63]

The tension between aesthetic conservation and wilderness approaches to national park management were most evident when Albright wistfully described the feeding grounds: "It was a great sight to stand above the feeding grounds and watch the bears of both species feeding, cuffing each other, mothers sending cubs up trees, a coyote sneaking in to get a snack, gulls flying about looking for chances to dive in for a share of the provender. . . . Why should this show not go on?" Here, it is clear that for Albright, the evening entertainment at the bear feeding grounds—compressed interactions to show as many visitors as possible in the shortest amount of time how nature worked—was a far more efficient use of resources than maintenance of "purely natural conditions." At the feeding grounds, the public had been able to observe the interactions and behaviors of no fewer than four species at different hierarchical levels in the food chain on a nightly basis (black and grizzly bears, coyotes, and seagulls), all accompanied by educational interpretation by park personnel.[64] Never mind wildlife as spectacle; to Albright's way of thinking, this was ecology as spectacle, served up for a crowd in a manageable amount of time in an accessible space. The people enjoyed themselves and learned something, the bears got fed and stayed away from the campgrounds as a result (according to Albright), the garbage went away, and all it took was a big pile of bear bait. Why throw away one of the park's most valuable resources (the pleasure and experience afforded by bears) and provoke public anger for the sake of a newly emerging abstract ideal of a far less tenable nature?

Newton Drury and Edmund Rogers, however, had had enough of trying to salve bear bites with anecdotes. A woman was dead, the NPS was being sued over it, and ecology taught that the natural world was a series of interconnections that might work just as well in the absence of active human intervention—and that the national parks might be ideal places to see nature in action. Parks, they believed, ought to be wild areas, not circuses or zoos where people went to view the humanized "antics" of animals. Thus, the dumps stayed closed and efforts to wean bears from campground garbage and roadside feeding continued. So did Albright's protestations.

In the minds of many visitors returning to the park after World War II, Yellowstone likely existed just as it had before the Depression, when the park operated a zoo and feeding grounds and had tacitly encouraged roadside feeding. Drury and Rogers knew they would have to make a special effort to convince returning crowds that not feeding the bears was a positive change. Fearful that members of the public would be both outraged to discover the feeding grounds closed and excited to feed bears themselves, they planned to intensify educational efforts to "correct" nursery and fairy-tale images that perpetuated an old-style narrative of the Yellowstone bear.

One significant and uncommonly correctible source of irritation was the Union Pacific Railroad's annual schedule circulars, a fantastic, colorful series that had been designed for decades by Walter Oehrle. The brochures typically showed anthropomorphized bears engaging in various human activities. In fact, Oehrle created his pictures by drawing humans where the bears would soon be, then adding bearlike characteristics to the figures. It was the 1946 circular that caused particular trouble. The bears were shown preparing the park for the postwar renewal of rail service, and a passel of happy bears greeted the summer's first train to West Yellowstone, Montana, welcoming tourists with shouts of "Welcome Back!" Although the rail lines may have been relieved to return to business as usual, the usual business was not what NPS officials were hoping for when it came to bears and people in Yellowstone. Acting Director Hillory Tolson requested that Regional Director Lawrence Merriam urge the UP to modify its message: "We hope that special attention may be devoted by the Yellowstone Park staff to correcting the unfortunate impression which has been given by the Union Pacific Railroad publicity that the tourists should expect to renew convivial relations with the 'friendly' Yellowstone bears, which relationship was interrupted by the war."[65] The UP continued to produce the Oehrle circulars until 1960, but never again depicted tourists and bears in such close concert.

In terms of changing visitors' ways of seeing bears, NPS managers also decided that stopping the bear feeding shows was not enough; rather, the landscape of the feeding grounds needed to be turned back into natural habitat for bears. In September 1944, Director Drury expressed his feeling to Secretary Ickes that the Canyon bear show, which had been the last in the national park system, had displayed bears in an entirely unnatural manner. Drury believed the practice had clearly violated the NPS Organic Act as well as the wildlife policy established by Director Cammerer in 1939, stating that presentation of animal life in parks to the public should be wholly natural. In light of this legacy, the Otter Creek bear feeding grounds, Drury believed, should be removed and the area relandscaped. A plan to demolish the feeding grounds, and thus erase the evidence of NPS-sanctioned feeding from the park landscape, was recommended to Director Drury on September 26, 1945, by Regional Director Merriam, who deemed it to be of such importance that he wanted the project completed before the 1946 season in spite of shortages of funding and staffing. On October 4, Drury responded that Merriam should arrange with Superintendent Rogers to "obliterate, so far as possible, all developments pertaining to the feeding of bears at the Canyon feeding area at the earliest possible date."[66]

Park officials agreed not to issue a press release notifying the public of these plans, or of concurrent plans to remove all directional signs relating to the Antelope Creek buffalo pasture, whose previous inhabitants now freely roamed the park. Anyone who inquired about the absence of these former landmarks was simply to be informed that the areas were no longer being used for their earlier purposes. In late May 1946, with the feeding grounds already in a deteriorated state from five years' disuse and neglect, park personnel removed fencing, guard rails, signs, the stairways leading to the area's log seats (also removed), a retaining wall, two pit toilets, and the small building where water had been heated for hosing down the concrete feeding pad each night. Removal of the pad itself was postponed until drier weather would permit bulldozer operations; it is still visible today.[67]

The razing of the Otter Creek feeding grounds placed a palpable strain on what had historically been a congenial relationship between Director Drury and former director Horace Albright. Drury had notified Albright of the plans to demolish the facility in October 1945. In November, in response to Albright's apparently negative and accusatory reply, Drury demonstrated that his tolerance for Albright's continual public and private criticism of the park's new wildlife policies had reached its limit, telling him, "Maybe we are wrong, and should have temporized longer, but I 'have to call 'em as I see them,' and take the consequences. . . . In any event, Supt. Rogers assures me that if there is a reversal of the present policy, he would recommend the feeding grounds on another site."[68] Given the unlikelihood of a "reversal of the present policy," it is hardly surprising that Albright was upset to hear about the demolition of Otter Creek.

Because he had been largely responsible for shaping the agency and its ideals, the NPS's sudden eagerness to erase the traces of his philosophical legacy may have hurt Albright personally and deeply. The razing obliterated the ultimate monument to his style of aesthetic conservation, in which park officials had actively helped to sustain the lives of bears while serving them up for human entertainment. The destruction of the Otter Creek facility represented more than a desire for the new picnic ground that replaced it: it signified the NPS's resolve not to return to the old ways of thinking about itself and its duties to the public.

Just in case there was any doubt that the NPS had done the right thing, the agency solicited comments from scholars and environmental leaders from around the nation in December 1945 about the closure of the feeding grounds. A year later, Drury wrote to A. T. Wilcox of the Michigan State College, "Throughout the year 1946 this Office did not receive a single protest against this policy, nor a request that the feeding of bears be resumed. . . . This dearth of audible signs of nostalgia has surprised us." However, researcher William Sanborn, in his 1947 dissertation on the park's educational program, found that "great numbers of visitors express disappointment that the bears are no longer fed by the Service." Later that season, the park's biologist stated that law enforcement rangers were having a hard time preventing visitors from skirting barricades and gathering at the still existing dump grounds (the public viewings had ended, but the park continued to use open-pit dumps for trash disposal until the early 1970s) in order to watch the grizzlies that still went there to feed, thereby creating their own unsanctioned bear shows. Efforts to stifle these "informal bear shows" were perpetually ineffectual, and they continued at least into the 1960s.[69]

Through visitor education, the park also continued to focus on its own message to help solve its "bear problem." In the late 1940s, the NPS's communications war chest included press releases and local newspaper stories, written by employees, about how feeding bears was dangerous to both bears and tourists. Officials also placed the Naturalist Division (formerly the Educational Division) in charge of a collection of "pictures of the type we like to have published."[70] In 1947, drawings of bears interacting with people were replaced in the park's broadside by a photograph of a black bear staring back at the camera from a spot at the forest's edge in a manner consistent with Rogers's desire to remake the ambiguously natured bear into a wild animal.

Superintendent Rogers's plans for dealing with the park's bear problem during the summer of 1951 included enforcing the no-feeding regulation among the park's employees, fencing the rear of the park's food establishments, continuing to trap troublesome bears, and undertaking a "more vigorous policy of prosecuting" visitors who flagrantly fed the bears. Complete enforcement was deemed logistically impossible for the time being; Rogers intended to formulate further enforcement plans after seeing how the season went.

Visitor education and reinforcement of the "Bears Are Wild Animals" theme were also important elements of the plans for 1951. To support his plans for improved enforcement, Rogers asked for 350,000 copies of a circular titled "For Your Safety" to be printed on four-by-five-inch sheets of red paper (or on white paper with red lettering) for distribution at the park's entrance stations. "For Your Safety," which was used in some version at least through the summer of 1956, asked visitors to "observe strictly the regulation which prohibits FEEDING, TOUCHING, TEASING OR MOLESTING BEARS. This regulation has not been taken as seriously by some visitors as the danger from bears warrants. Please help us, and make action under Federal regulations unnecessary, by observing this regulation throughout your stay in the park." It further admonished that "THERE ARE NO TAME BEARS IN THIS PARK. THEY MAY APPEAR HARMLESS BECAUSE THEY HAVE LOST MOST OF THEIR FEAR OF MAN — BUT THEY ARE ALL WILD AND OFTEN DANGEROUS ANIMALS."[71]

The park also introduced a flyer called "Dangerous," which featured a drawing of an enraged bear waving its front legs in the air and roaring, displaying an impressively enormous set of pointy teeth. This would come to be known as the "horror bear" image. Owing to his longtime recognition that the transient nature of the park's visitors, coupled with their preconceived notions about what to expect from the park's bears, made education difficult, Rogers wished that dissemination of bear warnings could be made on a national basis, but acknowledged that the best the park could do was to try for newspaper and radio coverage in the adjacent states that was favorable to the park's message.[72]

At the start of the 1950s, after more than a decade of hard work and innovation on the part of Superintendent Edmund Rogers, the image of the dangerous bear had arrived in Yellowstone. Its establishment represented the first step toward meaningful change in the heretofore too-close relationship between people and bears in the park, and it was hoped that the new image could be reinforced in the near future with hard-line enforcement of the no-feeding rules. However, like many of the best-laid plans, these would prove easier to put onto paper than into practice.

In 1951, concerned citizen William Wandall sent Superintendent Rogers a comic strip from the *Philadelphia Inquirer* in which "Colonel Potterby and the Duchess" were depicted in the act of befriending a roadside beggar bear. Victor Cahalane contacted the cartoon's artist, Chic Young (creator of the more enduring "Blondie"). Cahalane conceded that Young could not "be expected to know that our rangers are getting prematurely gray over the chances that tourists take with the supposedly tame but actually wild and powerful bears." He suggested the following as a way that Young could mitigate any damage done: "How about giving your public a cartoon which will show some aspect of the real relationship between people and park bears? Following is the text of one of the signs we have posted in Yellowstone . . . it may lead to an idea."[73] Cahalane then reproduced the text of the sign for Young's perusal:

NOTICE TO BEARS
BEWARE OF SABOTAGE

We want to warn you that certain humans in this park have been passing the biscuits and soda pop to some of your brothers. Keep your self-
respect—avoid them. Don't be pauperized like your uncles were last
year. You remember what happened to those panhandlers, don't you?
Do you want gout, an unbalanced diet, vitamin deficiencies, or gas on
the stomach? Beware of "ersatz" foodstuffs—accept only natural foods
and hunt these up yourself. These visitors mean well but they will ignore the signs. If they come too close, read this notice to them. They'll
catch on after awhile.

THE COMMITTEE.

IF YOU CAN'T READ, ASK THE BEAR AT THE NEXT INTERSECTION

Young's response to Cahalane's proposal is unknown, but it seems curious
that a sign that took a comic approach and anthropomorphized bears by
pretending they could read would be introduced under Superintendent
Rogers, who wanted to convince visitors that Yellowstone's bears were
dangerous wild animals. The explanation may be that by the 1950s the NPS
was willing to try just about anything to change visitors' attitudes toward
bear feeding.

Historically, the use of humor in bear warnings had tended to backfire, its
medium consistently proving to be more engaging than its message. In 1940,
the park had experimented with humor in the form of a cartoon that showed
a bear rebuking a tourist for feeding him. That summer, Rogers told Director
Cammerer that the cartoon was an effective tool in convincing people not to
feed bears and requested that it be reproduced on card-sized paper so that
rangers could pass it out to people caught feeding. In April 1941, he asked for
one thousand copies of the cards, but by the end of that summer their actual
efficacy was being questioned. Victor Cahalane was informed that although
the park's managers were confident that people feeding bears now knew better than to do so, visitors still seemed to be doing it for the thrill of it, or to
show off. In addition, the cards were being coveted as souvenirs by people
who fed the bears purposely in order to acquire them.[74]

In short, visitors were more inspired to own comic messages such as cards
and signs than to obey them, thus turning such items into mementos instead
of deterrents. "Notice to Bears" was no exception. In fact, a visitor from New
York City wrote the superintendent that she had been "very much amused by

your sign concerning the fact that the public should not feed the bears. Would it be possible to secure one of those that read 'Bears Beware' etc.?" There was little humor in Acting Chief Ranger Frank Sylvester's negative reply to her request.[75]

In light of the continuing problems and casual visitor attitudes toward bears, a social science researcher attempted in 1952 to ascertain just what Yellowstone's visitors did and did not know about bear feeding. That summer, Donald Bock, of the Colorado A&M School of Forestry, administered "A Survey of Public Opinion Concerning the Yellowstone Bear Feeding Problem," probably the first study of the subject conducted since park biologist Walter Kittams had interviewed visitors he encountered in the act of feeding bears a few years previously. Like Kittams, Bock found that the majority of visitors he contacted were aware that feeding was against the park's rules, but didn't really know why. Most who had an idea believed that danger to visitors was the only reason for prohibiting feeding.[76] In a statistic that might call into question the truth-in-reporting practiced by Bock's respondents, 72 percent of his subjects claimed that neither they nor anyone in their parties had fed the bears, but 92 percent said they had seen others doing it. Sixty-four percent believed that the practice of feeding violated national park principles, but several of those who did not were emphatic in their negative responses.

Perhaps most interesting, 39 percent said they would rather have seen fewer bears in a wild state than more bears along the roadside, echoing George Baggley, Arno Cammerer, and Olaus Murie.[77] Although growing concerns about the "unnaturalness" of feeding had been an important factor in the park's determination to eliminate the practice, and Bock's numbers showed that a significant contingent of visitors probably would have been amenable to such a philosophical explanation of why they shouldn't feed bears, the park's antifeeding messages during the 1950s and 1960s failed to argue that people shouldn't feed wildlife on principle.

In fact, there is little evidence that any of the park's educational efforts were helping to discourage people from feeding bears. The number of bear-related personal injuries reported in the park rose from 38 in 1951 to 109 in 1956—the second-highest number reported in the park's history—and there is no indication that antifeeding efforts were succeeding. There also seemed to be more begging bears on the roadsides than ever. In 1956, a visitor wrote Edmund Rogers to ask what in the world was going on in Yellowstone, as he had only seen eight bears during a 1939 visit and had returned with his children in 1956 to see an astonishing seventy-one.[78]

In the absence of a definitive, convincing explanation of why they shouldn't feed bears, several visitors wrote to suggest that the situation could at least be made benign if people fed bears only what was "good for them." A visitor from Davenport, Iowa, was incensed to arrive at the park in the summer of 1951 only to discover that bear feeding was illegal and that bears that repeatedly injured people or raided campground garbage cans were shot. According to him, "Yellowstone wouldn't be Yellowstone without the bears and the ability to be near them and feed them, etc." He offered some suggestions on proper methods of feeding and concluded with the suggestion that if the NPS was concerned about the health of the bears, it should provide people with a list of what was and was not good for bears to eat.[79]

A woman from Tucson, Arizona, wrote to say that she and her family had had a lovely visit to the park, but were a bit perplexed about the bear situation, to which she felt she could lend some insight. She explained that, initially, she and her family had "believed what the rangers told us concerning the eventual extermination of the bears, if people continued to feed them." But then they heard other visitors justifying feeding by "explaining that the park officials really wanted the bears to be fed . . . and that the children should not be denied this pleasure."[80] Not sure who was correct, the woman thought a bit and suggested what seemed to her a fair compromise:

> Use an inexpensive by product to make small biscuits that can be safely fed to bears. Then put several of these biscuits in each . . . scrap sack that is given to each tourist as he enters the Park. On the outside of the bag could be printed the following message, in large gaudy lettering:
>
> > Feed the bears ONLY what you find in this bag.
> > These "Bear biscuits" are harmless to bears.
> > Throw them from your car, and move on.
> > Never get out of your car to feed a bear.
> > He might harm you and scratch your car.
> > "Bear biscuits" are not good for humans.
> > Use the empty sack for scraps. Please do!

This visitor was obviously paying attention while in the park—she understood that feeding was dangerous to humans, to their property, and to the health of the bears, and found a solution that would even improve park cleanliness. But she hadn't gotten the idea that the practice of feeding was philosophically undesirable and triggered a host of indirect negative effects related to habituation—perhaps because it wasn't being communicated.

In 1959, a woman from Mill Valley, California, suggested a similar solution to the problem of campground trash disposal. Although garbage collection had been made more frequent in recent years, the park's campgrounds still lacked effective bearproof containers, and so under cover of darkness sometimes "resembled . . . what London during the blitz might have been like: bizarre noises and screams all around, occasional loud bangs, lights shining in all directions" when the bears came to collect their nightly booty. She wrote:

> Instead of relying on the unsightly, unpleasant, and un-photogenic garbage can method, why not . . . Provide a separate container for "Edible Garbage": or, better yet, be straightforward about it and label it "BEAR FOOD." It would not take long to educate the visitors to put edible scraps into the proper container, and then take pleasure in actively helping to keep our Bear Friends well fed and happy. . . . It would be well to hand each visitor a list of suggested items to feed or not to feed. . . . This should in no way interfere with the wise policy of warning people against hand-feeding the wild animals, including Bears. . . . I should like to think that on our next visit . . . there will be a chance that . . . our Bears may rise above being lowly garbage pickers.[81]

Like the visitor from Tucson, this woman recognized that hand-feeding was dangerous for humans and for bears, but attempted to solve the problem by ensuring that humans provided only nutritious nuggets. She even picked up on the idea that garbage-eating bears were "demeaned" bears, but the idea that providing bears with easy access to human foodstuffs was contrary to maintaining "natural" conditions did not emerge.

Confusion was evident, perhaps arising from the continued contradictions between official park regulations and their consistent nonenforcement. In spite of its creative adventures in messaging, the park was still not backing up its educational efforts with law enforcement in any meaningful way in the 1950s. If anything, feeding still seemed to be on the rise, concomitant with the postwar surge in visitation brought on by the return of the family vacation and the arrival of the American car culture. In a 1951 memo, the park's acting superintendent informed the NPS director that there were so many people feeding the bears that only the most flagrant offenders could be prosecuted—four people who had actually left their cars to hand-feed them.[82]

Former seasonal ranger Jim Caslick, stationed at Lake during the summers from 1951 to 1953, remembered that in those three summers of patrolling bear jams in Yellowstone, he never wrote a single ticket for bear feeding, nor was he ever reprimanded for failing to do so in spite of the fact that his ticket book was regularly inspected by a supervisor who knew that his seasonal staff devoted a substantial amount of their time to getting the bear jams moving. Although 95 percent of Donald Bock's subjects had reported knowing that feeding was against the rules, it appeared to some seasonal rangers that no one knew. Visitors would continue feeding even in the obvious presence of a ranger with no sense of worry about getting caught.[83]

As usual, bears that broke the rules did not enjoy the same leniency. In the absence of a formal bear management plan for the park, bears were dealt with and lethally controlled as was deemed necessary by the park's district rangers, instead of in accordance with a prescribed set of guidelines. According to Caslick, ursine visitors to the Fishing Bridge campground were trapped and relocated three times and then dispatched. As had been the case for decades, rangers kept track of how many strikes a particular bear had against it by marking offending animals with paint: "We had the three paint colors . . . and Bruin got three chances at Fishing Bridge Campground. First time we trapped him, one color . . . next incident . . . the second color. Take him back into a remote area again. Same procedure the third time. If he came back the fourth time, he was trapped, and that was his last move. A bear trapped in the campground that had been previously painted three times was then disposed of. I guess if there was a bear management policy, that was it."[84]

Most of the problem bears at Fishing Bridge in those days—the bears that were painted—were black bears. Grizzlies, thought to be a more serious threat to human safety, were dealt with somewhat differently in Caslick's experience: "We had a grizzly on occasion as well. That was sometimes handled in a more direct way, depending upon history of incidents and all . . . we had some night incidents in which I held the flashlight, and the district ranger settled the grizzly bear problem in the campground—on the spot [by shooting the bear]."[85]

A later description of bear management methods during the 1950s indicated that they were, indeed, marked by a lack of messing around, that "bears that could not be successfully transplanted were destroyed or shipped to zoos," period. It hardly seems curious, then, that this was one period when rumors percolated that the NPS had embarked on a large-scale project to exterminate the bears of Yellowstone. In a memo dated September 24, 1951, new NPS director Arthur Demaray voiced concern over the fact that "rumors are beginning to come to us expressing apprehension over the destruction of 'large' numbers of bears in Yellowstone Park, including the thought that bears are destroyed on the slightest provocation." Demaray pronounced as "too drastic" the park's stated policy of instructing all district rangers "to avoid any delay in removing bears which persisted in frequenting developed areas and causing difficulty or which in any way appeared to be a threat to persons or property."[86]

It was true that the forty-four bears killed in 1951 were more than twice as many as had been killed in 1950. Pressed for an explanation, Acting Regional Director James Lloyd fell back on the old notion that Yellowstone's bears were simply "overpopulated." Lloyd speculated that the park had had to kill more bears in 1951 because it hadn't killed enough in the preceding seasons. He hypothesized a direct correlation between high numbers of bears killed in one season and low numbers of visitor injuries in the following season, indicating a belief that in spite of all the attention paid to visitor education efforts, the underlying philosophy of bear management was still that the best defense is a good offense, and that meant killing bears. Lloyd also revealed the degree to which interventionist wildlife policies had become standard practice during these years: "While we have not investigated bear conditions on the ground in Yellowstone and do not have all of the facts at hand, it appears to us that the Yellowstone bear problem is just another case of a surplus of park wildlife. There is no reason that we know of why bears, like other park animals, if uncontrolled, will not overpopulate their ranges."[87] Lloyd went on to predict that for the NPS to avoid future lawsuits, Yellowstone's rangers would have to exercise even more vigilance (i.e., kill more bears) after roadside feeding was ended.

Lloyd's idea that bears would "overpopulate their ranges" if not controlled alluded to the park's ungulate management strategies of the time, in which Yellowstone's bison and elk herds were regularly culled, either by relocating or killing what were determined to be "excess" animals relative to the presumed "carrying capacity" of the land. Ironically, it was that very management practice that sixteen years later would bring about policy changes that served as the catalyst for two decades of virulent controversy over the fate of Yellowstone's bears. Until that time, though, managers would repeatedly reiterate their intention to intensify bear control measures, that is, to solve the problem by killing more bears.[88]

Edmund Rogers retired in 1956 after spending more years at Yellowstone's helm than any other superintendent in the park's history. Under his tenure the park had undergone extraordinary changes. The bear feeding grounds were closed, and administrators had made strides toward demythologizing the relationship between bears and people. Aesthetic conservation had essentially been abandoned in favor of a brand of preservation that was influenced by movers and shakers in the wilderness movement. The Depression and war years had offered opportunities for change, and Edmund Rogers had seized them. Yellowstone's "bear problem" was far from fixed, but the groundwork for changing the thinking that had allowed it to exist for so long had been laid.

3

Funny Bears and TV Stars

New superintendent Lemuel "Lon" Garrison, who arrived in 1956, inherited Edmund Rogers's bear problems but failed to make any significant progress in alleviating them. In fact, in many ways, the immediate postwar era seemed to usher in a new era of people-pleasing in Yellowstone. The most important example of this was a massive development project called Mission 66, a ten-year, multimillion-dollar plan aimed at constructing and improving park facilities in order to accommodate the increasing numbers of visitors to the national parks in the postwar era.

The World War II years had been lean ones for the National Park Service, and when America returned to the parks it discovered roads and facilities that had not only been left to dilapidate due to wartime shortages of funding and staffing but also were never intended to accommodate the exploding numbers of visitors who had been set free by the postwar boom in expendable income, car manufacturing, and baby-making. Prior to the war, Yellowstone's highest number of visitors in a single season had been 581,761 in 1941. A short seven years of severe neglect later, visitation topped 1 million for the first time in 1948, and by 1955, still without substantial budget increases and facilities rehabilitation, it had increased by another 368,000. In the summer of 1953, writer Bernard de Voto toured some of the more famous parks and described what he had observed in the October issue of *Harper's* magazine: low pay, inadequate budgets, and disintegrated facilities suffered by both visitors and employees. De Voto excoriated Congress for this sorry state of affairs, in which "much of the priceless heritage which the Service must safeguard for the United States is going to hell," and in light of his belief that increased appropriations would not be forthcoming, provocatively proposed that as many of the national parks should be closed as it would take to reduce the working size of the system to a number that current appropriations could feasibly fund. He suggested starting by closing the system's "jewels"— Yellowstone, Yosemite, Rocky Mountain, and Grand Canyon National Parks—and thereby succeeded in communicating his point: How could the United States be trusted to lead the postwar world when it couldn't even safeguard its own precious heritage?[1]

The NPS agreed, at least in the sense that the conditions described by de Voto were indeed poor. In January 1956, NPS director Conrad Wirth proposed to President Eisenhower and his cabinet a visionary, ten-year, $154 million capital improvements program designed to bring park facilities into line with anticipated visitor needs. Mission 66 was a study in optimism and accommodation, built around values of recreation, modernism, the nuclear family, and American pride. It was also ideologically obsolete before it was physically complete, and in the end was held up by some as a symbol of everything that was wrong with the NPS.

Yellowstone's proposed piece of the Mission 66 pie amounted to $70 million in combined government and private funds to be invested in road and trail improvements, buildings, utilities, and concessioner facilities. The park's superintendent, Lon Garrison, was named chairman of the Mission 66 steering committee, making Yellowstone ground zero for Mission 66 improvements, which most famously included the construction of a highway cloverleaf at the Old Faithful junction—in the style of the new interstate highway system—and the replacement of Robert Reamer's fabulous but structurally unsound Canyon Hotel with a new collection of facilities built in the Modern style. Like Albright before them, Wirth and Garrison both believed in what Garrison called "the paradox of protection by development": the idea that the best way to protect fragile resources was to develop the parks in such a way as to channel and control the crowds that flocked to them, which meant comfortably accommodating their numbers. Under this "paradox," undeveloped areas would still be set aside for wilderness and better preserved by the presence of what amounted to small cities in the frontcountry.[2]

Paradox also defined the park's approach to communicating to visitors about bears under Garrison—the paradox of deterrence through embrace. The policy was not terribly successful. By 1957, for instance, the photo of a black bear at the forest edge introduced in the park's 1947 broadside had been inexplicably replaced with an image of exactly what park managers presumably did *not* want to see—a black bear standing on its hind legs, leaning on a car and sticking its paws into an open window, looking for a handout. This photo was accompanied by instructions that ran completely contrary to the image: "On foot, give all bears a wide berth; if one approaches your car, stay in it, with windows closed. Park bears are wild animals. Do not tease, molest, or feed them." In 1959, this hold-up bear was gone. In its place was another roadside bear, sans automobile but clearly begging just the same, with the identical accompanying text describing Yellowstone's bears as "wild animals." This image and text were used at least through 1961.

The use of humor in bear warnings continued under Garrison, and was a source of internal controversy among NPS managers. In the summer of 1958, the park introduced yet another sign with a comical feel, this one reading, "BEAR MOOCHERS AHEAD—KEEP AWAY—DO NOT FEED." This warning was placed liberally throughout the park in conjunction with the more stern "DANGER—FEEDING BEARS IS PROHIBITED." In February 1959, Garrison attributed the sharply decreased number of personal injuries in 1958 (39, as opposed to 91 in 1957) to these new signs and what he described as "a more aggressive control of bears."[3]

That summer, being caught feeding a bear in Yellowstone earned visitors either a warning note or a talking-to. And there were a lot of feeders around; in November of that year, Yellowstone's acting superintendent reported that rangers had issued 1,200 written warnings in the summer of 1959, and that for every written warning, rangers had given 3 to 5 verbal warnings.[4] Trying to maim or kill a bear was treated as a marginally more serious offense than trying to feed a bear. Two men were fined a total of $60 for throwing firecrackers at bears in 1959, and another received a $300 fine and suspended jail sentence for shooting a bear at the Indian Creek campground. No arrests were made, or tickets issued, to people caught feeding bears. In 1957, when 908 written warnings and 3,800 verbal warnings were issued, four people had appeared before the U.S. commissioner assigned to Yellowstone on such charges. Two were given suspended sentences, and the other two were fined $5 each.

Fewer people were injured in 1959 than in 1955–1957, but it was suspected that this reduction was not because feeding had decreased but rather because people were being more careful about it after having seen the new signs ("Danger—Feeding Bears Is Prohibited" and "Bear Moochers Ahead—Keep Away"). Just two years later, however, the same "Bear Moocher" signs that had twice been identified as a specific reason why injuries had dropped were blamed for a jump in numbers of injuries, which rose to sixty-nine in the summer of 1960. In 1961, Regional Director Howard Baker informed Director Wirth that "we believe roadside signs such as 'Beware—Bear Moochers Ahead' instills [*sic*] a sense of levity rather than one of seriousness in the visitor." This swift turnaround of opinion regarding the use of humor indicated not only disagreement over its effects, but more importantly that the NPS didn't really have any idea why injuries fluctuated from year to year, or how to judge the efficacy of any of its individual efforts. Furthermore, grizzly bear researcher John Craighead had complained to Lon Garrison that people were so frequently visiting the Trout Creek dump hoping to see informal "bear shows" that they were interfering with research observations there.[5] As usual, the situation was not showing any signs of marked improvement.

In November 1959, the idea of actually enforcing the park's regulations arose again. A $50 fine for feeding was proposed but met with the typical lack of consensus regarding whether it would be effective, whether it was enforceable, and whether it was even fair to the visitors who got so much pleasure out of feeding and came to the park expecting to do it. The park's chief ranger favored posting signs warning that a fine would be imposed on those caught feeding, but the park naturalist opposed "unenforceable regulations." The chief naturalist was also skeptical: "This may be 'heresy,' but I hope the time never comes when there are no bears sitting by the roadside inviting a handout or in the campgrounds taking advantage of the careless camper. This is the normal nature of the black bear. It is a tradition of Yellowstone and some 1,000,000 annual visitors love it. . . . The judicious reduction of dangerous animals . . . seems to be the answer for [the] 1960 season."[6] The park's administration was still split between those who favored a solution that called for disciplining humans and those who favored the continued discipline of bears, and continued to locate the problem with the animal and its "nature" rather than with visitors or their long-established system of interaction with bears.

That summer, a servicewide Bear Management Program and Guidelines (BMP) was disseminated from the office of NPS acting director Hillory Tolson. In its educational components, the BMP didn't differ all that much from what Yellowstone had already been doing for years. The plan urged that visitors be flooded with improved antifeeding information and messages, including printing warnings, instructions, and general information on such things as menus, match folders, store receipts, garbage cans, and picnic and campground tables.[7]

In other ways, the 1960 BMP did differ from past efforts. First, it formalized the process of bear management and provided for a fairly uniform implementation of servicewide policies, thereby reducing the potential for the

sorts of problems that had arisen in the 1940s, when some parks had eliminated their bear shows before others. Second, it put in writing the circumstances under which a bear could and should be killed, requiring that all possible efforts be made to ensure that bears eliminated for misbehavior were
indeed the offending bears. Finally, the BMP stated that antifeeding regulations should be "vigorously enforced." Consequences for violators could
range from a warning or ticket to an appearance before either the district
ranger or the U.S. commissioner assigned to the park, and repeat offenses
should not be tolerated. Whether a warning or a ticket was in order was up to
the individual ranger, who was encouraged to consider the circumstances
surrounding the specific incident.

The definition of "vigorous enforcement" was apparently left open to
interpretation. In Yellowstone, Garrison instructed his rangers to continue
to issue written warnings to all violators upon their first offense, except in
extreme cases—for instance, if a visitor refused to stop feeding after receiving the warning. Two hundred sixty-nine warnings were issued. Only repeat
violators were to be ticketed or summoned before the commissioner. By the
official count, 89 bears were removed from Yellowstone during the summer
of 1960; a letter from Acting Regional Director George Baggley to Director
Wirth placed the number of "bears killed" at 107. There were a staggering 358
incidents of property damage and 69 bear-related injuries that year. In addition, the dollar amount of actual or pending tort claims against the federal
government involving physical and property damage by bears in national
parks had reportedly reached $1 million. Together, these numbers of property
damages and management removals of bears were the highest ever recorded
in the park's history. In response, the park's chief ranger recommended that
for the remainder of the year, rangers should "continue a vigorous live-
trapping program in the campgrounds and the destruction of every bear we
live trap," for the protection of campers and the good of the bears.[8]

Bear deaths would lessen, but not by much, after the BMP took effect in
Yellowstone in 1961. This was partly because although the BMP nominally
strove to eliminate only problem bears, the program was predicated on the
theory that if the NPS were to actively kill all of the "spoiled" bears and simultaneously remove the conditions that led to such spoliation, then it
could swiftly establish "conditions whereby bears will be presented to the
public in normal numbers and without artificialities." From 1955 to 1965 the
official record counted 349 bears killed in control actions—the highest number recorded in any single decade of the park's history. Ninety-two percent
were black bears.[9]

Perhaps due to the scale of the problems in Yellowstone, Garrison took some liberties with the program's guidelines in regard to control actions. Whereas Tolson's directions called for bears to be destroyed only: "a) When they return to roadsides and campgrounds after being marked and moved out and continue to destroy property or injure persons without provocation. This action will require documentation and prior approval of the District Park Ranger," and "b) In an emergency situation when the situation cannot be handled quickly in any other way and there is danger of injury to persons or extreme property damage," Garrison abbreviated those instructions to read, "Destroy all bears which: a) return to roadsides or campgrounds after being marked and moved out, and b) when unable to handle the situation quickly in any other way." In 1961, Acting Superintendent Luis Gastellum again concluded that the park would never be able to completely stop feeding, and that the best its administration could hope for would be to reduce the number of injuries associated with the practice.[10]

The park continued to experiment with antifeeding messaging, and although Regional Director Howard Baker and others advocated a strict tone of sternness, the NPS had already lined up its next foray into humorous warnings. This would be the most compelling, confounding campaign yet, and it starred a national celebrity.

Hanna-Barbera had introduced America to Yogi Bear in 1958, when he appeared in several episodes of *The Huckleberry Hound Show*. Hailed as "the first break-out superstar of the Hanna-Barbera canon," Yogi, his pal Boo Boo, and the long-suffering Ranger Smith rocketed to stardom during the 1958–1959 and 1959–1960 television seasons, when they were featured in such cartoon shorts as "Pie Pirates," "Be My Guest Pest," "Bear on a Picnic," "Big Brave Bear," "Buzzin' Bear," and the timely "Space Bear." After just two short years, Yogi became too popular to continue to take a backseat to anyone. He got his own show on January 30, 1961, when *The Yogi Bear Show* debuted on 130 television stations across the nation. If, as Umberto Eco tells us, the original has to be idolized in order for the reproduction to be desired, then it is an unmistakable (if dubious) tribute to the fame and mystique of the Yellowstone bear that Yogi's creators were able to delight viewers with a full thirty-five half-hour episodes, all of which were loosely centered around Yogi's figuring out new ways to dupe Ranger Smith and steal "pic-a-nic" baskets from hapless visitors to Jellystone Park in an effort to sate his perpetual pangs of hunger.[11]

Although Yogi was never depicted on all fours, lapping up treats from a big pile of garbage, and he never physically attacked any of Jellystone's visitors, some of the show's themes did hit relatively close to the actual situation.

A few of the episodes focused specifically on Ranger Smith's efforts to change the bears' diet, and drew on some of the real reasons that the NPS was using to explain why feeding the bears was a bad idea. In episode 6, a doctor determined that Yogi's unceasing consumption of human goodies had made him ill, and instructed him to adopt a strict diet of nuts and berries. Yogi responded by feigning a suicide attempt, causing Ranger Smith to relent and offer him a picnic lunch.

Episode 15 played off the NPS's historical equation of begging bears with lazy panhandlers who had become accustomed to being "on the dole" and lost the will to "earn their own living"—a socially loaded image that began to appear commonly in NPS correspondence during the Depression years and remained in NPS discourse at least into the 1980s. In this episode, the park made begging illegal, stating that cash must be paid for what had once been handouts. Yogi countered by constructing a wishing well and using the accumulated coins to purchase his food. In episode 31, Ranger Smith attempted to deter Yogi's raids by rigging his refrigerator with a paint bomb, a likely allusion to the practice, common since the 1930s, of identifying repeat offenders by painting colored stripes on them. Yogi fell victim to the trap and, angered, again feigned suicide, leading Ranger Smith to relent once again. Yogi also pretended to kill himself in episode 20, when Ranger Smith was replaced by "Iron Hand" Jones, a ranger bent on enforcing the park's rules against bears' eating from picnic baskets.[12] For all his ineffectual foibles and seeming mean-spiritedness in trying to deny Yogi human food, Ranger Smith always proved in the end to be television's version of a benevolent steward of the park and its bears. Unfortunately for the real-life NPS, that meant that he almost always succumbed to Yogi's desires when the real trouble started.

Yogi's appearance on the American scene could easily have been taken as a threat to the NPS's efforts to stop bear feeding in Yellowstone, as his television adventures certainly did little to further the agency's goal of changing the image of the Yellowstone bear from clever clown to dangerous wild animal. If the NPS thought it had had problems with Colonel Potterby and the Duchess, what would it do with a jovial, hat-and-tie-wearing bear who habitually sauntered up to visitors, outsmarted them in hilarious and distinctly nonthreatening fashion, and had his antics broadcast in Technicolor into thousands of American living rooms on a weekly basis?

If you can't beat 'em, join 'em. Citing the need to "hit the other segment of the public who may find the message more meaningful through the cartoon approach," Superintendent Lon Garrison wasted no time in drafting Yogi into the NPS ranks in late 1960, when he contacted Hanna-Barbera with an idea for a pamphlet "without any commercial tie-in" that would feature Yogi advising visitors on how to store their food in order to keep it safe from bears.[13] The company agreed to design the pamphlet and print 100,000 copies at its own expense for distribution to the public. In the resulting leaflet, Yogi also warned visitors that "Park Bears Are Dangerous," and that they should keep a safe distance away from bears and keep their windows rolled up at all times. The brochure also included a poem, signed by Garrison, in which Yogi's admonishments were reiterated in rhyme.

The effect of all this was probably similar to that of Bart Simpson warning kids to respect their elders. Garrison himself expressed apprehension that the use of the pamphlets would be considered "jocular or a cavalier treatment of what we agree is a serious problem," and the park's chief law enforcement officer had already stated his opposition to the "use of comedy bears" in warning signs. But on April 21, 1961, Acting Superintendent Luis Gastellum approved the pamphlet. He acknowledged the role that Yogi and Boo Boo had played in perpetuating harmful misconceptions, but still argued, "We feel that by providing material and some suggested objectives we can help direct Yogi in his appeal to visitors to do what is right."[14] Rather than fight against Yogi's star power, the NPS hoped to channel that power in its own favor by making Yogi say words that managers condoned rather than words that made them pull their hair out.

In the end, incorporating Yogi Bear into a pamphlet may just have been another creative attempt to grab visitor attention, as many park managers doubted that people ever bothered to read the literature they were handed on their way into the park. In 1947, researcher William Sanborn had found that when one hundred visitors were asked if they were aware that there was a bear warning stamped onto the back of their entrance permits, only twelve knew that there was anything there, and only eight knew that the wording had anything to do with bears.[15] In 1962, rangers were instructed to ascertain whether victims of injury or property damage had read the literature they had received at the gates.

Whether or not the Yogi pamphlet was successful is debatable. Injuries dropped slightly in the summer of 1961, but as the case of the "Bear Moochers" sign had proved, simply assuming causal relationships between park media and visitor behavior was not a sound management practice. What we do know is that the pamphlet didn't last very long. There are no references to it in the record after 1961, and in 1977, the park was still looking for ways to "counteract the Yogi/Smokey/Teddy bear image."[16]

Although employed by the U.S. Forest Service (USFS) rather than the NPS, Smokey Bear has nonetheless played a strong role in shaping park visitors' ideas about bears as well as about conservation, making him well worth a slight detour here. A complex figure, Smokey was first introduced by the USFS in 1945 to replace fellow cartoon character Bambi, who had been on loan from Disney since 1944, and proven to be a popular symbol for fire prevention. In a curious twist of fate, Smokey acquired a real-life creation myth in 1950, when a bear cub in New Mexico's Lincoln National Forest was orphaned after a careless passerby tossed a cigarette and started his forest home ablaze. According to *The True Story of Smokey Bear,* a comic book distributed by the USFS, firefighters looked around when the smoke had cleared and discovered that the only living thing left within sight was a black bear cub desperately clinging to a charred tree. They took him to a warden at the New Mexico Game and Fish Department, who nursed him back to health.[17]

Suddenly, the USFS had a scenario that mimicked a classic dime novel, but in reverse—a real bear whose real story could add to the aura of the already existing fictional Smokey Bear. Accordingly, they turned the story of the real Smokey into the biography of the cartoon Smokey, hybridizing the real with the fictional to powerful effect. Smokey endures to this day, though his message about the unequivocal evil of forest fire has been modified through the years.

The "real" Smokey was ultimately sent to live at the National Zoo in Washington, D.C., but it is the cartoon Smokey who has remained cemented in people's minds as the familiar half-man, half-bear who walks around in a pair of denim jeans, carries a shovel, and sports a hat (whose style has ever since caused the "flat hat" worn by NPS personnel to be known colloquially as the "Smokey hat" and created a good deal of confusion over exactly which federal land agency actually claims Smokey). How Smokey started out as a "real" bear and grew into a man-bear is never explained, and was perhaps made more plausible by the popularity of fellow cartoon heroes such as Batman, who was called to his career out of a need to avenge a specific childhood trauma. The cover of a 1969 version of *The True Story of Smokey Bear* depicted the full-grown Smokey in the foreground, experiencing a vision of his tortured past; in the background, a bear cub clung to a blackened tree amid a blazing fire.[18]

Getting back to Yogi, it seems likely that his Hollywood persona proved stronger than his NPS message. If anything, using Yogi may have created more confusion about how visitors should think about bears by further obfuscating the differences between Jellystone and Yellowstone, Yogi and the "average" (Yellowstone) bear, and bears and humans; a bear who not only sports a hat and tie but is also an effusive talker and cunning schemer is clearly an anthropomorphized bear. A little boy from Louisville, Kentucky, proved that a syncretism between Yellowstone reality and Jellystone imaginary was cemented in some aspects of the public mind when he sat down in September 1961 to write the following cryptic letter, which he addressed and sent via U.S. mail to "Yogi Bear, The Cave, Jellystone National Park, Wyo."[19]

YOGI BEAR STEALS THE PICNIC BASKET

DEAR MR BEAR

I DON'T THINK THE RANGER WILL LIKE IT.

Not only did this boy's letter get delivered to Yellowstone (albeit with 4 cents postage due), it even generated a response from "Yogi" himself, drafted by park personnel who answered the letter as though they were Yogi and signed it with a drawing of a bear's footprint labeled, "Yogi's Mark."[20]

As Yogi, the author of the response explained that the park's rangers had been doing such a good job of warning visitors about him that he hadn't had a chance to eat too many goodies lately, and that other park bears had been causing trouble for Yogi and Boo Boo by injuring people and stealing food from cars and tents. Yogi also claimed to know Smokey Bear, but told the boy that he hadn't seen him lately because Smokey had been out fighting fires all summer. Yogi's letter was accompanied by the two antifeeding brochures that were distributed to visitors that summer: Yogi's brochure and the "Dangerous" flyer with the "horror bear" image. Although their conjunctive use was explained by Garrison as an attempt to use diverse styles in order to reach all of the park's visitors, taken together they sent conflicting visual messages that unquestionably served to reintroduce the friendly-and-scary duality of Yellowstone's bears that Superintendent Rogers had wanted to eradicate.

And then came Disney. In 1961, Disney's "Yellowstone Cubs" was filmed in the park for broadcast on *The Wonderful World of Disney* in 1963. In late 1961, an article appeared on the UPI wire indicating that bears had become so scarce in Yellowstone that Disney had been forced to bring its own bears from California to appear in the movie. W. H. Browning of the Montana Chamber of Commerce told reporters that "he was informed [Disney] had been able to find only one bear in the entire park since the last of August." The article attracted the attention of a Billings, Montana, resident who forwarded it to U.S. senator Mike Mansfield (Montana), who asked NPS director Conrad Wirth for an explanation. Superintendent Garrison told Mansfield that if fewer bears had been seen in 1961 it was because (1) it had been a plentiful summer for natural foods, (2) roadside refuse collection had been made more frequent, (3) visitors were being "informed, cautioned, and restrained" against feeding, and (4) the park had "increased our removal of nuisance or rogue bears by live-trapping and transplanting to remote areas of the parks."[21] He also explained that Disney had never intended to use Yellowstone bears in its movie. The company had brought its own bears because it needed trained bears to perform the stunts required by the film's script.

And what a script it was. The film opened with scenes of the cubs frolicking in the park's backcountry in the company of their mother. In the style of a nature documentary, a narrator explained various aspects of life as a black bear cub. When the bears entered the frontcountry, however, trouble ensued. While raiding a visiting family's vehicle for food, the cubs found themselves locked inside a trailer that was subsequently pulled away. Meanwhile, rangers tranquilized and moved their mother after she attacked a man who "teased" her by pretending he had no more marshmallows to feed her (i.e., who fed her in the long-established "wrong way"). By the hour's end, the cubs, which Disney called Tuffy and Tubby, had drunk from a bottle dropped by an unsuspecting baby camper, ransacked campground garbage cans, and operated an industrial potato-masher while in the process of destroying the kitchen of the Old Faithful Inn. Perhaps most memorable, however, was the scene in which Tuffy and Tubby successfully engaged the motor on a speedboat and piloted it around Lewis Lake at full throttle. In short, the film was a classic Disney docu-fantasy.

In many ways, however, "Yellowstone Cubs" was also a contradictory cautionary tale, and serves as a document of both bear management methods and attitudes toward bears at the time. The Yogi Bear antifeeding warning, distributed that summer, was featured in one of the film's opening sequences, showing a line of cars waiting at one of the park's entrances. When each car reached the kiosk, a ranger handed the visitors a folder of information about park wildlife; the Yogi brochure visibly stuck out the top. Next on the screen was a shot of the warning sign erected at park entrances at that time, which stated:

Regulations Prohibiting Bear Feeding Enforced
Bears Are Dangerous and Destructive
Keep Car Windows Closed When Near Bears or Parked
Keep Food Away from Bears

REMEMBER
All Wild Animals are DANGEROUS

Of course, the antifeeding regulations were *not* meaningfully enforced in 1961, as the next sequence demonstrated. In a scene that typified the ambivalence both toward bears and rule enforcement of the time, the voice-over narrative alternately warned against the dangers of feeding Yellowstone's roadside bears and celebrated the spectacle of it, proclaiming that the cubs "usually put on the best show," but that it was dangerous to come between a "she-bear" and her cubs. Bears ate cookies from hands stuck out of car windows, and a woman got caught in a bear embrace while petting and feeding. That, the narrator asserted, was "too much for the ranger" who was there patrolling the bear jam the whole time, and he decided it was time to get the traffic moving. Cartoony music played beneath the narrative, setting a festive mood.

Like the Yogi flyer, "Yellowstone Cubs" prominently featured NPS personnel as a means of giving the film documentary credibility, demonstrating the complicity of the NPS in its production. Rangers were shown at the entrance kiosk, at the bear jam, and throughout the rest of the film in pursuit of the cubs and their mother. Rangers were also depicted shooting the cubs' mother with a tranquilizer dart of sucostrin, whose use had been recently pioneered by researchers in the park. They then relocated her and painted her head upon release.

The combination of these more "realistic" sequences—which appear to be in concert with the historical record and starred actual NPS personnel doing their actual jobs—with the fictionalized and fantasized portrayal of the bears shown elsewhere in the film resulted in a kind of seamless docudrama in which the simultaneous celebration and condemnation of bear feeding, comic and frightening depictions of its results, and strict statements of the regulations but absence of their enforcement made it difficult to discern proper from improper behavior and to know where fantasy and reality met and diverged. Of course, such was not the film's purpose, but overall, the NPS's active participation would have sent into living rooms across America the timeworn message that feeding Yellowstone's bears had no dire consequences unless one was truly careless. Choosing to have his employees take part may have been another of Garrison's efforts to use as many kinds of media and messages as possible to communicate the antifeeding message to the broadest possible audience, but exactly what that message was seems once again to have been lost in the telling.

If the recorded numbers are any indication, it would appear that the park's efforts to convince people not to feed bears by popularizing the no-feeding theme had failed. During Garrison's eleven-year administration, an average of 52 people each year were injured by bears, and there was an average of 228 reported incidents of property damage annually. Strictly for comparison, there were annual averages of 49 injuries and 64 incidents of property damage during Edmund Rogers's previous administration of twenty-one years.

Of course, annual visitation was higher during Garrison's administration and, as others have pointed out, making any judgments based on the "official numbers" of recorded bear-related injuries, property damage incidents, and bears killed in control actions is a sketchy proposition.[22] First, there is no guarantee that the numbers are accurate. Visitors may have underreported incidents, and rangers may have been more careful about recording them under some administrations than others (if at all). Second, changes in the degree of stringency exercised about transporting versus killing bears in control actions occurred as different plans were put into action. Fewer bears might have been killed in control actions in one year than the next, but this difference was not necessarily indicative of improvement in the overall bear situation. A different policy may have been put in place, or again, it is possible that the numbers were not accurately recorded.

That said, the numbers, exact or not, are likely in the ballpark, and can be used to chart general trends. Furthermore, they are all we have to go by. Even with the possibility that those recorded numbers didn't entirely reflect reality, it seemed that despite all of the creative efforts launched under Lon Garrison, the park's visitors and its bears had carried on business as usual.

However, if Garrison's administration was notable for mixing reality and popular fantasy in its inventive, if unsuccessful, attempts to solve the bear problem, it was also notable for its interest in and approval of a scientific research project that on a number of levels (both positive and negative) would prove to be the most important and influential in the park's history. Back in 1951, Acting Regional Director Lloyd had been correct in stating that the park really didn't have much scientific information about bears on which to base management decisions. Except for occasional studies, most notably by Olaus Murie, Curtis Skinner, and Milton Skinner, not much scientific study of

Yellowstone's bears had been done by the 1950s, and the information that was available was primarily about black bears. What about the park's grizzlies?

In the mid-1950s, twin brothers John and Frank Craighead started talking with park naturalist David de L. Condon about the possibility of answering that question, using Yellowstone as their study area. Condon, who was passionate about park wildlife but frustrated by his continually dwindling research budget and increasing workload (in 1955 Victor Cahalane had finally resigned from the park service in protest over the paucity of funding for scientific research in the parks), believed that a continued lack of information about the grizzly and its habits and needs might well lead to its disappearance. Accordingly, he was enthusiastic about the prospect of a cooperative study in which the park service could provide the Craigheads with some financial and personnel support, facilities, and the environment for their work, while the Craigheads could conduct the research, produce the study, and provide the NPS with information and management recommendations. The brothers began their now-famous grizzly studies in 1959 under a joint agreement between the NPS; the Montana Cooperative Wildlife Research Unit, led by John Craighead; and the Environmental Research Institute, led by Frank Craighead.[23] In the end, the years of that partnership (1959–1971) would prove to be a watershed of both knowledge and acrimony, in large part because they coincided with cultural waves and NPS policy changes that would permanently affect the public's ideas about the agency and the bears of Yellowstone.

Acting Superintendent Capt. George Anderson's maid, Ellen, feeds bears kept chained outside his home at Mammoth Hot Springs, 1890. National Archives, Yellowstone National Park.

An emaciated bighorn sheep kept at E. C. Waters's Dot Island zoo, early 1900s. Note people peering through the slats. National Archives, Yellowstone National Park.

The Otter Creek feeding grounds were the most elaborate in the park. Log benches made up amphitheater seating for 250 spectators. As many as seventy grizzlies fed at once on the garbage provided at Otter Creek, where many hundreds of people at a time watched the show. National Archives, Yellowstone National Park.

Black bear Juno in his pen at the Mammoth zoo, 1920s. National Archives, Yellowstone National Park.

"Lunch Counter" for bears, Old Faithful feeding grounds, 1920s. National Archives, Yellowstone National Park.

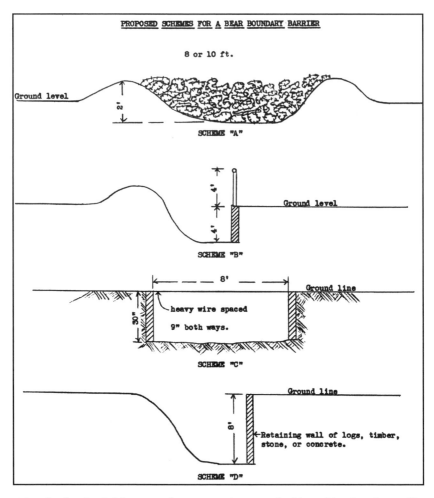

PROPOSED SCHEMES FOR A BEAR BOUNDARY BARRIER

8 or 10 ft.

Ground level

2'

SCHEME "A"

4'

4'

Ground level

SCHEME "B"

8'

Ground line

heavy wire spaced
9" both ways.

30"

SCHEME "C"

Ground line

8'

Retaining wall of logs, timber,
stone, or concrete.

SCHEME "D"

After the death of visitor Martha Hansen in 1942, the idea of fencing the park's campgrounds gained appeal. Above is a 1945 schematic of a proposed "dry moat" that would be less conspicuous than chain-link but still keep bears and visitors apart at night. National Archives, College Park, Maryland.

DANGEROUS

PARK BEARS and other animals are WILD

They cause many injuries to visitors

TO PROTECT YOU, OUR REGULATIONS PRO-
HIBIT FEEDING OR MOLESTING THEM

Watch them from a safe distance

PULL OFF THE ROAD AND STAY IN YOUR CAR

NATIONAL PARK SERVICE
UNITED STATES DEPARTMENT OF THE INTERIOR

Form 10–108
(June 1957)   (OVER)

In 1951, this bear warning was introduced under Superintendent Edmund Rogers, who believed that the park needed to change the messages it was sending visitors about bears if the bear problem was to be solved. Telling visitors that bears were dangerous was a departure from past policies. Yellowstone National Park Bear Management Office.

NOTICE TO BEARS
BEWARE OF SABOTAGE

We want to warn you that certain humans in this park have been passing the biscuits and soda pop to some of your brothers. Keep your self-respect—avoid them. Don't be pauperized like your uncles were last year. You remember what happened to those panhandlers, don't you?

Do you want gout, an unbalanced diet, vitamin deficiencies, or gas on the stomach? Beware of "ersatz" foodstuffs—accept only natural foods and hunt these up yourself.

These visitors mean well but they will ignore the signs. If they come too close, read this notice to them. They'll catch on after awhile.

THE COMMITTEE.

IF YOU CAN'T READ, ASK THE BEAR AT THE NEXT INTERSECTION

In 1951, the park experimented with humor as a way to convince visitors not to feed bears. Signs like this one were posted at various locations around the park. Yellowstone National Park Bear Management Office.

Superintendent Jack Anderson objected to the obvious markings used by John and Frank Craighead for purposes of grizzly bear research in the park. The markings were one source of a bitter feud between park managers and the brothers whose reverberations lasted for decades. Yellowstone National Park Bear Management Office.

PARK BEARS ARE DANGEROUS

**PARK BEARS and other animals are WILD!
WATCH THEM FROM A SAFE DISTANCE**

Feeding Park bears isn't right,
Ones that look harmless
    can bite,
They think it's great fun,
    Till the handouts are done,
Then they grab for
    whatever's in sight.

To protect you, Park regulations prohibit feeding or molesting wild animals. Please follow instructions. Wild animals can cause serious injuries.

Pull off the road,
And stay in your car,
ROLL ALL THE WINDOWS UP
    TIGHT,
It's better to be safe and watch
    from afar,
Than risk damage, or
    injury or fright.

KEEP CAR WINDOWS CLOSED!

"Look out, you kids," says Yogi Bear,
"For my outlaw cousins are everywhere.
These roadside beggars look mighty sweet
but all they want is lots to eat.
They'll eat most anything they can
including chunks out of your hand.
Get in the car when a bear shows up,
close the door; keep the windows shut.
Keep your grub hung way up high
between two trees when bears go by.
And if you think that you're in danger
just go and ask a friendly ranger.
Beware outlaw bears along the way
They can't be trusted any day."

Lon Garrison
Superintendent
Yellowstone National Park

**NATIONAL PARK SERVICE
UNITED STATES DEPARTMENT OF THE INTERIOR**

TV's Yogi Bear says:
"The best operation,
In this situation,
(When bears are prowling
    around)
Is to keep all your stuff
Locked up where it's tough
For a Yellowstone bear
    to scrounge."

FOOD STORAGE SUGGESTIONS FOR CAMPERS

As a rule, campers who keep a clean camp, and use a minimum of odorous foods are less bothered by bears than those campers who do not keep a clean camp and allow garbage to collect. However, any food or food container that emits an odor is a natural target for bears. Food left on tables or in open boxes is a definite invitation to bear damage.

1. Food should not be stored on a table or in your tent.

2. Seal surplus food in clean wrapping material or in airtight containers.

3. Keep your food as cool as possible.

4. Metal chests with good locks make fair storage receptacles, although experience has shown that not all metal chests are bear-proof.

5. Campground and back-country campers often suspend their supplies between two trees out of a bear's reach.

6. Burn all garbage and food containers, including cans, in back-country camps.

© HANNA-BARBERA PROD.

Park managers continued to experiment with humor in bear warnings under Superintendent Lon Garrison, who in 1960 agreed to draft Yogi Bear into the NPS ranks with this flyer. Its use in conjunction with the "Dangerous" flyer likely contributed to confusion about what the park was really trying to tell visitors about bears and the act of feeding them. Yellowstone National Park Bear Management Office.

Grizzly No. 264, extremely popular with visitors and photographers for her majestic appearance and high visibility at the park's roadsides, was killed by a vehicle in 2003. National Park Service/Jim Peaco.

Bear No. 264 was widely mourned by her "fans" and in the park's local communities. This photo was taken in Gardiner, Montana. National Park Service/Jim Peaco.

The advent of digital photography has forever changed our ways of seeing what's "real." Collection of author.

4

Science Versus Scenery

The Wilderness Bear

The 1960s brought a period of transition whose importance to the National Park Service is hard to overstate. The decade began with the Mission 66 project well underway, with Yellowstone superintendent Lon Garrison as its chair. By the time John F. Kennedy arrived in the White House to succeed President Eisenhower, however, new ideas about Americans' relationship with their environment were taking hold and finding their expression in the new administration. Kennedy chose as his secretary of the interior Stewart Udall, a former Arizona congressman who would hold the post for nine years. Udall wasted no time in letting NPS director Conrad Wirth know how he felt about Mission 66 and its dubious implications for natural values in the parks. Citing the NPS's enabling legislation, Udall told Wirth that "it is certainly the clear intent of Congress that the natural and wilderness features of the parks must not be impaired. . . . I am a strong believer in wilderness preservation and you can depend on me to scrutinize all programs and activities of the National Park Service with this viewpoint clearly in my mind."[1]

This decisive attitude shift regarding what was most important in the parks—human accommodation or wilderness values—was indicative of the political rise of the wilderness movement. Active since the time of John Muir, the movement had gained momentum during the late 1950s, when "the quantity and quality of their [advocates'] fury became sufficiently potent to influence the political process." The watershed had come with environmentalists' 1955 defeat of the Echo Park dam project proposed within Dinosaur National Monument at the border of Colorado and Utah. The project's abandonment was largely achieved through the efforts of the Wilderness Society, led by Howard Zahniser (later author of the Wilderness Act), and the Sierra Club, led by David Brower. The groups sent mass mailings, produced a motion picture and a book about the area's wilderness qualities edited by famed Western writer Wallace Stegner, wrote articles for their organizations' magazines, submitted editorials and open letters to newspapers, and got attention from national periodicals such as *Life, Collier's, Newsweek, Reader's Digest,* and the *New York Times.* They ended up victorious when it was determined that public protest had reached such magnitude that the presence of Echo Park on any dam bill would ensure its defeat in Congress.[2]

Why had the Echo Park dam proposal touched such a nerve in postwar America? In part, pleas for wilderness preservation had taken on a sense of urgency that they had not possessed prior to World War II, the atomic bomb, and the start of the Cold War. Suddenly "the last hour" for preservation had arrived, and our "survival" depended on whether we chose to seize it or ignore it. Whether we would leave our future generations a verdant, healthy earth or a wasted, desolate one became a question posed by some writers, many of whom also emphasized that all of humanity was a single species and shared a single earth. In 1961, Olaus Murie asked of environmentalism, "What does all this mean—this love of flowers, birds, mammals, earth features of all kinds? . . . Do we not need some sort of companionship with Nature's world to make better people of us? On the radio, in the newspapers, everywhere, we learn about . . . political hatred of all kinds . . . but there are hopeful signs. We have learned that those who seek the wild places, who really see some of the beauty of this world, have a much more generous feeling toward a neighbor. As Thoreau said, 'in wildness is the preservation of the world.'" Given the tenor of Murie's prose, it would hardly seem out of place if he had tagged "from nuclear annihilation" onto the end of Thoreau's famous quotation, to which he seems to have lent a rather contemporary interpretation. The popularization of the "one Earth" concept was later solidified with the first photos of Earth from space.[3]

It was out of this climate that the NPS received one of the most influential policy statements in its history, in the form of a collection of recommendations from the Secretary's Advisory Board on Wildlife Management. Called "Wildlife Management in the National Parks," or the "Leopold Report" after Chairman A. Starker Leopold, the document's purpose was threefold: to determine what the goals of wildlife management in the national parks should be, to determine what kinds of wildlife management policies would best enable the NPS to meet those goals, and to identify methods for achieving them. In the end, the Leopold Report provided the agency with a specific guiding ideology: a rebirth of the land as it was before the arrival of modern civilization—in short, primitivism. A return to primeval wilderness, or as close to it as possible, would be the NPS's new driving objective. The report recommended that the agency's primary management goal should be to maintain or re-create "the biotic associations in national parks . . . in the condition that prevailed when the area was first visited by the white man," that is, the creation of "a reasonable illusion" of primitive America. Parks should be made to "look natural," even if achieving that goal required substantive manipulation of existing landscapes. As an example of what needed to be done, the authors offered, "If the mountain men who gathered [in Grand Teton National Park's Antelope Flats] in rendezvous fed their squaws an antelope, a twentieth-century tourist at least should be able to see a band of these animals. Finding out what aspect of the range needs rectifying, and doing so, would appear to be a primary function of park management."[4]

Restoring the primitive scene, according to the report, would require planting and removing trees along roadsides, obscuring all "observable artificiality," creating simulated buffalo wallows in order to spur native plant growth, and reintroducing certain wildlife species in order to "enhance the mood of wild America." Above all, the NPS should accomplish these transformations "invisibly," meaning that the signs and traces of management efforts should be concealed from the public—much as scene production is achieved at Walt Disney World. This irony was not lost on critics such as wilderness advocate Adolph Murie (brother of Olaus), who called the report "the most extreme anti-park policy statement I have yet encountered. Is a scene *natural* when you chop trees down or plant trees! Is that an honest presentation! Do we want to make Disney Lands out of our roadsides!"[5]

Despite Murie's objections, the Leopold Report represented a huge turnaround from the management paradigm embodied by the Mission 66 program. Two years before the scheduled completion of Mission 66, the language and recommendations of the Leopold Report became a guiding NPS policy. They were implemented in conjunction with those from another 1963 report, this one from the National Academy of Sciences (NAS), known as the Robbins Report. The purpose of the NAS committee was to examine the state of research in the national parks, which was found sorely lacking. According to the Robbins Report, lack of proper research had created significant potential for ecologically unsound management decisions, leading to fragmented knowledge and a muddling of administration, operations, and research management. The committee laid out a plan by which to define those management divisions, and recommended that the NPS embark on an in-service program of "mission-oriented research"—research specifically designed to address park-related issues and geared toward improving management and interpretation of park values. Such research programs should not be conducted with a view toward single species management, but rather for the preservation of the "total environment"—a criterion that set the NPS's research mandate apart from those of other institutions and agencies. For this reason, the committee stated, independent research in the parks should be encouraged, but should not serve as a substitute for NPS-led research.[6] The report left open the question of exactly what role the opinions and findings of independent scientists should play in agency decision-making—a point that would soon become pivotal in Yellowstone.

The NAS committee immediately recognized the problematic nature of that which the Leopold Report had taken for granted: namely, how one time period could be deemed more "natural" than another. It also called for avoidance of artificiality, but with a more hands-off approach. "The Committee recognizes that national parks are not pictures on the wall," wrote the Robbins Report's authors. "They are dynamic biological complexes with self-generating changes. To attempt to maintain them in any fixed condition ... would not only be futile but contrary to nature. Each park should be regarded as a system of interrelated plants, animals and habitat (an ecosystem) in which evolutionary processes will occur under such human control and guidance as seems necessary to preserve its unique features."[7]

In Yellowstone, the resultant changes in policy during the late 1960s and early 1970s instigated the rise of new bears and new narratives. Funny bears and TV stars were assuredly gone. This period would see the advent of the wilderness bear and a new emphasis on science and, in the end, produce a monumental struggle of science versus scenery. When new superintendent Jack Anderson arrived in Yellowstone from his previous post as superintendent of Grand Teton National Park in 1967, he brought biologist Glen Cole with him to serve as supervisory wildlife biologist. In Grand Teton, Cole's observations of elk herds had led him to develop a theory of "density-dependence" of wildlife populations. This was the idea that factors crucial to survival, such as the amount of forage available to a herd of ungulates, become more influential as a population grows in size, depressing the growth rate of the population by affecting birth or survival rates.[8] In other words, if left to their own devices in an ecologically complete habitat, elk populations, at least, would control or "regulate" their numbers so as to remain within the carrying capacity of their habitat. In essence, this was the idea that has come to be applied to other wildlife and known as "natural regulation" in the NPS.

Although he didn't invent the concept, Cole's ideas about natural regulation led him to lean in the direction of Adolph Murie when it came to the kinds of management advocated in the Leopold Report. Whereas the report had recommended that the parks use manipulative management techniques to create a natural "scene," Cole wondered if a natural scene wouldn't be the ultimate result of doing the opposite—in essence, allowing "nature" to "take its course" in the parks.[9] This issue, among others, soon led him to be greatly concerned over the research methods and conclusions of John and Frank Craighead, who had been conducting grizzly bear research in the park for several years under an agreement entered into with the previous superintendent, Lon Garrison.

In 1958, the Craigheads and their project had seemed like a dream come true for Yellowstone's managers. One reason was the unprecedented scope of the project, for the first time allowing researchers to judge the long-term effects of management actions and policy implementation and promising to provide NPS officials with sufficient data for making scientifically sound management decisions. Park staff were initially eager for the Craigheads to propose management recommendations based on their findings.[10]

From 1959 until 1971, John and Frank Craighead and their team of researchers studied the nature, numbers, and needs of Yellowstone's grizzlies. The Craigheads were pioneers in the field of radio telemetry, which allowed them to identify individual bears and track not only their movements but also their lifeways over long periods of time. In addition to radio collars, the Craigheads used small metal ear tags and brightly colored ear streamers to mark bears for identification and classification. Marked animals had a number tattooed on their armpit or lip so they could be identified even if they lost their other markings. In order to be collared, tagged, and/or tattooed, bears had to be immobilized and sedated with tranquilizing drugs. Here again, the Craigheads were at the forefront of technological innovation. Over the first nine years of their project, the group captured and marked 235 grizzlies; followed the careers of individual bears from year to year; recorded changes in the social organization of the bear community; and tried to determine the size, composition, and growth trends of the population and the diverse factors, both natural and imposed, that influenced it.[11] The bears that fed at the park's backcountry dumps were the primary subjects of their research.

However, under Jack Anderson, whose marching orders were to implement the recommendations set forth in the Leopold and Robbins Reports, minimizing "observable artificiality" in Yellowstone meant intensifying efforts to end the public spectacle of roadside feeding and closing the park's open-pit dumps, where grizzly bears still came to feed on a regular basis.[12] In essence, this meant re-creating the "natural bear" in Yellowstone. Believing that weaning bears from garbage slowly by closing the dumps gradually would only lead to more generations of bears learning to eat trash for a living, and that grizzlies that dined on human garbage became habituated to humans, the park's administration decided that the best course of action would be to close all of the dumps as soon as possible—to get the bears off garbage in a "cold turkey" manner.

This decision concerned the Craigheads, who, after eight years of studying the park's grizzlies, believed that such swift and drastic action could result in "tragic personal injury, costly damages, and a drastic reduction in the number of grizzlies."[13] If closure was to happen, they favored a gradual approach accompanied by the introduction of "ecocenters"—backcountry carrion feeding stations where the park would drop dead ungulates from helicopters, with the dual goal of both providing grizzlies with supplemental nutrition in the wake of the dump closures and concentrating them away from developed areas and the park's boundaries, outside which they were not protected. The Craigheads made these recommendations in a 113-page draft report, "Management of Bears in Yellowstone National Park," which they submitted to park managers in 1967. In it, they also advocated that in order to optimize the grizzly's preservation, the NPS should reduce the number of grizzlies killed in control actions, work with agencies and landowners outside the park boundaries to provide increased protection, and allow scientists like themselves to continue research and managerial assessments.

The release of "Management of Bears in Yellowstone National Park" seems to mark the point at which relations between the Craigheads and the NPS began to sour. Part of the park's original written agreement with the brothers required them to prepare a management plan for Yellowstone's grizzlies; as early as 1964, Cole's predecessor had argued that that section of the agreement should be deleted because the park was responsible for preparing its own management plans. Several of the "Management of Bears" report's recommendations conflicted with the new management policies being implemented in the park, including the nascent concept of natural regulation. When Anderson circulated the draft report among his resource management staff at Yellowstone, their response was generally negative.

Chief Naturalist John Good wondered whether there was "some way we can get off of the road we seem to be on which leads to manipulative management of more and more species as time goes on? If we can't find another road Yellowstone's vignette of primitive America will be about as valid as Disneyland's Grand Canyon . . . and our claims to ecological management will be suspect to say the least."[14]

Research Biologist Bill Barmore opined that he didn't think Yellowstone "should have to sacrifice its reason for being—preservation of the primeval for the enjoyment of people—just to save the grizzly bear by encouraging unnaturally high densities in the park. . . . It shouldn't be the purpose of Yellowstone to be a grizzly refuge." Cole himself felt that the recommendations about phasing out the dumps and providing supplemental carrion feeding stations in order to accommodate the needs of grizzlies were tantamount to creating artificial concentrations of the bears, and thus departed "so greatly from park objectives that I won't even comment." NPS deputy chief scientist Robert Linn wrote, "It seems to me to be unscientific to recommend augmentation of population numbers when the entire idea is to present a natural population."[15]

In addition, park officials considered research and management functions to be separate. Because the park was responsible for devising and implementing its own management plans, it was not seen as appropriate that the Craigheads should be actively making recommendations for management, that is, telling the NPS what to do.[16] Against the Craigheads' recommendations, the NPS proceeded with plans to quickly close Yellowstone's open-pit dumps. At Trout Creek, one of the park's two major dump facilities, trash was separated, with combustibles being incinerated (an action the Craigheads had recommended), which resulted in reduced amounts of organic matter being available for consumption by grizzly bears.

In addition to ensuring that the park's bears ate a natural diet and were not artificially concentrated into certain areas, "presenting a natural population" came to mean ensuring that what visitors saw in the park conjured notions of the primitive and wild. The Craigheads suggested, at one point, that one of their proposed ecocenters be located on the east side of the Yellowstone River in Hayden Valley, where visitors could watch grizzlies feeding on the carrion from a safe distance. To the park's managers, however, that proposal sounded a bit too reminiscent of the park-sponsored feeding shows of years past. In fact, in his field notes from a 1968 visit to the park, during which he had specifically discussed the idea with Anderson and Cole, Adolph Murie wrote that the two NPS officials had agreed with Murie's own feeling that "tourists did not deserve to see bears from [the] roadside."[17]

Instead, Cole felt it was essential that the park provide an opportunity for visitors to safely see grizzlies in a nonmanipulated setting, or at least be aware that the animals existed in the park, because "the primary purpose of parks is providing visitors with the opportunity to see and appreciate natural plant and animal scenes as they would have occurred in primitive times." For those times when no representative grizzly was willing to oblige the visitor by spontaneously appearing in a primitive scene, Cole proposed that interpretive signs informing visitors of the bear's unseen presence be erected at either end of Hayden Valley. The signs would be accompanied by the following text: "The Hayden Valley is the home of the grizzly bear and other native animal life. Enjoy these scenes of primitive America from your car, or by staying on the roadside. Foot travel off roadsides is prohibited to assure your safety and to avoid disturbing the wild animals." Regardless of whether they ever actually saw a bear, Cole wrote, visitors would be enriched just by knowing they had driven through grizzly habitat.[18]

Along with clearly reiterating the tenets of the Leopold Report, Cole's text had another, perhaps serendipitous effect: it replaced the friendly, reliable roadside bear and the dangerous, "horror" bear of the past with the potentially dangerous, mysterious, imaginary bear—one whose power lay in its ability to generate excited anticipation over an encounter with the unknown. The imaginary bear, still evoked today, is less cheaply entertaining than the roadside beggar bear but far more potent. Taking the form of diaphanous suggestion rather than experienced reality, the imaginary bear is an empty vessel to be filled by visitors with a wealth of meaning and possibilities far more expansive than those of the past. In essence, it represents the difference between the predictable, packaged experience of old and a new, unpredictable kind of experience more akin to what one would get on a wilderness adventure than on a trip to the circus.

According to the Craigheads, however, it wasn't just interpretive bears that Cole wanted to imagine into the landscape, it was an entire population of real bears. One of the key disputes arising between Yellowstone's managers and the Craigheads was over the brothers' contention that the vast majority of Yellowstone's grizzlies utilized the dumps for food at one time or another. Because of this, the Craigheads reasoned that if food sources to which the bears had become accustomed over generations were suddenly removed, the grizzlies would move into nearby campgrounds to seek garbage, which would lead to their removal from the ecosystem either by relocation or lethal control, ultimately resulting in the extinction of Yellowstone's grizzly population.[19]

Cole felt that two distinct grizzly bear populations lived in the park—a population of "garbage bears" that used the dumps and were tracked by the Craigheads, and a "backcountry" population that did not use the dumps and were not tracked. Accordingly, Cole reasoned that the effects of swift dump closures on the park's overall grizzly population would not be as dire as the brothers predicted. In his view, grizzlies that were habituated to garbage and could not adjust to its absence were doomed anyway, and would be replaced by others in a naturally regulated population. Dump closure was an all-or-nothing proposition; the idea of phasing them out was "an impossible research design for evaluating a practice which must either be *continued* or *eliminated*."[20]

In response to the cool reception given their report by park managers, the Craigheads took their case to the media, releasing the document publicly and consenting to several newspaper interviews. When two women were mauled to death on the same night by grizzlies in Glacier National Park in the summer of 1967, John Craighead told the *Great Falls Tribune* that the deaths were the result of the NPS's recently implemented policies to reduce the amount of garbage available to bears in that park. By June 1968, A. Starker Leopold was expressing his concern over "the hostile situation at Yellowstone between the Craighead boys and the Park Service." He suggested that an ad hoc committee be formed to review the Craighead project and figure out how to make the most of what the brothers had learned lest the knowledge fall victim to bad blood and go unused.[21]

In 1969, that committee presented its findings. The NPS's Natural Sciences Advisory Committee, led by Leopold himself, released "A Bear Management Policy and Program for Yellowstone National Park," whose goal was to recommend how the park could best restore the grizzly to natural foods by closing the dumps while minimizing human injuries and bear deaths. The committee suggested a number of fairly familiar policies in preparation for the closures, including better sanitation, public education, increased patrols, scare devices, fencing, and campground closures and relocations. In addition, it advised Yellowstone's managers to study bears' reactions to dump closures, recommended ways to deal with intransigent animals, and urged continued research and early publication of the Craigheads' findings. Echoing the Craigheads, it also recommended that during the transition period of dump closure, the park should establish backcountry feeding stations by dropping carrion into remote locations by helicopter in order to draw bears away from occupied areas.[22]

Based on the results of the committee's report, Yellowstone's managers released their "Program for the Protection and Management of Grizzlies over a

Transition Period to Restore Bears to Using Natural Foods." The program in-
corporated most of the committee's recommendations, with one glaring
omission: the carrion drops. The transition program called for the park's
dumps to be closed swiftly, with the grizzly population foraging entirely on
natural foods by the park's centennial year of 1972, with no feeding stations
in the plans.[23] The open-pit dump at Rabbit Creek (in the Old Faithful vicinity) was slated for closure in 1970, and the final dump, Trout Creek (in Hayden Valley), in 1971.

Then, on June 10, 1969, a 475-pound grizzly bear mauled a visitor at the
park's Fishing Bridge campground—a pretty little five-year-old girl from St.
Paul, Minnesota, named Daphne Jax. Jax had been returning from a trip to
the restroom about 8:30 P.M. when she rounded a corner and surprised an
old male grizzly that wrapped its jaws around her chest and shook, then
dropped her. She suffered a broken rib and punctured lung, but made a fine
recovery after a couple of weeks in the hospital. The bear was shot dead
about an hour after the attack. Jax remained cheerful throughout her hospital stay, but declared to the press that she did not like bears and, as a result,
had no desire to return to Yellowstone. Ever.[24]

As the story was pieced together, it became evident that the bear had not
attacked Daphne out of starvation due to the reduced garbage available at the
dumps (as some suspected), but rather had been agitated prior to encountering her; a couple of screaming children had been pelting the grizzly with
rocks and bottles. In the course of running away from them, the bear ran directly into the little girl. Nevertheless, John and Frank Craighead repeated
their claim that the NPS's decision to swiftly close the dumps had forced
grizzlies into campgrounds in search of food. Newspapers all over the intermountain West picked up the story that the NPS was directly to blame for
Jax's mauling. Anderson responded that, in fact, the purpose of the garbage
reduction had been to keep bears *out* of campgrounds and that everything
possible had been done to mitigate the dump closure, including installing
bearproof trash cans throughout the park, cutting off other unnatural food
sources, and warning visitors of the dangers posed by bears. He also maintained that campers, not the bear, were to blame for the attack.[25]

A week after the incident, in a memo to Anderson, Glen Cole reiterated
his position that the park's frontcountry "garbage bears" had no value or
place in the park, and that because of the dangers they posed to humans,
"retaining such bears will jeopardize the preservation of a truly wild grizzly
population in Yellowstone. . . . I would recommend no hesitancy in destroying adult animals that have become too wary to trap or immobilize

and habitually frequent campgrounds." At the same time, the park's administration was under pressure from the Craigheads to stop killing grizzlies. Park managers had recorded 34 management removals of grizzlies since the brothers began their research in the park, with the numbers rising following the arrival of Anderson and Cole in 1967. In 1969, 10 grizzlies had been removed; another 10 would be removed in 1970. In 1968, for the first time ever, more grizzlies had been killed than black bears. The same would happen in 1970 and 1971, as new policies directed rangers to deal with each and every grizzly bear spotted in or near a park campground. The researchers' frustration was palpable at the loss of potential data that occurred each time one of their study bears was killed, rather than tranquilized and relocated.[26]

One new management policy with which no bear expert disagreed was the Anderson administration's decision to force changes in visitor behavior relative to the park's roadside black bears. Finally recognizing that it might be easier to teach humans not to feed bears than to continue trying to teach bears not to seek human foods, Yellowstone's 1969 Bear Management Policy (BMP) outlined specific goals for education and enforcement, which would no longer be crippled by the "wink-wink, nudge-nudge" approach favored in the past. Warning literature passed out at entrance stations was to be "bluntly and honestly worded including notification of strict enforcement of the no feeding regulation," and they meant it—feeders finally began to be consistently ticketed and prosecuted. Prior to that time, though warnings had numbered in the hundreds, Yellowstone's rangers had issued only 10–12 actual citations for bear feeding each year. In the summer of 1969, 89 citations were issued, with offenders fined $10 each.[27]

Although 89 tickets was probably still just a drop in the bucket compared to the total number of feeders out there, this more regular enforcement of the rules against feeding was, by all accounts, an immediate success. Between 1967 and 1971, bear-related injuries dropped from 61 to 7. Between 1969 and 1971, the number of citations issued for bear feeding dropped from 89 to 34, and Yellowstone's roadside begging bears went from being a common to a rare sight. Regardless of this precipitous decline, Glen Cole suggested in 1971 that the situation could be further improved if the park issued press releases publicizing the names, home states, and fines charged to violators and billed them for the cost of relocating problem bears.[28] Though there is no evidence that this idea was put into practice, the number of annual injuries continued to fall, and has never again reached double digits.

And so what had for so long been considered unthinkable and impossible—getting Yellowstone's visitors to stop feeding Yellowstone's bears—was finally achieved in just a few short summers by enforcing a regulation that had existed in some form for seventy years. It also may be that, as was shown by the earlier surveys, people were fairly ready to stop feeding by the late 1960s, when environmental attitudes were changing; perhaps people were adopting the notion that the bears possessed inherent value beyond providing entertainment to park visitors.[29] From that time on, the primary focus of active bear management in Yellowstone shifted from black bears to grizzly bears. This emphasis remains largely the same today.

Also in 1969, keeping a clean camp became the law in Yellowstone, rather than a recommendation for visitor convenience. Unfortunately, compliance with this regulation was impeded by the same sorts of problems that for decades had slowed enforcement of the no-feeding rule. For one thing, the information provided to the public did not reflect the transition from recommendation to requirement. In 1972, the actual rule, "All food or similar organic material must be kept completely sealed in a vehicle or camping unit that is constructed of solid, nonpliable material, or must be suspended at least 10 feet above the ground and 4 feet horizontally from any post or tree trunk," became little more than friendly advice on the information distributed to park visitors: "Yellowstone is bear country. Maintain a clean camp and keep food in the trunk of your car."[30]

The results were evident. Park maintenance personnel estimated that they were discovering anywhere from 25 to 50 ice chests left out each night at the park's major campgrounds. To compound the problem, some rangers appeared reluctant to enforce the new rule due to the seeming unwillingness of the park's commissioner to deal with such cases. By mid-July, rangers had issued only three citations for failure to properly store food in campgrounds, despite innumerable violations.[31]

Enforcement of the no-feeding rules was a key component of the park's program to encourage primitive presentation and re-create a "natural" bear population in keeping with the goals of Superintendent Anderson's administration. With all the energy being devoted to natural appearances in the park, it seems fitting that, beginning in 1969, the park administration's dispute with the Craigheads finally culminated over the issue of how Yellowstone's bears *looked* once they had been tagged and collared for the Craigheads' study. In that year, citing aesthetic reasons and the need to make the park presentable for its upcoming 1972 centennial, the NPS razed the old building that had housed the Craigheads' in-park laboratory, forcing them to move their headquarters to a location outside the park boundaries, in West Yellowstone, Montana. Four months later, aesthetic reasons made the park's administration reluctant to allow the brothers to extend their telemetry studies to a herd of elk that frequented the roadside along the Firehole and Gibbon rivers because "neckbands and radio transmitters used to date are very conspicuous and animals so marked are seen and photographed by large numbers of visitors."[32]

The stage was set for a fight of science versus scenery, and concern about marking scenic elk soon turned into concern over marking grizzly bears. Anderson expressed unease over the "prevalence of conspicuously marked wildlife throughout the park" to John Craighead. Furthermore, he wrote, "we wonder if the continuous use of park wildlife to develop, test and improve biotelemetry systems represents too great a conflict with our attempts to portray natural conditions for visitors. . . . Something . . . seems to be lost in viewing our grizzly bears with either colored streamers hanging from their ears or brilliant radio collars." Anderson was supported in his opposition to research marking by Glen Cole and Adolph Murie, who in a 1968 visit with Anderson and Cole had expressed his negative views on the use of such "gadgetry" in national parks and wilderness areas. Several years later, Cole himself would recommend against allowing the use of collars in wolf research at Isle Royale National Park, explaining, "I personally have difficulty with the concept that wolves must be captured and marked in order to study *natural* processes." Cole suggested ways in which researchers could acquire their information by less intrusive, nontechnological means.[33]

The necessity of creating a natural appearance in the park was the reason park staff most consistently used to justify NPS actions that proved frustrating to the Craigheads throughout their next and final two years in Yellowstone. The park's impending centennial only increased Anderson's determination, and the importance of optimizing the park's natural appearance by the summer of 1972 was repeated like a mantra in his communications with the brothers. Although it might be suspected that Anderson had simply latched on to an ancillary issue as a means of ridding himself of the Craigheads' increasingly problematic presence, Anderson was consistent on the subject of what he perceived to be visual intrusions in the park's wilderness landscape. Road signs concerned him as much as wildlife markings, and shortly after it was erected, Glen Cole's interpretive grizzly bear sign in the Hayden Valley was recommended for removal by C. K. Townsend, chairman of Anderson's Sign Committee. Townsend, who believed that the sign's primary goal was to encourage visitors to view wildlife from the safety of their cars rather than wandering around searching for it, asserted that it was having the opposite effect, as was evidenced by the increasing numbers of social trails at its site and along others of Yellowstone's roadsides. He also argued that the sign was redundant because visitors could receive the same message by tuning in to one of the park's informational radio messages at the same location. Townsend concluded by expressing the rather militant view that "every sign in the park is an intrusion on and distraction from the natural scene."[34]

In early 1969, when the Craigheads asked to extend their study past 1971 in order to more fully assess the effects of dump closure on the park's grizzly population, Anderson informed Regional Director Fred Fagergren not only that he did not wish to grant that extension, but also that the park would "additionally require that no new bears or other park wildlife be conspicuously marked and markers be progressively removed from any animals not essential to the study." Fagergren responded favorably to Anderson's suggestions. In April, Anderson told John Craighead that "the conspicuous marking of park wildlife seems to have reached the point where it detracts from the scenic and esthetic values obtained from viewing wildlife. . . . We realize our wildlife . . . affords an unusual opportunity to immobilize and mark animals at will, but these are also animals that will be seen and photographed by thousands of visitors each year." Anderson concluded by advising Craighead to find an area outside the park to continue any studies involving telemetry after 1971.[35]

Craighead agreed to relocate the team's studies of elk and black bears to an area outside the park and to end the grizzly study in 1971, but took issue with Anderson's claims that the tags, streamers, and collars worn by grizzlies had caused sufficient aesthetic disruption to warrant ending an eleven-year, $1 million research project at such a crucial point as that which would directly follow the final dump closures, which were imminent. He told Anderson that 256 grizzlies had been marked over the course of the study, but never more than 100 at any given time.[36] Craighead also asserted that the grizzly was seldom viewed by visitors—that even the study team had seen only a few marked grizzlies in well-traveled areas of the park—and pointed out that past researchers had conspicuously marked the park's much more visible roadside black bears without eliciting similar complaint from the park's administration.

In fact, Craighead was right—past park managers had used tagging as a political asset in the past. Former superintendent John McLaughlin, who served briefly between Lon Garrison and Jack Anderson, had received complaints about the effect of ear tags on the visual experience, but had taken the side of science. When one visitor wrote to complain about seeing bears with tagged ears, McLaughlin had explained that the park's administration had decided to "sacrifice natural appearance" for the sake of carrying out an effective study. When another wrote to complain of ursine campground marauders, ear tags were specifically referred to as a sign of positive changes to come: "Research is helping—maybe you saw a tagged bear during your visit."[37]

Craighead also told Anderson that in his experience, more people were interested in seeing marked animals and learning about research than were opposed to this practice. It is hard to determine how many protests about marked bears Anderson may have received, but one truly stands out in the record—a set of song lyrics written by Helen Heaton, a college professor from Stevens Point, Wisconsin. Set to the tune of a song called "Beans in Your Ears," the text was as follows:

> We drive up to Yellowstone often each year,
> Expecting to peer at the elk and the deer,
> To build us a campfire and singe all our hair,
> And feed us a bear,
> And feed us a bear.

> The last time we went we were somewhat surprised
> At what greeted our eyes,
> I swear I'm not fibbing,
> Those bears were all wearing those bright colored ribbons,
> Those bears all had tags in their ears,
> Those bears all had tags in their ears.

> We wondered if Vogue magazine had been there,
> Giving fashion advice on what bears should wear.
> We finally decided the tags were prepared
> To honor the outstanding bear,
> To honor the outstanding bear.

> The bears that are wearing those ear tags of yellow
> Are feeling quite mellow
> Like satisfied fellows.
> They ripped up the tents of a troop of boy scouts
> And ate up their ninety nine trout,
> And ate up their ninety nine trout.

There were bears wearing ear ribbons made of plain white,
Who patrolling the campground the previous night,
Found nothing to satisfy their appetite,
So they gave some poor dude a bad bite,
Gave some poor dude a bad bite.

In some bruins' ears there were ribbons of red.
Those arrogant bears gave the dudes haughty stares.
We wondered about them till some friendly stranger
Said those bears have bitten a ranger,
Said those bears have bitten a ranger.

You might not believe it but I'll swear I saw
The South District Ranger shake a big grizzly's paw,
Cause it and the others wearing ribbons of blue,
Had bit them a Craighead or two,
Had bit them a Craighead or two.

The garbage dump bears had no ribbons at all,
They just sat in the dumps on their furry fat rumps.
They're ashamed to be seen on the road all this year,
For they've no colored tags in their ears,
For they've no colored tags in their ears.

We appreciate research and what one can learn
But we are starting to fear that the next thing we'll hear
Is the Craigheads have got them a grant for next year
To tag all the dudes in their ears,
To tag all the dudes in their ears.

We think Mother Nature's adornment will do.
Bears don't need those ribbons
Of red, white, and blue,
So Dear Mr. Ranger, we'll give you three cheers
For removing those tags from bears' ears,
For removing those tags from bears' ears.[38]

Regardless of whether the park's administrators were thrilled to hear that one of the professor's annual goals in Yellowstone was "to feed us a bear," they agreed with her feelings about tagging, and in the summer of 1971, rumors reached John Craighead that Yellowstone's rangers had received verbal instructions from Anderson to remove the markings of any bears captured in control actions.[39] Incensed, Craighead reminded Anderson that the markers were crucial to the Craigheads' research, and that the Craigheads' own data showed that "far less than 1%" of Yellowstone's visitors ever saw a marked grizzly—a statistic that he felt invalidated Anderson's claims that color markers were severely disruptive to the visitor experience. Anderson responded that only four color streamers and one metal ear tag had been removed, the tag by mistake, and countered that 1 percent of Yellowstone's visitors was still "25,000 persons that are short-changed in seeing the grizzly as it occurs naturally."[40]

In August 1971, the NPS submitted a revised Memorandum of Understanding (MOU, the agreement governing the terms of the Craigheads' studies in the park) to the Craigheads, under which they would be permitted to continue several studies in the park. This new version contained changes that the Craigheads perceived to threaten their academic freedom, most notably a clause requiring that all manuscripts be submitted to the NPS for review prior to their publication. It also stipulated that the brothers were to obtain some of their information from the NPS rather than collecting it themselves. The Craigheads elected not to sign the MOU, and the formal association between them and the NPS was finished. The brothers expressed their reasons for refusing to sign the MOU to the public through the press, and it was perhaps this episode more than any other that earned the NPS a persistent reputation, deserved or not, for resistance to and attempts to censor independent research.[41]

Despite the Craigheads' protests, park managers had closed Yellowstone's dumps on schedule, in accordance with the transition plan. Operations ceased at Rabbit Creek in 1970 and at Trout Creek in 1971, in time for the much anticipated centennial summer of 1972. All interested eyes were on Yellowstone, the Craighead controversy raged on, and at the height of that visitor season a grizzly bear attacked and killed twenty-five-year old Harry Eugene Walker of Anniston, Alabama, who was camped illegally in the Old Faithful area. The results were singularly gruesome, and the story again made rich fodder for the press. Harry Walker's family sued the park for $500,000, claiming negligence and wrongful conduct. The suit blamed Walker's death on the park's bear management policies, specifically the dump closures, and alleged that the NPS had failed to properly warn visitors of the dangers posed by bears. The plaintiffs' star witness was Frank Craighead, who testified on their behalf for a full day and a half. In 1975, U.S. District Court Judge Andrew Hauk ruled against the NPS, awarding the Walker family $84,417.67. The ruling was overturned in the following year on the grounds that the NPS couldn't possibly be held responsible for ensuring that all of its 25,000 daily visitors received their warning literature and were fenced into their campsites at night (as per one of Judge Hauk's recommendations)—especially those who chose to camp in unsanctioned areas.[42]

Despite the publicity generated by the Walker situation and the specter of ravenous, bloodthirsty Yellowstone grizzlies it created, bear-related injuries recorded in the park had actually reached an all-time low in 1972, with a total of eight, six of which were not caused by grizzlies. As park managers continued to strive to create a more natural "wilderness" bear, they also strove to get visitors to experience the park's more wild places. Author Paul Schullery remembered that during these years, which coincided with the first Earth Day and the height of the back-to-nature and backpacking crazes of the 1970s, the belief was that getting people out of their cars was the best way to bring out their preservationist urges: "The message wasn't necessarily that you have to hike to [Kingdom Come], so much as you have to get out of your car and connect a little bit, even if you just walk a hundred yards down the trail." George Wilson of the *Washington Post* put it a bit more emphatically: "The biggest frustration of all for Yellowstone managers is the 'togetherness in the wilderness' nesting instinct of the visitors. . . . Superintendent Anderson and his colleagues hope to find a way to persuade more of Yellowstone's visitors to move off the well-worn paths and discover the wilderness."[43]

In the same way that they had conceived of, re-created, and now managed the park as a "total environment," rather than for the benefit of a few select species or features, park managers started to conceive of, re-create, manage, and promote the act of seeing the park as a "total environment," rather than one that specifically catered to the desires of the passive eye. It was no longer enough for visitors to just hum along in their cars until sitting in traffic meant that there were bears to be fed and photographed ahead. The new wilderness visitor would quit the car and get into the backcountry, experiencing the park on a more complete, deeper level.

Accordingly, a number of new interpretive programs in Yellowstone encouraged visitors to consider their place in Yellowstone with solemnity as well as revelry, and to start thinking of the park as an ecosystem. These programs communicated a broader, heavier sense of humans' capacity to affect the environment, and the environment's power to affect people, than had been seen before. In 1969, a program called "The Living Land," previously limited to a description of Yellowstone's flora, described "the plants and animals of Yellowstone, their dependence upon one another, and man's role." The evening program, "Our Sacred Lands," went from explaining "the heritage of our National Parks" in previous years to "talk[ing] about this park and others, and what open space and wild land can mean to our lives." In 1971, "The Living Land" became "This Wild Land."[44]

In addition, two new interpretive installations asked visitors not only to see themselves differently, but also to experience the park without "seeing" it at all—the Grant Village listening chairs and the Three Senses Nature Trail. At the Grant Village visitor center, the "listening chairs" were a collection of egg-shaped body helmets that catered to the ear rather than the eye. Designed so a person could crawl into one of them and be isolated from the rest of the visitor center, the chairs were positioned so that visitors could look out the window (presumably into the wilderness) while listening to an audiotaped program. When the listener pressed a button, a wave of ethereal, "primevil [sic]" music started to flow through the helmet, swelling to an expansive theme and then diminishing beneath the voice of a narrator who had been specially chosen because of his ability to facilitate the "wilderness mood": "You are on the threshold of one of the last great remaining wildernesses in America. A scant few yards from the controlled environment of this visitor center, man is an intruder. He walks the forest floor, climbs the rock-strewn ridges and paddles across the sparkling lakes as one tiny thread in the huge web of life which surrounds him." The recording's hypnotic narrative instructed visitors to conjure up the archetypal memories shared by their primeval ancestors, then chanted, "The need is real. Periodically you must return to the wilderness . . . you must renew your oneness with natural things . . . you may never understand why the wilderness rejuvenates; why you revel in its beauty and feel humble in its vastness. But . . . you know you do. And you know . . . that for some inexplicable reason you need wilderness as you need food and water. For you are MAN—and you are of the wilderness."[45]

The listening chairs postulated wilderness as a basic human need—the need to flee the modern world and retreat to the environmental womb from whence we all came, rooted in Jungian urges of mysterious origin. They de-emphasized human domination, instead depicting humans as tiny buoys floating in a vast wilderness ocean. Although the overall message was not new—Olaus Murie, for instance, had written that "wilderness represents man's original home" back in 1960—this was a new kind of NPS interpretation, not only in its form but in its message. The script for the listening chairs was also devoid of dates and "other specific data," promoting instead the larger idea of human universality rooted in primeval nature. Its potential narrators were carefully screened for their abilities to convey vocal qualities that Superintendent Anderson associated with wilderness.[46] The Grant Village listening chairs forced visitors to encounter Yellowstone through senses other than sight—to connect with their environment through sound and imagination rather than visual pleasure.

In the Lower Geyser Basin, the Three Senses Nature Trail did the same. Although it was conceived as an interpretive trail for the blind (the first of its kind in the NPS system), the timing of its appearance located the Three Senses trail within an experiment geared toward prodding the visitor away from passive sight-collecting (i.e., the "checklist" approach to national park visitation) in favor of a more holistic, qualitative park experience. Fitted with a series of signs connected by a metal rope whose text appeared both in print and in Braille, the trail asked visitors to experience Yellowstone through senses other than sight for a few minutes. Each sign instructed visitors to close their eyes and follow the metal rope with one hand until it bumped into the next sign. While walking, they should concentrate on a sound, smell, or tangible feeling that the previous sign had told them to be alert for along the way. Located on the park's Fountain Flat Drive, the trail wound through a small thermal area where visitors feasted their ears on hissing steam and bubbling water, inhaled the sulfuric reek of thermal gases, caressed the nubbly bark of evergreens, and generally learned that there was more to a trip to Yellowstone than just seeing a bear and snapping a shot of Old Faithful.[47]

The interpretive de-emphasis on sight as the dominant sense utilized by visitors in their Yellowstone experiences was consistent with the management policies recommended in the Robbins Report, emphasizing focus on the system as a whole rather than on individual components. Not everyone was convinced, however. Many wrote to complain, to ask why the NPS didn't want to let people see bears anymore, to inquire what was wrong with bears eating at garbage pits anyway, to suggest that the park institute a series of feeding stations for bears (à la the Craigheads' ecocenters) lest they die out in the absence of garbage-food, and to offer the idea that perhaps bears could be kept in a confined space where they could be safely viewed. Newspaper articles claimed to speak for the public with headlines and statements such as "Park Tourists Miss Begging Bears," and "Ask 99 out of 100 People What They Want to See Most and It's the Bears." Park officials responded to the question, "Where are all the bears?" by informing the public that

Yellowstone's bears were still alive and well and living in the park, but were no longer as easily seen because they had lost interest in begging as a result of the law enforcement and relocation programs begun in earnest a couple of years before, and now served the higher purpose of spiritually elevating visitors lucky enough to see them: "When bears are not fed, they quickly adapt to taking natural foods, and while fewer are seen by visitors, those that are seen will be more representative of wild bears in a natural habitat, uncorrupted by man."[48]

Pierre Bourdieu has written that there is distinction in distancing oneself from a source of pleasure; that "high taste is in part based on the degree to which one abstracts oneself from one's emotional reaction to things." The "pure aesthetic is rooted in an ethos of elective distance from the necessities of the natural and social world," and "good taste" represents a break from life on the ground—rather, it represents life lived in the plane of artificial construct, distant from the body and its needs.[49] The wilderness way of seeing bears—as creatures whose ability to thrill lies in their innate wildness, rarity, and status as a symbol of the wilderness setting they require—subjugates the corporeal to the intellectual. In a sense, wilderness itself is about restraining individual desire for the sake of a higher moral purpose; resisting the urge to develop, to kill, to leave one's mark, out of an appreciation for the socially constructed sanctity of the land and the geographical escape from the more tangible everyday that it provides. In this context, feeding the natural bear becomes morally unthinkable, the act of the crass and unenlightened who are incapable of the restraint practiced by the more highly evolved. This ideal could be seen at work in the park's new bear message.

In their interpretive offerings and resource management policies of the early 1970s, park managers promoted an ethos of holism—the extraordinary idea that even in a land of exceptional curiosities, no single component of environment or experience should be favored over another. This approach not only was ideologically synchronous with the park's controlling policy documents and the idea of natural regulation but was also reflected in the park's 1972 Master Plan, a document that redefined the park's very purpose and goals in accordance with the new policies.

Minimizing human impact on the environment was a significant goal of the plan, which called for moving camping and overnight facilities to gateway communities near the park and instituting public transportation, instead of private vehicles, as the primary mode of visitor transport. The Master Plan, still nominally in effect today, also amended the park's mission to accurately reflect the goals and beliefs of the day:

Yellowstone National Park . . . was "dedicated and set apart as a public park or pleasuring-ground for the benefit and enjoyment of the people" and "for the preservation, from injury or spoliation, of all timber, mineral deposits, natural curiosities, or wonders . . . and their retention in their natural condition." Thus it was stated in 1872, at a point in this Nation's history when only a handful were convinced that America's natural resources were limited and that the public could not have its cake and eat it too. Today, with the Nation and the park facing an environmental crisis, it should be apparent that to have both is to have neither. In light of this, the original purpose must be translated in terms of contemporary connotations; as such it should read: To perpetuate the natural ecosystems within the park in as near pristine conditions as possible for their inspirational, educational, cultural, and scientific values for this and future generations.[50]

The "updated" mission statement clearly iterated that Yellowstone was a place for wilderness experience, not mass recreation. It also hinted at a formal shift in management philosophy from principles of aesthetic conservation to those of preservation, in light of what its authors recognized as significant changes in the world, and in the needs of the national parks, since the time when the park's Organic Act was originally penned. Also written into the plan was the intention to "restore the natural regime" in the park, which included ceasing the use of pesticides, allowing fires to burn unsuppressed in certain areas, reestablishing predators as a population control method for the northern elk herd, and instituting catch-and-release fishing.[51] To their great credit, the park's managers were true to these big ideas—they supported each with corresponding actions.

The results of these actions were also big, and their success was open to interpretation. Part of restoring the natural regime had meant closing the park's dumps, which had happened on schedule. As the Craigheads had predicted and Cole had expected, grizzly deaths had become more and more frequent as dump operations slowed and ceased. Today's managers estimate that between 1967 and 1972, 229 grizzlies died in the Greater Yellowstone Ecosystem (GYE), partly because as bears spread out to meet their needs, they were killed outside the park. It was not solely the decision to swiftly close the dumps that caused this result, however. At the time of the closures, natural foods available in the park had reached an all-time low because of other wildlife management policies, including the culling of ungulate herds and fishing regulations that were too liberal, leading to overharvesting of the Yellowstone cutthroat trout, a primary staple of the grizzly's natural diet.[52] The culling program ended in 1967, but fishing regulations were not revised until after the release of the Master Plan. Other influences included climate trends, poaching outside the park, and nearby cattle and sheep ranching that attracted bears.

Despite the myriad factors that may have contributed to the grizzlies' decline, the Craigheads maintained that the blame rested primarily with the NPS. In 1973, *National Wildlife* published an interview with Frank Craighead called, "They're Killing Yellowstone's Grizzlies." In it, Craighead predicted imminent extinction if present population trends continued, reinvigorating the rumor that the NPS was engaged in an extermination campaign against the grizzly. In January 1974, Frank Craighead refined that prediction for the *Billings Gazette*: "Craighead: No Bears by 1990." Agency officials, for their part, continued to reassure the public that the NPS was not "killing Yellowstone's grizzlies"; that in fact, "nowhere else is the general public seeing more bears and other wildlife than in Yellowstone." In that same year, *BioScience* published Glen Cole's article, "Management Involving Grizzly Bears and Humans in Yellowstone National Park, 1970–1973," based on the results of Cole's own studies of Yellowstone's grizzlies. In it, Cole asserted that the park's bear management program was right on track, and in fact had proven successful so far.[53]

Understanding the wholly different measures by which each camp was defining success or disaster is key to understanding why the park's managers and the Craigheads could each be convinced that the other was utterly wrong. The NPS perceived its primary bear management goals to be maximizing naturalness and keeping visitors safe, which meant getting bears off human and onto natural foods and reducing the number of bear-related human injuries. In those terms, the program had, in fact, been a success. For the Craigheads, encouraging and maintaining a healthy and viable grizzly bear population was the paramount concern, and in those terms the NPS's bear management program appeared to be failing miserably. Cole had acknowledged the differences in these views in a January 1970 cover letter to the editors of *BioScience,* explaining, "It is recognized that different interpretation can be made if the park's attempts to maintain a grizzly population under natural conditions and provide for the safety of visitors are not considered to be related or primary objectives."[54]

It was also clear that personal differences were contributing to the professional disagreements between the NPS and the Craigheads. In a November 1973 article for the *National Observer,* reporter Michael Malloy wrote,

"Everyone agrees the bear war could have been settled in a spirit of scientific objectivity. But a Craighead supporter says it has been turned into a personal feud by 'that simpering sycophant, Glen Cole,' and a Cole supporter says it has been turned into a personal feud by 'those arrogant, deceptive sons of bitches,' the Craigheads."[55]

Differing goals and personal conflicts may have helped make Yellowstone's managers slow to embrace what was perhaps the Craigheads' most important contribution to American environmental history: the popularization of the Greater Yellowstone Ecosystem (GYE) idea. Central to the Craigheads' work was the recognition that grizzlies and other wildlife with large home ranges didn't observe park boundaries, meaning that the lands surrounding the park were just as crucial to grizzly conservation as the park itself. However, Yellowstone's managers considered Yellowstone's grizzly population to comprise only the bears that appeared to consistently remain within the park's boundaries; in their view, bears that wandered outside the park for significant periods were not part of the Yellowstone grizzly population. Back in 1967, in his response to the Craigheads' management recommendations, Glen Cole had expressed concern that "differences between the resident Park grizzly population and surplus individuals that permanently emigrate outside boundaries [were] not considered" in the report, arguing that census records showed that the park itself had served as an "'ecological unit' for preserving a representative population of grizzly bears."[56]

Cole was not only scientifically skeptical of the GYE concept, he was also concerned about the potential political ramifications of its adoption. In his 1967 memo, he stated that the problem with lumping the "two populations" together was that it would lead to "attributing all hunting mortality outside [park] boundaries to Yellowstone's population which should not be done." In other words, if bears that died outside the park's boundaries were included in the park's population census, the NPS would be held unfairly responsible for mortality numbers over which it legally had no control. Cole maintained that an established distinction between grizzly bears whose home ranges were within Yellowstone and "other bears that are either emigrants or have part or all of their home ranges outside park boundaries" should be recognized.[57]

The passage of the Endangered Species Act of 1973 ensured that the NPS would publicly butt heads with the Craigheads over the issue of whether or not to recognize the GYE as the proper ecological unit for determining the numbers and health of the park's grizzly population. In March 1974, Yellowstone's research biologists Douglas Houston, Mary Meagher, and Glen

Cole presented a united front against the inclusion of Yellowstone's grizzlies on the federal government's list of threatened and endangered species. Although it might sound surprising that the NPS would oppose the listing of a species that it was charged with preserving, the reasoning was familiar: the bears that made their permanent homes within Yellowstone were separate from those that lived outside it, and the bears in the park faced no threats from NPS policies or hunting.[58] Thus, it would not be appropriate for that population to be listed as either endangered or threatened.

In that same year, however, a National Academy of Sciences committee, formed to evaluate Yellowstone's bear management program at the request of the Wyoming congressional delegation, agreed that the park and its adjacent areas should be considered a single ecosystem for purposes of managing the grizzly bear. Known as the Cowan Report for the committee's chair, ecologist Ian McTaggart Cowan, the committee's findings criticized the park's research program, determined that Cole's population estimates were unsupported, and concluded that the grizzly population had probably declined since the dump closures. Although the committee ultimately concluded that Yellowstone's grizzly population was not "in immediate danger of extinction," Cole disputed the specific results of this report, arguing that it included data collected before the dump closures and relied on the Craigheads' census numbers. He also asserted that Yellowstone's grizzly population "is either reaching or has reached carrying capacity," and that the committee's conclusion that the park's research was inadequate for grizzly management in the "Yellowstone Ecosystem" as defined by the Craigheads was not warranted, because the park's research had been carried out on "park bears."[59]

Cole also worried that considering the park and its adjacent lands as a single unit would have the effect of diluting the urgency of the bears' situation outside the park: "As they have been defined, ecosystems for grizzlies combine parks and preserves, where the preservation of representative population units seems assured, with other areas which have remnant numbers of bears and many conflicting human uses. Combining such different situations obscures the precarious states of the grizzly in areas outside parks or preserves, and surely confuses the attempts to classify the species as threatened or endangered in areas where this would be appropriate."[60] In November 1974, he asked U.S. Fish and Wildlife Service director Lynn Greenwalt to remove his name from a list of reviewers for "A Review of the Status of the Grizzly Bear in the Lower 48 States, with Recommendations for a Federal Position," a document investigating the question of whether the grizzly bear should be placed on the Endangered Species list, due to his continued disagreement that the GYE was the proper population unit for evaluating Yellowstone grizzlies.

Despite NPS opposition (as well as Cowan's unpublicized personal change of opinion regarding the percentage of the bear population that may have been underrepresented in the grizzly number estimates used by both the committee and the Craigheads—leading him to the conclusion that there were more grizzlies than either had believed), Yellowstone's grizzlies were included on the list with the rest of the grizzlies of the lower forty-eight states in July 1975. They were listed as threatened rather than endangered—a move that Fund for Animals executive vice president Lewis Regenstein deemed a "sell-out."[61]

If the long fight between the park service and the Craigheads had any happy result, it was the creation, in 1973, of the Interagency Grizzly Bear Study Team (IGBST). Organized by the Department of the Interior, the IGBST is "a centralized research group that promotes data collection and analysis on an ecosystem scale, prevents overlap of effort, and pools limited economic and personnel resources." The group conducts research and provides data needed for short- and long-term management of grizzly bears in the Yellowstone area.[62] Initial IGBST members were the National Park Service, U.S. Forest Service, and U.S. Fish and Wildlife Service. Since 1974, the Idaho, Montana, and Wyoming Departments of Fish and Game have been included. The U.S. Geological Survey's Biological Resources Discipline currently administers the IGBST.

As an independent research unit reporting to several different agencies with several different mandates, the IGBST seemed to be the answer to everyone's wishes regarding Yellowstone grizzly research. The group's goal of preventing "overlap of effort" spoke to the Craigheads' contention and long-standing complaint that Glen Cole's studies had duplicated and interfered with their own, while the idea of pooling economic and human resources maintained the aspect of the Craigheads' research that had been most attractive to the NPS: not having to foot the entire bill. Most importantly, the study team aimed to satisfy those who believed that park science had to be performed by researchers not directly responsible to the park's superintendent.

The IGBST was initially prohibited from radio-collaring grizzlies in Yellowstone, but its former head has claimed that when he told Superintendent Anderson that the team could learn things that even the Craigheads had never known, Anderson began to reconsider. By greatly expanding the

Craigheads' study population and using more collars and improved technology, the study team discovered not only that there was just one free-ranging Yellowstone grizzly population, but also that the home ranges of individuals within that population were larger than even the Craigheads had suspected. With these findings, the GYE concept indubitably arrived in Yellowstone National Park.[63]

The Politics of Peril

In 1975, Yellowstone superintendent Jack Anderson retired from the National Park Service. Supervisory Wildlife Biologist Glen Cole left Yellowstone soon after. Together they had led the park into a new era of bear management and of bear–visitor relations. They had re-established the natural bear in Yellowstone and seen bear-related injuries drop from 61 in 1967 to 3 in 1975. The struggles had been difficult, even ugly. Those that lay ahead would prove no easier for the park's new managers. The grizzly's addition to the Threatened Species list in 1975, and the dire population estimates that would follow, ushered in the idea of the imperiled bear, hanging on to survival by the tips of its claws. The mid-1970s and early 1980s were a time of strong counter-narratives to the NPS's official messages about bears, when vocal critics publicly challenged the soundness of "natural regulation" as a management practice. The imperiled bear, vulnerable as it was, also proved extremely malleable during this period and was shaped into a symbol of vanishing wilderness, a monster of almost supernatural proportion, a pariah for Sagebrush Rebellion-era critics of the U.S. government's land management policies, and finally a component part of an ecosystem—and narrative—defined by science.

Under new superintendent John Townsley, relations between the Craigheads and the park improved, and the press war between the brothers and the NPS briefly ended. Internal problems replaced public arguments. Although the bear management program required vigilant enforcement for success, black bear researcher David Graber and his assistants noticed a "substantial level of violations of the 'bear/food' regulation" in July 1976, leading Graber to conclude that compliance (and thus enforcement) had decreased since the previous summer. Park biologist Mary Meagher concurred with Graber's assessment in her annual evaluation of the park's bear management program for the following year. Meagher, who had previously warned that the most difficult part of a preventive program was its maintenance, cited employee attitudes that had resulted in "inadequate and careless operational mechanics; a tolerance for build-up of a moderate level of bear problems; and an insistence on repetitive moves (rather than control kills) of problem bears."[1]

The park's messages to visitors about bears remained similar to those of recent years. A list of typical questions and their proper responses, devised by park managers to help employees respond to inquiries about the bear population, provides some insight into what types of messages visitors were receiving. The talking points explained that people who wanted to know where the black bears had gone should be told that black bears no longer frequented the roadsides because they were no longer fed there, and because those animals spotted at roadsides were "selectively removed" by park personnel. The adage that "you will see fewer bears in Yellowstone from now on (compared to the roadside circuses of the past), but those seen will be truly wild" was repeated. Visitors who wanted to know the "proper" number of grizzlies in Yellowstone were told, "The 'correct' number is the number that occurs naturally, that is, without artificial foods." The black bear population was estimated to be 650, the grizzly population 250 (though the latter were admittedly difficult to count). Continued enforcement of established rules and policies was named as the best way to prevent additional removals from each population.[2]

If the park's official bear narrative was a bit vague in the mid-1970s, it had at least two competing counternarratives that were anything but. One was offered by "Save the Bears of Yellowstone" (STBOY), led by Dale Brandemihl of West Yellowstone, Montana, which surfaced in 1976. In its literature, STBOY not only mourned the disappearance of the grizzly bear from most of its native range but also railed against encroaching development in the Yellowstone area, depicting a national park in which commercial burger stands, gas stations, and skyscrapers overwhelmed natural beauty. Brandemihl's flyers also pointed out that although it had been common to see thirty bears a day in the park in 1966, ten years later it was "almost impossible" to see one from the road due to the NPS's policy of removing roadside bears. Conflating visible roadside begging with liberty and opposed to the drugging, trapping, and occasional destruction associated with bear research and treatment of problem bears, Brandemihl was intent on "see[ing] what steps can

be taken to allow the bears of the park to roam free once again" and "intro-
ducing . . . alternative practices concerning ways to handle a Bear problem
when one exists, other than to just execute them and not worry about it."
Brandemihl told the *Billings Gazette* that he would bet his life that there were
no more than 65–110 grizzlies left in the GYE, but he was unable to substan-
tiate this claim with any more than a "feeling that there were only a handful
of grizzlies left in the park."[3]

In 1978, Brandemihl told the *Gazette* that he planned to conduct his own
research on the park's bear population. When asked why, in that case, park
managers had never heard of his organization, he explained that he had been
afraid to tell them about his activities lest he be "thrown out like the Craigheads."[4] Nevertheless, he claimed that STBOY hoped to publish its first report on Yellowstone's bear management by November of that year, establish
a research base at Hebgen Lake, and put a stop to all research that required
bears to be drugged and handled. To raise money for his organization, whose
volunteer "researchers" and "directors" he refused to publicly identify,
Brandemihl donned a bear suit and walked the streets of West Yellowstone
holding out a tin cup.

Regardless of its fringe status, STBOY's existence for at least three years in
the mid-1970s elucidated some key issues in the Yellowstone bear debate and
beyond, touching on several topics that would soon become part of a
broader public discourse. These included a general sense of local mistrust toward the NPS, genuine concern for Yellowstone's bears, growing worries
about development and habitat encroachment in the GYE, and questions
about the appropriateness of handling bears in a wilderness setting. All of
these concerns would be taken up by more mainstream environmental
groups in the coming years.

Coming from another arena entirely but also providing a counternarrative
to official messages was a film that banked on the popularity of 1975's *Jaws* and
shamelessly imitated its plot. Describing its subject as "18 feet of gut-
crunching, man-eating terror," *Grizzly!* in 1976 cast a bear, a biologist, and a
park ranger in a clichéd struggle of man versus hostile, murderous Nature,
telling a story of people and bears in the national parks that was about as far
from the romantic wilderness of the Grant Village listening chairs as it could
possibly be. People concerned for grizzly conservation weren't encouraged by
the message that the movie sent to its audience. Writer Bill Schneider, who actually sat through a screening of *Grizzly!*, wrote, "Every time *Grizzly* tore up
somebody, all those children in the theater cowered, screamed, and hid their
eyes. Mauling after mauling, they seemed to build up an intense hate for this

terrible beast. And when the hero blew the bear to bits, they let out a cheer resembling the reaction to the home team pulling out the game at the last second. . . . The crowd went home thinking this was the grizzly bear." Local bear biologist Charles Jonkel acknowledged that the film could "hardly help our grizzly management efforts."[5] It is unlikely that this B movie had much widespread influence, but it did tap into a reinvigorated image of the "horror bear" that would be played out in the popular press over the next few years, often simultaneously with the imperiled bear, fighting for its life in the face of human threats to its existence.

At Yellowstone, public education warning people to keep themselves and their food away from bears continued in its common forms, including brochures, warning signs, in-park radio broadcasts, and reminders at campgrounds and interpretive programs. In a 1977 report, however, Starker Leopold and Purdue University biologist Durward Allen pronounced such traditional media and their messages "grossly inadequate" throughout the park system. They called for antiquated communications to be replaced with multidimensional educational programs designed to reach members of the public long before they ever arrived in the park, to be disseminated through movies, television, and magazines. They also advocated an intensified system of warnings to visitors once they arrived in the park. All in all, they wrote, "a major effort to reach the average citizen seems to be in order [if we are to] counteract . . . the common characterization of the bear as a friendly buffoon." Again, Yogi, Teddy, and Smokey Bears were named as culprits in cultivating that image, along with television's Grizzly Adams and his friend Ben.[6]

Leopold and Allen recommended that the NPS produce a professional film to teach ordinary individuals about the habits of bears, their place in wilderness, and their management. The film should include a summary of the NPS's program to preserve the bear in its natural state and "be a convincing notice to the public that the National Park Service is in earnest about meeting its obligations in an important wildlife field"; that is, it would counteract the allegations of unprofessionalism and mismanagement that had been leveled against the NPS in the media as a result of the Craighead experience. They found the warning signs and brochures distributed to visitors to be "generally trite, casual and unconvincing," and urged that the public must be convinced of the danger posed by bears and that frightening people was not an inappropriate means of achieving that goal. Education should be conceived with the objectives of protecting "the people from the bears; the bears from the people; and the National Park Service from tort cases in the event of mishap." Those final words would later be turned against them.[7]

The very system of bear warnings that Leopold and Allen had criticized became a topic for national debate later that year, when NBC Nightly News ran a segment on grizzly attacks in the national parks since 1967. "With the growing crowds of people visiting the national parks," correspondent Bill Brown told the nation, "grizzlies began to attack more often. . . . In the past eleven years, five people have been mauled to death, and dozens badly hurt." Brown reported two possible explanations for the rise in grizzly–human conflicts: campground foraging resulting from servicewide dump closures and the contemporaneous increase in backcountry hiking.

He then interviewed former Yellowstone visitor and mauling victim Melvin Ford, who was in the process of suing the NPS for $225,000 on the basis that he had not been warned of the danger posed by grizzlies in the park, and that his ignorance had led to his injuries (though according to park officials, rangers had spoken with Ford on the evening of the attack and advised him to put away the ice chest he had left out on the ground. This ice chest, still out, attracted the grizzly that mauled Ford at about 3:30 A.M.). Brown then talked with another visitor who told a similar story and finished by expressing contemporary environmental anxieties about humans overrunning the earth, its wilderness, and its resources, ominously stating, "Bear experts predict more maulings. They say, in the face of invasion from humans, the grizzly has no place left to go."[8]

In response to this segment, and accompanying stories aired by local affiliates, many people took pen in hand to tell the NPS that they couldn't believe what they had just seen on TV. Apparently the years of warnings had finally started to reach beyond the park's boundaries:

How can these people say they were not appropriately warned about the bears when all you see around the park are signs emphasizing animal crossings and fire hazards as well as do not try to feed the bears. This information has been put out as long ago as the Yogi Bear Show 20 years ago! These people will have to suffer with their injuries both mentally as well as physically and for that I sympathise but for their stupidity I have no sympathy.[9]

The news about the bears . . . is the most ridiculous thing I ever heard. You automatically know your [sic] in the animals domain and that's what its all about. . . . If these people want Cony [sic] Island tell them to go to New York. . . . Who needs to be warned about bears at all in this area?[10]

The people say they were not warned. That is a lot of baloney. There are all kinds of warning signs all over the place. . . . It is time people woke up to the fact that they should leave the bears alone. Stay out of their territory or take the punishment.[11]

How can these people blame you and your staff for these grizzly attacks. I agree that is a horrible thing . . . but really whose fault is it. . . . In most cases, it cannot be your fault because of signs posted and verbal warnings and what not. Then it seems to me that in most cases, the blame has to lie on the people who venture up into bear country.[12]

Though the news broadcast had evoked the spirit of both the STBOY and *Grizzly!* counternarratives, it was the former that these writers embraced, at least in one aspect—the idea that people who "invaded" bear country should accept some risk for being there. This perspective was embraced even by grizzly researcher Barrie Gilbert, who famously opposed the killing of the grizzly that mauled in him in 1977.[13]

As public concern and sentiment for Yellowstone's grizzlies grew, their population was sinking drastically. In the summer of 1978, the IGBST had announced that it had no data to indicate a possible population crash; by September 1982 the team's leader, biologist Dr. Dick Knight, stated that the grizzly situation was "critical." In the next month, the *Livingston Enterprise* announced that IGBST members were reporting that Yellowstone's grizzlies were "more threatened than ever," probably numbering fewer than two hundred animals. The *New York Times* also publicized the story. According to the press, the Craigheads and others blamed the NPS for the crash, saying that they had been predicting it for years as a side effect of the swift dump closures and what they felt were the NPS's skewed population figures based on Glen Cole's dual population theory. Park biologist Mary Meagher feared that if things didn't start turning around in a hurry, "we will find ourselves being told what to do about the bear, which may not be rooted in biology and sound agency decisions."[14]

Controversy about the park's brand of science and management soon reached unprecedented heights, with not just the Craigheads but plenty of other people as well trying to telling the NPS what to do. In the February 1983 issue of the *Atlantic Monthly,* an article appeared that told the Yellowstone grizzly story to a whole new audience. In "The Last Bears of Yellowstone," author Alston Chase alluded to a number of social factors that may have contributed to the grizzly's decline in the GYE (e.g., black bear baiting, sheep grazing, poaching, and habitat reduction), but the upshot of his argument was that none of them would be so important if the park's bear policy hadn't "forced" the bears out of the park in search of food when the dumps were closed.[15]

Overall, Chase's article, packed with such quotable claims as "[Yellowstone's] bear program will be a total success when they have eliminated all bears" and "There is not a shred of truth in what you . . . have been told," read like an amicus brief in support of supplemental feeding.[16] Chase affirmed the Craigheads' contention that because people were a component part of the GYE, it was not "unnatural" for bears, as instinctual foragers, to consume their garbage, nor was it unnatural for people, who had been significantly manipulating bear behavior for at least a century, to replace that garbage with carrion "ecocenters" in the sudden absence of the dumps.

"The Last Bears of Yellowstone" was also a denunciation of "natural regulation," which Chase depicted as a failure, unacknowledged as such by an agency whose hubris was too great to allow it to admit it. Chase portrayed natural regulation as the fairy tale of radical environmental daydreamers, an unattainable utopian vision whose goals were made impossible by the unfortunate existence of humanity but were funded with its tax dollars. He also recited Leopold and Allen's statement of goals for education and warnings— "Protect the people from the bears; the bears from the people; and the National Park Service from tort cases in the event of mishap"—and offered it as proof that Yellowstone's managers had pursued their chosen course of action because they were a cadre of lawsuit-fearing ideologues.[17]

To his credit, Chase raised important questions about natural regulation as a management practice. In terms of bear management, what did natural regulation really mean, and how were its parameters defined? Was supplemental carrion feeding really less "natural" than repeatedly translocating bears and killing them? By whose standards and definition? And what of the roles that humans had traditionally played in the ecosystem? Humans were in Yellowstone and had been for thousands of years, yet to Chase and others they seemed to have no place in an NPS management philosophy that proposed to "restore" the ecosystem.

Coming on the heels of the 1979 publication of Frank Craighead's *Track of the Grizzly,* which included a "tell-all" final chapter, "Bureaucracy and Bear," chronicling the park's Anderson years from the Craigheads' perspectives, "The Last Bears of Yellowstone" fanned the flames of a controversy that, in 1977, Interior Secretary Cecil Andrus proclaimed had "come and gone."[18] To have the Craigheads and the NPS incessantly arguing in the media was one thing, but to have a third party take up the Craigheads' position in a popular national magazine was another. In 1983, Alston Chase's claimed status as an unbiased observer of the situation in Yellowstone may have lent credence to his story in the public mind. Even for those—perhaps especially for those—who had never heard of John and Frank Craighead, or given Yellowstone much thought, it might have been easy to believe the worst.

Chase's view convinced a resident of Plainsboro, New Jersey, who wrote President Reagan "to protest the federal 'eco-system' philosophy that has caused the wholesale slaughter of bears in Yellowstone Park" and urged Reagan to "fire all the ideologically deranged, impotent federal bureaucrats and managers who have blood on their hands for murdering the bears. . . . I don't want my taxes going to those who would squelch science, free speech and the rational support of our American wildlife." He offered a couple of examples of whom Reagan should fire and demanded that the park feed the grizzlies, as the Craigheads had recommended. The students of an environmental studies class at a Kansas City Country Day School also parroted Chase's main points in a set of letters urging the NPS to feed the bears. A man from Westminster, Colorado, did the same, reciting Chase's statements as though they were indubitable fact and recommending that supplemental feeding be introduced in Yellowstone.[19]

These letters represented a new kind of complaint for Yellowstone's managers—one based not on personal experience with the park but rather on a text about the park. Authors of such letters tended to repeat ideas and information that they had read or heard as though they were commonly accepted facts rather than the theories or opinions of individuals, making the author of the letter sound as if he or she were an expert on the matter. In most cases, it seemed that, as the NPS would later say of Chase, "he is certainly entitled to his opinion, [but] it remains unclear . . . why he is qualified to sit in judgment of [the] broad array of professional wildlife managers, scientists and conservationists [that supported the park's policies]."[20]

Ironically, it began to seem that actually possessing the proper qualifications made one suspect rather than trustworthy in the minds of some members of the public. By the early 1980s, a nexus of events had occurred on national and local levels that helped inflame traditional American wariness of government, especially when it came to Western land issues. Following the domestic turmoil of the 1960s and 1970s, in conjunction with the loss of faith in government wrought by the Vietnam War and the revelation of a series of government cover-ups that culminated with the resignation of President Richard Nixon, and compounded by the economic recession and "energy crisis" of the mid-1970s, the nation was sinking into what President Jimmy

Carter infamously identified as a "malaise." In the West, Carter's energy proposals, which purported to protect the environment but allow for oil and gas development in times of "critical need," were interpreted as "tantamount to declaring large portions of the West 'national sacrifice areas'" by both environmentalists and a growing coalition of commodity interests that would soon be popularly known as the Sagebrush Rebellion.[21]

Political scientist R. McGreggor Cawley has written that because it "marked the beginning of a period in which virtually every assumption about federal land policy underwent challenge and reconsideration," the Sagebrush Rebellion has proved as important to the history of U.S. federal land policy as the conservation and environmental movements. As a movement with no official leadership, its goals were established by its discourse, which in the late 1970s took the form of legislation passed in several Western states declaring the intention to "take back" control of federal lands within their boundaries. Employing the rhetoric of "conventional wisdom," or "common sense," the Sagebrush Rebellion (like its ideological cousin, Wise Use) was motivated by self-interest and, more importantly, the belief that the environmental community had managed to insinuate a preservation bias into federal policy-making.[22]

With the election of self-avowed everyman, sagebrush rebel, and big-government foe Ronald Reagan to the presidency, the tide began to turn, and the rebels established a foothold on the national political stage. On a smaller scale, Frank Craighead and Alston Chase had used the national media to convey the notion not only that the NPS was fallible but also that its managers were arrogant, untrustworthy examples of federal bureaucracy at its worst. When federal land management decisions became fodder for popular magazine articles within this combined context, it became easy for some to believe that their own unstudied opinion of how the national parks should be managed was just as valid as that of any NPS manager. This attitude became well enough known to Yellowstone's managers in subsequent years that it earned a nickname: "barroom biology."[23]

In response to the new crop of angry letters, Regional Director James Thompson and Yellowstone's new superintendent, Robert Barbee, assured those concerned that "the survival of the grizzly bear is among the highest of our priorities" and that the NPS was "fully committed to . . . reversing the apparent long-term decline of the Yellowstone grizzly population and to achieving a viable, self-sustaining population." Barbee further explained that the objectives of the park's grizzly bear management program were research, implementation of science-based management practices, and interagency cooperation aimed at achieving a regional grizzly research and protection program.[24] Though the image of the imperiled bear would hang on, the scientific narrative would come to dominate the park's bear messages, and still does today.

Bob Barbee's arrival at Yellowstone had been welcomed by scientists and administrators alike. Barbee, who in his master's thesis had explored possibilities for translating the ambitions of the Leopold Report into management practice, knew well the challenges that managers faced under the philosophy of natural regulation, placing him in an excellent position to be able to respond to Alston Chase and others critical of NPS policies.[25] During his tenure, Barbee weathered some of the stormiest controversies the park had ever seen, including the defeat of the Noranda gold mine, proposed for location near Cooke City, Montana, just outside the park's boundaries; the fires of 1988; and the decision to reintroduce the wolf to Yellowstone. In the years prior to those events, however, the park's grizzlies remained its hottest topic.

Although roadside feeding had been essentially eradicated, the debate over bear feeding in Yellowstone continued in the form of arguments over supplemental feeding of grizzlies. In 1983, the question of whether the park itself should feed the bears was again at the forefront of the grizzly debate. Advocated by the Craigheads and popularly supported by Chase, the idea was mentioned as being a possibility "during critical periods" in the park's Environmental Impact Statement (EIS) for its Bear Management Program, released that year. Later that year, the Senate's Committee on Environment and Public Works, of which U.S. senator Alan Simpson (Wyoming) was a member, held a hearing in Cody, Wyoming, to discuss the status of the grizzly bear. Afterward, Senator Simpson asserted that the results of the hearing had shown that in the wake of the dump closures, "the survival of the grizzly in the lower 48 states may well depend on a . . . plan to increase the protein level in the grizzly's diet. . . . We should provide supplementary feeding options only when it is proven to be critically necessary—and at least in one case—the grizzly bear—we may be certain that it is."[26]

Supplemental feeding was discussed at meetings throughout 1983 by an ad hoc committee of the Interagency Grizzly Bear Committee, consisting of Dick Knight, John Craighead, Mary Meagher and Chief Ranger Gary Brown from Yellowstone, and representatives from the Wyoming Department of Fish and Game and the U.S. Fish and Wildlife Service. Despite John Craighead's continued arguments that bears needed ecocenters, and that because humans were a natural part of the ecosystem, it would be natural for them to provide bears with food, the committee (including Craighead) unanimously recommended against supplemental feeding in December 1983.[27]

Unfortunately, defining the problem in terms of dump closure for so long may have artificially limited the search for solutions to the boundaries of the dump conversation, trapping the Craigheads and the NPS on a to-feed-or-not-to-feed carousel whose spinning blurred the surrounding landscape of change and possibility. Researchers in and around Yellowstone had long suspected that if the area's grizzly population was in decline, the closure of the park's garbage dumps might not be the sole, direct factor driving that decline. Poaching in the surrounding national forests was an increasing problem, as was the number of bears being destroyed for killing livestock on the multitudinous sheep grazing allotments contained in the GYE's grizzly habitat.[28] As Bill Brown had reported, backcountry use was increasing in the GYE during these years, due to a popular boom in camping and hiking, and perhaps most importantly, more people were not only visiting the GYE but living there: new development and road construction were depleting habitat.

Along with these social factors were a variety of possible biological influences, including trends in climate and natural foods availability that had the potential to negatively affect survival and reproductive recruitment. Considered together, all of these factors suggested a web of complexity that made the idea that Yellowstone's bear management program was solely responsible for the decline appear unlikely. As Mary Meagher wondered at one point, "Could the Great Bear Controversy have become a marvelous smokescreen to divert our attention from real and complex population influences?"[29]

Despite the evidence to the contrary, the hypothesis that the dump closure had caused the bears' decline, making supplemental feeding the obvious solution, was an appealing way of explaining things. It postulated a one-to-one, cause-and-effect correspondence between action and result, and offered up an immediate and practical fix: feed the bears. It was "simplistic . . . active, it 'does something.'" To combat the attractiveness of simplistic solutions such as supplemental feeding, park personnel designed some interpretive offerings to help communicate to the public the message that the survival of Yellowstone's grizzlies depended on more than supplemental nutrition. In August 1983, longtime ranger Ted Parkinson told a group of nine hundred visitors that poaching and summer-home development were the two biggest threats to the grizzly's survival in the GYE.[30] Clearly impassioned, Parkinson also emphatically railed against what he called the "bum, beggar, panhandling bears" of the past, and explained that after Yellowstone's managers

started thinking a little bit, used our big brains, our marvelous brains, then at last we understood what was wrong with man's food, then we made the new . . . rule in Yellowstone—no more bear feeding! And that was intended, first, to protect the bears. Second, to protect the park visitors from getting injured. So now we still have just as many bears in Yellowstone as we ever had, but they're [screaming here] *not along the highways!* They're out in the backcountry, *earning a living,* doing what they are *supposed to do.* And I like it that way, don't you? [woman from audience: "Yes!" clapping].

Based on the rapturous applause that followed, Parkinson's heart-rending stories of Yellowstone's bears and the ways they had suffered in the days of roadside and dump feeding, coupled with his evangelical delivery, had won him an amphitheaterful of converts. The concluding moments of his program emanated the atmosphere of a camp meeting, with the audience being urged to testify about the evils of the past and redemption in the present—and doing so.

Less fervent, but just as timely, was a script that John Good wrote to accompany a slide show aimed at educating local junior high school students (and possibly, by proxy, their parents) about Yellowstone's grizzlies and their current management. The script described the historical relationships between people and bears, and then the more recent history of bears and people in Yellowstone. State and federal agencies, the children were assured, had studied and worked with grizzlies for years, and at long last come up with a plan to preserve them. The presentation argued against supplemental feeding and in favor of the park's recent initiation of temporary closures of "human use adjustment areas," or Bear Management Units (BMUs), which restricted human access to certain places in the park during certain periods in order to minimize bear–human interactions, prevent human-caused displacement of bears from their prime food sources, and decrease the risk of bear-caused human injury in areas with high levels of bear activity. These areas were closed to the public during key periods of grizzly activity, but there were different degrees and kinds of closure. In some areas, only off-trail travel, night hiking, or overnight camping were prohibited during certain periods. Other areas required a minimum party size and regulated the number of parties that could utilize them during a given week. In fact, only a few areas were simply closed to all travel for a period of time.[31]

The BMUs, introduced in the 1983 EIS, were immediately controversial with the local populace. One that caused particular ire among visitors was the closure of the campsites, shoreline, and streams of Yellowstone Lake during the cutthroat trout spawning period, roughly May 15 to June 15. Good fishing for bears means good fishing for people, and many anglers were disappointed and angered with the park's decision to "give the Lake shore to the bears until mid July." Wrongly assuming that the park had instituted the lake closures in order to encourage bears that had not been previously using the area to start doing so (as part of its "bear naturalization" program), one visitor concluded, "It would appear to me that the recent objective of the bear policy is to establish, or reestablish, the bears in the areas of Yellowstone Lake that have been significantly used by the public. This can only bring about increased confrontation and problems . . . one will have to move over. My vote is that the bears give ground."[32]

Others agreed. When the park announced plans to permanently close its 667-site campground at Fishing Bridge, local fury erupted. Located on the banks of Pelican Creek, a tributary that feeds into Yellowstone Lake just east of Fishing Bridge, the Fishing Bridge campground had long been one of the park's most problematic in terms of bear–human conflicts, so much so that it had been open only to people camping in hard-sided vehicles since 1977. Because of the high incidence of conflicts and resultant control actions that occurred there, the area had become a mortality sink for grizzlies.[33] Visitor facilities at Fishing Bridge had been scheduled for removal in 1979, but, largely owing to the protests of the Wyoming congressional delegation, the removal had not yet occurred.

When Barbee proved steadfast in his conviction that the campground must go, it seemed to some local residents that the park's administration was favoring the "rights" of bears over those of people. At a public hearing in Gardiner, Montana, to discuss the campground's removal, a woman dramatically held up a postcard of the park's Roosevelt Arch and pointed out that its famous inscription, "For the Benefit and Enjoyment of the People," didn't "say a word about grizzly bears."[34] For some, Yellowstone's grizzlies had become a political symbol of the federal government's rule of tyranny over Western public lands, manifested through the NPS's desire to prevent people from accessing them so that they might be preserved as wilderness for trees and wildlife—just as Horace Albright had feared back in 1945.

At the same time, human use of that wilderness was generally increasing. In combination with the park's change in bear policies, the increase in backcountry travel that had occurred since the 1970s meant new patterns of bear–human conflict in Yellowstone. The last reported injury from a roadside black bear had occurred in 1976, and though there were few bear-related injuries by the 1980s, those that did occur tended to result from surprise encounters between hikers and grizzlies in the backcountry and were more likely to be fatal.[35]

The year 1984 was not a good one for backcountry bear–human conflicts in Yellowstone. Five injuries, one fatal, resulted from encounters between grizzlies and hikers. The death of Brigitta Fredenhagen, a twenty-five-year-old visitor from Basel, Switzerland, remains mysterious to those charged with investigating bear–related injuries and deaths in the park. By all accounts, including her own journal, Fredenhagen had received plenty of information and warning about bears and "taken all precautions" against a bear attack. However, on the night of July 29, Fredenhagen was dragged 258 feet from her tent and partially consumed by a subadult grizzly.

Without evidence that Fredenhagen had disobeyed the warnings and advice given her, except perhaps that she shouldn't hike and camp alone, it was difficult for park personnel to apply what they learned about the attack to helping future campers avoid the same fate, except that her death was at least partially responsible for Pelican Valley's designation as a BMU.[36]

As it turned out, that decision provided researchers with an opportunity to scientifically judge the effectiveness of signage as a warning method. In his master's thesis research, Kerry Gunther found that in spite of Fredenhagen's death and the subsequent BMU rules requiring a minimum party size of four clearly posted at the trailhead, 279 of 337 parties (83 percent) observed entering Pelican Valley over the course of two summers included fewer than four people, and 20 percent of the hikers were, like Fredenhagen, alone. Gunther's observations led him to conclude that "bear safety recommendations are not very effective at influencing visitor behavior."[37]

This problem had been evident for years at the park's roadsides, where signs urging people to stay away from bears had proved ineffective. Also proving ineffectual in the 1980s were the park's attempts to shoo bears from roadsides through aversive conditioning. At that time, park policy dictated that roadside bears be treated by park personnel as though they were "fed bears," meaning that their presence was simply not tolerated. These animals were frequently slated for relocation, even if people were not feeding them. This practice posed a particular management problem in the case of grizzlies, because they required removal of more than one hundred miles from their point of origin in order to prevent their return. In many cases, this meant removal outside park boundaries, where they were likely to be killed by poachers or shepherds. As an alternative to relocation, park employees tried a form of deterrence in which a specialized gun was used to shoot a plastic can full of water at the bear's rump. Unfortunately, this amounted to spanking the bear for doing what it was supposed to do—foraging for natural foods. Like past attempts at aversive conditioning, these hazing efforts were generally unsuccessful as the bears quickly learned to recognize the trucks and uniforms of the hazers and would simply move out of range of the gun (approximately thirty yards) when they saw the rangers coming.[38]

Once again, park managers realized that it would probably be easier to make people stay away from bears than to teach bears to behave in the manner the NPS desired. Finding that people are more likely to ignore signs than to ignore people in uniform, Yellowstone's managers finally resorted to crowd management (today's method of dealing with bear jams). When a bear is reported to be foraging within sight of the roadside and cars start to stop, park personnel are sent out either to keep people in their cars or to ensure that they remain the mandated one hundred yards away, and to keep the traffic moving. Today, an average bear jam requires between four and six people to successfully manage it; in 2004, park personnel responded to 919 bear jams.[39]

The year 1986 saw another fatal grizzly attack, this time on a photographer who too closely approached a sow and her cubs. Also in 1986, Alston Chase's *Playing God in Yellowstone,* a book-length version of "The Last Bears of Yellowstone" that applied the same brand and style of criticism to a variety of natural resource management issues in the park, was published. The book's appearance was preceded, in January of that year, by *Outside* magazine's publication of "The Grizzly and the Juggernaut: How Enlightened Environmental Theory Has Destroyed the Great Bears of Yellowstone." "Juggernaut," the chapter from *Playing God* that dealt with the park's bear management (or mismanagement, as Chase would have it) program, was an expanded, updated, and rhetorically amplified version of "The Last Bears of Yellowstone."

Chase's premise was, again, that natural regulation was a misguided philosophical fantasy masquerading as ecologically based policy, and that although it was killing the grizzly population, the NPS was unwilling to abandon the theory because of agency arrogance and an unreasonable devotion to the cultural notion of "naturalness." According to Chase, the aesthetically addled NPS had by now managed to draw an impressive number of government agencies and environmental organizations into its web of self-deception and science-hate, as ostensibly evidenced by the fact that all of those organizations had expressed support of the park's general bear management practices as well as the decision not to implement supplemental feeding. As the author of the NPS's written response to the article put it, Chase seemed "unable to come to terms with the possibility that all these people . . . [were] convinced that his proposed changes simply [weren't] necessary."[40]

"Juggernaut" was populated by the same "hungry" bears, deluded government officials, and questionable information sources as "The Last Bears," and
even went so far as to question whether the GYE could support any bears at all
in the absence of supplemental feeding. It generated an apparently enormous
volume of angry mail to Superintendent Barbee's office; public response was
significant enough that Barbee had his staff formulate a formal reply to
Chase's article. Those who wrote to inquire about what they had read in *Outside* received a copy of Chase's article, numbered by paragraph; a letter from
Barbee thanking them for their concern; and the NPS's twenty-seven-page,
paragraph-by-paragraph response to Chase's accusations.[41]

That response acknowledged that there were practical limits to the goals
of natural regulation when implemented as management practice: "[Chase]
makes his case by setting up a strawman, claiming that the Park Service has
an idealistic, impractical goal of primitiveness for Yellowstone. If the agency
were as impractical and idealistic as he claims, there would be grounds for
criticism. However . . . there are recognized, practical limits to the degree of
primitiveness that can be achieved."[42] This statement is revealing of the more
pragmatic approach to natural regulation that was evolving in Yellowstone
and that would find its place in the coming era, when "adaptive management" would be introduced into NPS planning and policy—management
that is expected to change based on what happens as implementation pro-
ceeds and its results are monitored.

Though Chase and his views may have dominated the bear narrative at
the national level in the 1980s, there were several strong counternarratives to
his doomsday prognostications and conspiracy implications, especially at
the regional level and among niche audiences. According to Yellowstone historian and writer Paul Schullery, the most significant of these were the slide
shows and films of Steve and Marilynn French, whose presentations to the
public, to conservation groups, and to Yellowstone National Park staff were a
"powerful antidote" to the impression left by Chase that if the bears of Yellowstone weren't yet a relic of the past, then they soon would be. "Thousands
of people in [the Yellowstone] region, and around the country, were sitting
down in auditoriums to see the most startling and previously unimaginable
footage of those 'extinct' bears, in numbers, in the wild."[43]

The Frenches' film footage of wild Yellowstone grizzlies engaging in a
full complement of behaviors—from taking elk calves to mating to scram-
bling around cliffs, largely shot from the roadside—showed people that
contrary to what they had read in the press, Yellowstone's grizzlies were
still out there to be seen, and they were doing fine without the dumps.

Though the Frenches never tried to extrapolate their observations into population estimates, they were responsible for a shift in perception about the state of Yellowstone's grizzlies, produced scientific papers on the bears, and disseminated, through their Yellowstone Grizzly Foundation, a large volume of educational information, replete with photos of grizzly behaviors that in the past had largely been the exclusive purview of researchers and managers.[44]

The Frenches' own behaviors, practiced in the course of collecting their film footage, have proven no less influential than those of the bears they recorded. Their method was a combination of passion, optics, and patience that has inspired others to spend hundreds of hours watching and hoping, and served as the precursor to the way that wildlife watching is largely practiced in the park today. Again according to Schullery, the Frenches "made the bears more publicly accessible, even to park staff. They showed us how to find the bears that were already there."[45]

At the start, even the Frenches didn't know how to find grizzlies, and they were frustrated in their efforts until they enrolled in a Yellowstone Institute class taught by a bear researcher. There they learned to stop concentrating their efforts in lodgepole pine forest, as they had been doing to that point ("like other tourists familiar with the proverbial association between bears and woods," as writer Richard Conniff put it), and "all of a sudden bears were everywhere." After not having seen any bears in five years of looking, the Frenches saw thirty-two in five days. Word soon spread that they were filming Yellowstone grizzlies, and Superintendent Barbee asked them to come to Mammoth and share their footage with park staff. They subsequently presented their films at scientific meetings, where researchers who had been writing about bear behaviors they had never previously seen were amazed. The Frenches' dedication to observational natural history at a time when research technologies were advancing by leaps and bounds—they have accumulated thousands of slides and more than two hundred hours of film—made a marked difference in the perception of those fortunate enough to see it. According to Marilynn French, "one of the things that was kind of neat was that we were dispelling some of the myths."[46]

There were also literary alternatives to Chase's point of view in the 1980s, several of which combined natural history with social history. *Where the Grizzly Walks,* by Montana Fish and Game employee-cum-writer and publisher Bill Schneider, actually preceded "The Last Bears of Yellowstone" by six years. Published in 1977, *Where the Grizzly Walks* came too soon on the heels of the Craighead debate to make any claims about its resolution, concluding that "who was right seems less serious than what is right for the grizzly now and in the future." Schneider did, however, offer significant criticisms about how grizzlies had been managed in the past, and warnings about the cumulative threats posed by Greater Yellowstone Area recreational and resort development, sheep allotments, logging, fossil fuels extraction and other mining, road and power-line building, and fire suppression. The book, fueled by Schneider's passion for both grizzlies and the wilderness they require in order to survive, concluded with a multifaceted prescription for improving the bear's chances for recovery, including reintroduction to appropriate areas from which it had vanished, continued research, an end to scientific and bureaucratic squabbling, wildland fire use, intergovernmental cooperation with American Indian tribes, decreased tourism promotion, changes to mining laws, limits on wilderness use, improved land use planning in regard to resort and other recreational development, general resource and energy conservation, grazing without permission for predator control, more responsible media reporting, and public education with an aim toward fostering public tolerance and responsible behaviors.[47]

Paul Schullery's *The Bears of Yellowstone,* which first appeared in 1980, comprised three parts: the first a natural history of both black and grizzly bears in Yellowstone, the second a history of bear management in the park, and the third a collection of Yellowstone bear stories and lore, including an examination of "the power of these animals in our culture." Often written in the first person, Schullery's book was highly accessible as well as entertaining, and lacked the aggressive judgments that characterized so many portrayals of the park's history of bear management.[48] Schullery's personal, easy writing style, narrative flow, careful research, and appealing combination of communicating facts and ruminating on the meaning of bears in American society likely brought the park's bears, their story, and a concern for their welfare to a much broader popular audience than most other texts of its time.

The year 1982 brought Thomas McNamee's seminal *The Grizzly Bear,* an in-depth natural history based in the scientific literature about grizzlies, and a study of that science itself. McNamee's seamless, thought-provoking prose moved between telling the story of a female grizzly raising her new cubs and exploring both the threats to the bear's survival and the research and management that was trying to secure it, cognizant that it would be impossible to achieve an understanding of the grizzly without also investigating "the tangle of thoroughly *non*-nonhuman affairs encircling the grizzly bear." His narrative was sprinkled with firsthand accounts of research, management activities, and conversations with those who conducted them, providing a humanizing look at the people engaged in grizzly conservation and giving them a voice outside of scientific journals and conferences.[49]

In *Grizzly Years* (1990), Doug Peacock told the story of his two decades of tracking and watching grizzlies. Peacock, who served as his friend Edward Abbey's model for the monkeywrencher Hayduke, was drawn to grizzlies for a different reason from the other authors discussed thus far. Peacock tracked grizzlies not via telemetry for purposes of science, but rather by staking out carcasses and learning the habits of individual bears as part of a personal quest. *Grizzly Years* counterpointed Peacock's search for grizzlies with his experiences in Vietnam, which had ultimately led him to the bears. Explaining that he began filming Yellowstone grizzlies on the same day that the Khmer Rouge began its massacres at Phnom Penh, Peacock wrote, "From my slightly twisted point of view, preserving grizzlies . . . meant putting the brakes on a world gone mad." In compelling, vivid style, Peacock chronicled his searches, skewered federal bureaucrats for favoring people and politics over the needs of bears, and tried to articulate why he had made grizzlies a central focus of his life: "In Vietnam the primary predator was man. . . . The grizzly radiated potency. He carried the physical strength and thorniness of disposition that allowed him to attack or kill most any time he cared. But, almost always, he chose not to. That was power beyond a bully's swaggering. It was the kind of restraint that commands awe—a muscular act of grace."[50]

Unfortunately, none of these texts seems to have commanded the headlines and the forefront of the debate like Chase's did. It is likely that none touched a social nerve like Chase's sensationalist writings, which in retrospect seem to have been less concerned with spreading knowledge about bears and their welfare than with using grizzlies—again, the highly malleable imperiled bear—as a means to tap into broader cultural attitudes about government arrogance and incompetence, and the mistrust they generated.

Although the area grizzly population has rebounded in recent years, Yellowstone's bear management staff still receive the occasional letter from a citizen who would like to see supplemental feeding introduced for the park's grizzlies, and John Craighead and his coauthors supported reinstatement of the garbage dumps in their 1995 book, *The Grizzly Bears of Yellowstone: Their Ecology in the Yellowstone Ecosystem, 1959–1992.*[51] Supplemental feeding was seriously promoted by local politicians at least once more, in the 1990s, but it seems fairly safe to say that barring a change in the self-conception of the NPS and its mission, the dumps will not be making a comeback.

Bear management staff also still get letters from people who are upset either because they didn't see a bear during their visits or because they have apparently just read one of the accusatory volumes published over the past two decades or seen a television documentary and want to know just who the NPS thinks "gave it the right" to engage in what they have been told is the indiscriminate killing of bears. If there was a characteristic response to these letters during the Barbee era, it was to address the writer's concerns specifically and individually, rather than with a blanket line of rhetoric as had sometimes been typical during previous years. Also in contrast to previous years, Superintendent Barbee believed that "for all our knowledge and experience, we don't dare forget that we're public servants, not oracles. If we try to tell the public what they should like, we're stretching any definition of our authority, and getting into the father-knows-best syndrome. We have to be really careful there."[52] This philosophy represented a clear departure from the evangelical attitude sometimes demonstrated in the past.

In what may have been either a servicewide or park-level decision, Barbee's feeling that visitors needed to be left to make up their own minds about what they saw in Yellowstone was evident in the changing interpretation offered by the park's official map and guide (the broadside of today) throughout his tenure. The version of the map and guide distributed early in his administration, reprinted from one created during the Townsley administration, had waxed poetic not only about what visitors would see but also about how to properly experience and think about those sights:

Walk out into the cool, crisp air of an early fall morning. Hear the frosty meadows crackle as dim shapes invade their stillness and the mountains ring with the age-old, wild notes of bull elk issuing their thrilling challenges. This is Yellowstone, a tremendous block of wild mountain country in which thousands of furred and feathered creatures are living, mating, and dying in harmony with the natural rhythms that have ruled the land for millions of years.

In this natural scene, man is but a visitor who is privileged to share glimpses into the intimacies of nature—if he only has the time and patience. Here, roads, campsites, and hotels are enclaves of civilization in a wilderness world in which nature remains sovereign.[53]

By 1990, the map and guide was very different. One reason was that its much smaller size allowed for far less text, eliminating by necessity much of the flowery description of animals, places, and wilderness philosophy that had dominated the earlier edition. Gone were pronouncements about what Yellowstone "was" or "wasn't." Mood-setting suggestions such as "Stand on the lip of the Lower Falls; watch the bottle-green Yellowstone River break into frothy white jets as it drops away 94 meters . . . into the canyon below; listen to its constant wild roar; feel the spray on your face" were replaced by need-to-know facts: "Grandview Point affords a distant view of the 308-foot Lower Falls. Lookout Point affords a vista of Lower Falls, and a steep trail descends to a closer viewpoint."[54]

Emotion was excised from the park's narrative in favor of a more "objective"-sounding style. Bears that had previously been described as deceptively "sleepy"- and friendly-looking were now described as "wild and dangerous" animals that "appear tolerant of people, but may attack without warning." Visitors were also bluntly told that both black and grizzly bears had "seriously injured, maimed, and killed" people, and that "animals who receive handouts often become aggressive, cause personal injury, and must be destroyed." Bears were not mentioned in the section of the guide giving specific information about where to look for what wildlife, despite the fact that visitors still desperately wanted to know "where they had gone."[55]

In short, science had replaced sublimity. Indeed, the new political climate in which Barbee found himself demanded such a switch, as the great grizzly debate—and many others—had come to be defined by questions of science. Yet the answers would never be clear or easy. Underlying those scientific questions were (and still are) political undercurrents manifested through bitter battles over whose science was "better," and whose less tainted by personal agendas. Under the weight of those competing agendas, science, and the need for it, has ended up being no more universally accepted than any other narrative structure in Yellowstone.[56] However, science continues, for now at least, to be the park's dominant narrative relative to bears.

Today's Yellowstone Bear

In today's Yellowstone, bears have returned to the roadsides, where they still focus on obtaining food. But they're not begging. They're foraging—munching on grasses, chewing up wildflowers, turning over rocks and logs to dig in the earth for insects burrowed beneath them. A lucky visitor might even see a grizzly pulling apart a winter-killed bison carcass lodged in an icy spring stream. In contrast to the bears of old, the bears seen near Yellowstone's roadsides today mostly ignore visitors. And visitors seem all right with that—at least until they raise their cameras. At that point—even though they shouldn't—it's not uncommon for people to try to attract a bear's attention for a moment, seized by that old compulsion to look nature in the eye, and have nature look back. To ensure that today's visitors use their telephoto technology rather than their feet to obtain their "close-up views," and to minimize such inappropriate, unsafe interactions, park staff patrol as many bear jams as possible, and the laws designed to keep people and bears apart are diligently enforced.

Though the roadside presence of bears increases the need for staffing in order to prevent foolish behavior and injuries, it is also a positive sign for the park's bear populations, typically indicating that richer food niches in the park's backcountry have already been filled by more dominant bears. This situation pushes others toward less desirable territories that include roads and other areas populated by humans. Seeing bears in the park also allows visitors to know that they're still there—that grizzlies survived the frightening years directly preceding and following their Threatened Species listing, and that black bears survived the many years of double-digit control actions that characterized their era of roadside begging. Since 1975, more than 33,000 bear sightings have been reported in the park. In 2004 alone, visitors and park staff reported 2,609 bear sightings: 1,445 of those were grizzly bears.[1]

On the other hand, more roadside bears also means more bears killed by cars. In the summer of 2004, when poor natural food production led more and more bears to widen their foraging efforts, five black bears (including three cubs) were killed in collisions with automobiles—five times the annual average. In many such incidents, speed is a factor; people driving too fast is a perpetual problem in the park, and animals often suffer the consequences.[2] In the summer of 2003, one such collision claimed the life of one of the park's most popular bears.

Grizzly No. 264, a female, was born in the early months of 1991. From an early age, bear No. 264, who acquired her number during research capture operations, was unusually tolerant of humans. Her habituation was not only atypical but also inexplicable, as there was no clear reason for it—to managers' knowledge, No. 264 was never fed by people, and she did not exhibit begging behaviors. Throughout her life, bear No. 264's penchant for roadside habitat, as well as her size and majestic appearance, made her a favorite subject of frequent park visitors and wildlife photographers. She was seen by countless people and photographed countless times.

In the fall of 1992, No. 264 was spotted feeding on an elk calf near the roadside and then began running into people on trails around the Norris and Mammoth areas, and walking up behind unsuspecting fishermen. Her behavior was not aggressive—she might comfortably pass within five feet of people without taking an interest in them. After that first year, visitors and photographers who frequented the park began to seek out No. 264, causing headaches for the park's bear managers. But her proximity to developed areas made the usually labor-intensive art of wilderness photography much easier, and she provided people with unique opportunities for observing a grizzly engaging in its natural activities. Still, she tended to go about those activities in a curious fashion. Grizzly No. 264 was highly predatory, hunting and killing elk calves into the fall and early winter, long after they ceased to be the easy marks that newborn calves provide. She was also known to stash her kills near roadsides for a few days at a time rather than consuming them right away or burying them in more remote locations.

Bear No. 264 felt comfortable in the frontcountry, and tended to tolerate people whose temptation drove them to foolish acts around her. It was bear No. 264 that bluff-charged the man described in this book's Introduction, who thought roadside bears were "exempt" from the rules and walked up to pet her cub. She ran up to the man and used her enormous claws to paw the ground in front of him and warn him away from her cub, but did not do him any harm. On another occasion, she was observed chasing a tourist who had closely approached her with his video camera. Running is never a good strategy for avoiding harm from a grizzly, but that's what this man did after bear No. 264 turned to chase him away. When the man stumbled and fell, the bear simply stopped and looked at him. He got up and continued running; she followed along at the same distance as before the chase was interrupted. He was indescribably lucky, and she was extraordinary.[3]

Bear No. 264 had three litters of two cubs each, of which only two cubs survived. Whether they will exhibit the same tolerance for human presence is not yet known, but it would be unfortunate if they did. In June 2003, bear No. 264's level of comfort with frontcountry living cost her her life when she was hit by a car—a frequent and unsurprising cause of death for bears that spend as much time around roads as she did. Her injuries were terminal, and she was euthanized later that night at a veterinary hospital in Bozeman, Montana. Her death precipitated an unprecedented outpouring of grief among the local community and those who had come to be her ardent "fans," monitoring park radio calls to track her movements through the park.[4]

Sadly as her story ended, and despite her unusual proclivities, bear No. 264 presented us with potent layered meaning. Cherished for her majestic appearance in the landscape, she was also, minus the feeding, a kind of positive, twenty-first-century throwback to the days when visitors could count on bears obliging them by reliably appearing at the roadside: instead of food, humans had provided protection for the bear through such measures as the Endangered Species Act, and the bear had acted as a visual reward for those efforts—the system was working! Like those other highly visible, wildly popular Yellowstone wilderness symbols, the Lamar Valley wolves, bear No. 264 also made the park's vast wilderness accessible to everyday visitors by bringing it right to the roadside, in some small way refuting the belief that wilderness is the place where people aren't.[5]

In a larger sense, today's Yellowstone bears, and the renewed respect that most people feel for them, are reminders that there are places left in America where people do not command the food chain's top echelon. Many take comfort in that knowledge, and feel enriched by the vulnerability that comes with the opportunity to walk through an area inhabited by creatures larger and more powerful than we. In this sense, Glen Cole's imaginary bear—or more accurately, perhaps, bear of the imagination—is very much alive and still present in Yellowstone. It is the suggested bear whose silhouette we see at trailheads today, depicted in abstract rather than representational form, neither friendly nor overtly threatening, in itself communicating nothing more than the unpredictability of what an encounter might bring. Make note of the warnings and walk past the trailhead, and the imaginary bear appears and disappears through the trees as a vapor in the wind, nowhere and everywhere. Its potentiality excites and unnerves us more and more with each step farther into the woods. The suggested bear wanders a landscape of the mind, waiting to enter the landscape of the eye.

Treasured for the sense of wildness it infuses into a relentlessly developed world and for the possibility of its presence, rather than strictly for its entertainment value, the bear has also come to be recognized as a component part and defining element of the larger Greater Yellowstone Ecosystem. James Pritchard has noted that since the mid-1970s, ecological ideas have strongly influenced the ways Yellowstone's visitors have thought about nature when visiting the park, and the influence of those ideas is apparent in many ways.[6] Perhaps the broadest of these is the notion that seeing a bear, although highly desirable, is no longer a required element of a fulfilling trip to Yellowstone. Rather, bears' role in visitor experience is similar to their role in the ecosystem, where they are a highly important part of a larger whole whose meaning and significance far outweighs their simple presence.

In 2001, 150 randomly chosen Yellowstone visitors were asked (in a survey conducted for this research) to rank the importance of seeing a bear during their visit on a scale of 1 to 5, with 1 being not very important and 5 being very important. The overall average answer was 3.29—somewhere in the middle (this included a "minus 5" from a man traveling by motorcycle who was clearly less than interested in encountering a bear during his visit). Many people added that they would like to see one, "but it wouldn't ruin the trip if I don't," "but I won't commit suicide if it doesn't happen," or "but I know they're hard to see." These answers were given in spite of the fact that fully one-half of the visitors interviewed had stated, unprompted, that a bear was one of the three sights they most wanted to see while in the park (along with Old Faithful and wildlife in general).

Overall, the survey indicated that visitors come to Yellowstone today to see the things they have always come to see: extraordinary thermal features, wildlife—bears in particular, and beautiful scenery. The average importance of seeing a bear to the overall quality of one's trip would seem to indicate that although visitors still commonly associate bears with Yellowstone, seeing bears is no longer a driving reason for making the trip, in spite of the fact that they still appear to be one of the park's main attractions. The visitors surveyed still strongly associated bears with the park, but did not necessarily expect to see one during their visits.

Visitors are also not quite as sure of what it means to see a *Yellowstone* bear as they may have been in the past. When those same 150 visitors were asked what their "perfect picture" (photograph) of a Yellowstone bear would be, more people described an image of a bear standing in a river, fishing, than any other ideal picture. Interestingly, however, this is a sight that few people ever see in Yellowstone, because the bears usually fish in the early morning or after dark, in remote areas that are sometimes closed for bear management purposes. It seems likely that visitors were actually picturing the famous fishing grizzlies of Alaska's McNeil River Falls—images that have proliferated through TV nature shows and calendar art—when they described their perfect picture of a Yellowstone bear. This possibility indicates that today people's ideal image of a Yellowstone bear has less to do with a specifically Yellowstone bear than with a more general, fuzzy image of what a bear in the wild is supposed to look like and do. It seems that people aren't exactly sure what to expect of or how to visualize a specifically Yellowstone bear, which may not be a bad thing in light of the very specific images embraced in the past.[7]

That same survey also showed that on the whole, Yellowstone's visitors are not particularly bothered by seeing collared or otherwise marked wildlife. The debate over whether wild animals living in national parks and wilderness areas should be collared for scientific monitoring purposes has continued to rage since the Craighead brothers pioneered the technique in Yellowstone. Collars and other markers have gotten smaller and less conspicuous over the years, and in order to further minimize their visibility today's managers even frequently wrap collars in dark-colored tape. Nevertheless, there are those who still hold the line established by Superintendent Anderson, maintaining that any visible marking is deleterious to the viewing experience and makes the marked animal seem "less than wild" because it is an indication of interaction with humanity. In this way, collaring undermines the facade of untouched nature that many people attribute to national parks and wilderness areas.

Other critics point out that collaring requires that animals be drugged and handled, which has in the past proven to be potentially dangerous for both wildlife and managers. Advances in drug technology have greatly decreased the potential for hazard in recent years, but the possibility of injury or death during capture and immobilization or (in extremely rare instances) afterward still exists. Still others complain that the collars look uncomfortable and that the park should simply "leave wildlife alone" and "stop studying them to death," a rather common expression that originated in the days when animal deaths caused by immobilizing drugs were more common than they are today.

Proponents of collaring maintain that the amount and quality of knowledge that can be obtained from monitoring certain members of an animal population far outweigh the negative visual effects and small potential for danger. Innovations in global positioning system (GPS) technology have greatly increased the scope of that knowledge in recent years. Among other things, researchers can now learn the extent of an animal's range, measure its length of life, discover what food sources might hold it in a certain place for extended periods of time, track its reproductive history, and find out how it uses land throughout the day and night—all of which is valuable information for managers charged with making land use decisions within the Greater Yellowstone Ecosystem and protecting threatened species such as the grizzly.

When asked if they had seen any park animals wearing radio collars or ear tags, roughly 23 percent of 150 randomly sampled Yellowstone visitors (35 people) said they had. When those 35 people were asked if seeing a marking had affected their experience of viewing that animal, 77 percent (27 people) said that seeing the marking had had no adverse impact. Visitors who had not seen any animals wearing radio collars or ear tags were asked to imagine their reaction to seeing such an animal. Of those, 86 percent (97 people) believed that seeing an animal wearing a collar or a tag would have no impact on their experience of viewing that animal. Twenty-one of those people volunteered that they wouldn't be bothered because they knew why collaring was done, and believed it to be a positive thing. One man went so far as to say that seeing a collar would actually enhance his viewing experience for that reason.

Twenty-three percent of respondents who had seen a marked animal (8 people) said that seeing the marking had adversely impacted their experience of viewing that animal. Of those visitors who had not seen a marked animal but were asked to imagine their reaction, 14 percent (16 people) said they thought their viewing experience would be adversely impacted by the marking. These people were prompted to explain why this had been or would be the case. Answers included that the collar had made the animal seem less natural, with one adding that collared wildlife were unsuitable for wildlife photography; that the collar might be uncomfortable for the animal;

that wildlife should be "left alone"; and that wildlife should be "allowed to be free." Others said they would be bothered by seeing traces that the animal had interacted with humans, and two people said they would be bothered because they wouldn't know why the animal was wearing a collar.

Overall, more than four out of five visitors surveyed said that seeing an animal marked for scientific purposes either had had or would have had no impact on their experience of viewing that animal. In fact, in some instances, the long-held contention of some scientists that visitors' seeing marked animals was a positive by-product of research because it generated public interest in science and wildlife conservation proved to be true. The percentage of people who had actually seen a marked animal and been bothered by it, however, was higher than the percentage of people who had not seen a marked animal but thought they would be bothered by it, reminding us that there is a gap between how people imagine their reactions and what those reactions actually turn out to be. But even among those who had seen a collared animal, more than three out of four said that the marking had had no impact on their viewing experience, indicating that most visitors may not cling as tightly to an ideal of "pure, untouched" Yellowstone as may have been thought, or as actually did at times in the past.

The survey respondents were fairly well aware of the past history of bear feeding in Yellowstone, and 95 percent said they would not want to feed a bear in Yellowstone today, even if they had no fear of being caught and punished for it. When asked why not, 43 percent of all those who answered "no" cited safety reasons. Notable responses included, "A bear can attack me," "It might kill me or scratch my car," "You don't mess with bears," "I'm chicken," and "You can't have people going around getting themselves killed." The second-most popular explanation for not wanting to feed the bears related to the idea that bear feeding is bad for bears. Concerns cited in this category included, accurately, the popular adage, "A fed bear is a dead bear"; ten people explained that bears that gain access to human foods have to be either relocated or killed because they will invariably return seeking more and then become hazardous nuisances.

Other people knew that bears that were fed might become dependent upon human foods, and some worried that they would be unable to survive in the winter, "when there's no one there to feed them." Eleven percent mentioned the possibility that bears might even lose their natural instincts and skills for foraging altogether. A third supposition was that human foods would be unhealthy for bears; that they are "not the right food." In all, 32 percent of the people who said they would not want to feed bears alluded to the fact that to do so would be to the detriment of the bears. Other respondents were opposed to feeding because it was "unnatural" in some way, because bears were "wild," or would cease to be wild if they were fed.

Fifteen percent of respondents indicated that feeding had negative effects on people. The most common responses in this group had to do with the idea that people feeding the bears today will cause trouble for those who visit tomorrow, because they will leave behind a habituated bear that may cause property damage or bodily injury in its search for human foodstuffs. Other reasons for not feeding included "We just want to look, not to touch," "Wildlife should not be fed," a desire to follow the rules, "That's stupid" (once accompanied by "If I saw someone doing that, I would hit them"), "That would make it like a zoo," a concern that human feeding would disrupt the "cycle of nature," an overall feeling that feeding is "just not right," and a simple lack of desire to feed.

Of the 8 people out of 150 who said they *would* want to feed a bear in Yellowstone, 5 said they would do it in order to be able to get close to a bear. The remaining 3 said they would feed because "they're hungry," "it seems like the humane thing to do," and "I've just always fed animals. Like squirrels."

All in all, if one of the preconditions for civil obedience of a rule is that its constituency believes in its legitimacy, then the NPS appeared not to have a problem in regard to bear feeding, insofar as at least 95 percent of those interviewed agreed that there were legitimate reasons why people should not feed bears in Yellowstone and were aware of what some of those reasons are. This conclusion, however, should be taken with the caveat to mind the gap between decontextualized statements and contextualized action, and recalls Donald Bock's 1953 visitor survey, in which almost everyone claimed to have seen someone else feeding a bear, but almost no one would admit to having done it themselves. In a clear case either of conflicting internal philosophies or of saying what one thinks one should say and then what one really feels, one woman commented, "I know human food is not appropriate for wildlife—wildlife needs to be with the ecosystem as it is. Have they ever thought about selling food that could be used for that?"

The survey results also did not bespeak any need to reduce either the numbers of staff available to patrol bear jams or the wildlife warnings that are conveyed via interpretive materials, as this question did not address whether people would approach a bear without the intent to feed. In fact, two people, in the course of emphatically stating that they would want to stay far away from bears, named "50 feet" as being the proper distance—a full 250 feet closer than the 100-yard distance required by law. Other surveys have shown that as a group, Yellowstone's visitors tend to greatly underestimate the distance from which wildlife viewing can be safely conducted.[8]

Although people seem generally aware, at this point, of some of the reasons why they shouldn't feed bears, continued vigilance and education efforts will always be necessary—as Edmund Rogers recognized long ago, the transient nature of the park's visitorship means that there will never be a shortage of new visitors or people whose experience leaves them unprepared for what they will experience in Yellowstone. This is especially true today, when the breakdown of traditional boundaries that typifies the postmodern age means that invisible barriers of socially acceptable behavior are quickly losing their potency. The continuing need for both education and vigilance was shown by the fact that half of those who wanted to feed the bears were in the lowest age group, and by a decrease in awareness of past feeding as age decreased. Finally, it is clear that residual desire for bear feeding still exists. As long as people and wildlife come together in Yellowstone, there will be a continuing need for education and enforcement to ensure the well-being of both.

As law enforcement of human behavior remains diligent, so do efforts to ensure that bears that do become habituated aren't permitted to obtain human foods repeatedly—a situation that could easily lead to human injury. Working with wildlife managers from the park's surrounding states, park staff members trap bears that discover anthropogenic food sources in the park's local communities; bears that repeatedly obtain human foods often must be killed. In the park, bears that discover backpacks left along streams by fishermen or dropped on trails by spooked hikers, or that develop the habit of jumping on tents for food or fun, are also trapped and either relocated, sent to zoos, or destroyed. Although each case is different, bears are not repeatedly relocated as has been the case in the past, as this has not proven an effective strategy in ending habituation and its associated hazards.

Today, the park's overall message to visitors about bears is that they're wild animals; they're occasionally dangerous; and if people behave appropriately, the park is pretty safe for both bears and visitors.[9] If that description does little to spur the imagination, conjuring neither affection, terror, nor wilderness romance, then it is consistent with the rest of the park's contemporary narrative of the bear as simply an entity for the visitor to be aware of, and presumably to fill with his or her own meaning. Today's responses to visitor letters follow the example set by Barbee of specifically addressing the writer's concerns and typically include a brief, unimpassioned history of Yellowstone's bear management and the reasons for its changes over the years, as well as a list of suggestions about where and when bears can be viewed in the park.

Bear–related information is conveyed in many ways that cannot all be listed here. They include warnings printed in the "Yellowstone Trip Planner" that people can request long before they ever arrive at the park. Visitors passing through the entrance gate receive the park's map and guide (the equivalent of the old broadsides), which states, "*All wildlife,* especially bison and bears, can be dangerous; keep your distance!" It is illegal to approach within one hundred yards of bears. Bear warnings appear in the *Yellowstone Today* newspaper, also distributed at the entrance stations. Pamphlets are distributed at visitor centers; press releases remind the public about bears' emergence from hibernation and other significant events (e.g., maulings); and bear management staff present talks to between thirty and forty school groups each year, as well as providing annual training for the park's concessions staff and seasonal interpreters, who are required to include a safety message about hiking and camping in bear country at each campfire program they present. Like Leopold and Allen, bear managers envision a greater utilization of modern technology as a means of improving the effectiveness of communicating today's message; the Internet and more video- and television-oriented media, rather than newspapers and other strictly textual data, may be the most appropriate ways of communicating with today's generation of visitors.[10] Bear information appears on the park's website.

In regard to signage, current managers feel that simpler is better, and that the best signs are those that consistently remind people to be alert and aware and perhaps seek more information, such as those in the park's campgrounds that simply read, "You are in bear country."[11] Large (6-by-6-foot) signs posted just inside all of the park's entrance stations warn visitors that feeding or molesting animals is illegal, and that bears are dangerous and must not be fed. All of the park's campgrounds post red-and-white signs warning visitors that they are camping in bear country, that they must store all food in their vehicles, and that "all wildlife are dangerous." More warnings are found on campsite receipts; flyers; and campground bulletin boards, restrooms, and picnic tables. Rangers sweep campgrounds in routine food security patrols, equipped with informational flyers to distribute to those who still somehow fail to get the message. Food storage messages are also broadcast on the park's radio information stations.

Trailheads are marked with warnings, "Danger: Entering Bear Country— a Risk," and signs informing hikers that if they plan to camp, they must obtain a permit. Permits come with verbal warnings that safety is not guaranteed, along with advice about how to avoid an encounter, what to do if one does occur, what kinds of foods are attractants and how to store them, and where to and where not to sleep. Park staff inform backcountry campers of any recent bear activity in the area where they plan to hike and camp, and distribute the sixteen-page booklet, "Beyond Road's End," which includes similar but more detailed information. Visitors may also watch a video about how to safely camp and secure their food in the backcountry, where many campsites are now equipped with "bear boxes" as well as poles for suspending food between trees.

The signs that park staff post at trailheads to warn people that a bear has been reported to be frequenting the area feature a simple outline of a bear that represents a strong contrast to the cartoonish, humorous, or "horror bears" of the past. Experience has proven that people are less likely to steal the more simple-looking signs than the more detailed or more gruesome-looking ones. Temporary trail closure warnings, printed on 8.5-by-11-inch paper and laminated, feature a computer-generated standard clip-art bear rather than one specifically designed to convey a certain meaning or feeling about *Yellowstone*'s bears.[12]

The park's efforts to end feeding, eliminate injuries, and preserve its bears have proven largely successful. Since 1986, the annual number of bear–caused injuries in Yellowstone has fluctuated between zero and four, all restricted to the park's backcountry and all involving grizzly bears. Overall, the park averages one bear-related injury per year, usually occurring when a backcountry hiker surprises a sow grizzly with her cubs. During the 1980s, the average number of injuries was two per year; in the 1970s, six. Reports of property damage caused by bears have been reduced as well, with an average of seven per year throughout the 1990s. The average in the 1980s was twenty per year, and in the 1970s, forty-six per year. Fewer conflicts mean fewer removals. In the 1990s, one grizzly was removed from the park every three years on average, down from one annually in the 1980s and four annually in the 1970s. For black bears the numbers are even lower, with one removed from the park an average of once every five years in the 1990s and 1980s, and three annually in the 1970s.[13]

Though the numbers are based on research conducted decades ago, the park's black bear population is estimated to be 600 animals, and the grizzly population in the Greater Yellowstone Ecosystem has rebounded since the dark days of the early 1980s. It is estimated that there were 200 grizzlies in the ecosystem at the time of the bear's listing as a Threatened Species in 1975, and that number is thought to have dropped to an all-time low of between 170 and 180 between 1981 and 1983; now it stands at about 366, a number that is leading some to ask whether it is time for the grizzly to be delisted. In order for that to happen, the population must meet three recovery goals established in the U.S. Fish and Wildlife Service's 1993 Grizzly Bear Recovery Plan. Recovery parameters include:

1. *Females with cubs:* To have an average of 15 adult females with cubs-of-the-year (COY) per year on a six-year running average both inside the recovery zone and within a ten-mile area immediately surrounding it.
2. *Distribution of females with COY:* To have 16 of 18 recovery zone Bear Management Units (BMUs) occupied by females with young from a running six-year sum of observations; no two adjacent BMUs shall be unoccupied. Occupancy requires verified evidence (sightings of tracks) of at least 1 female with young (COY, yearling, or two-year-old) at least once in each of 16 BMUs over a six-year period.
3. *Mortality:* The six-year average of known human-caused mortality shall not exceed 4 percent of the current population estimate based on the most recent three-year sum of females with cubs, minus known adult female deaths. In addition, no more than 30 percent of the known human-caused mortality shall be females. These mortality limits cannot be exceeded during any two consecutive years for recovery to be achieved.

For purposes of quantifying the population, a grizzly removed from the GYE by any means—lethal removal, relocation, or shipping to a zoo—is classified as a mortality. In addition, a draft conservation strategy must be approved and signed by all involved state and federal agencies prior to any consideration of delisting. The states of Wyoming, Montana, and Idaho have completed plans providing guidance for grizzly bear management after delisting (if it occurs).[14]

However, the delisting process is not so automatic as simply ensuring that recovery goals are met and paperwork is in order. There are other factors to be taken into consideration; for instance, the potential for future grizzly habitat loss in the GYE. Yellowstone National Park comprises only 37 percent of the grizzly's bear's recovery zone; the GYE has a rapidly growing human population, and subdivisions built upon former ranchlands are common.[15] Also common is the tendency for local residents to feed bears, purposely or not. Unsecured garbage, improperly stored pet food, and bird feeders are the most common bear attractants in these places where many people choose to live in order to be near wild nature, but are not always willing to accommodate its presence when it becomes personally inconvenient. In the absence of active enforcement of local food-storage laws, problem bears are created, persist, and eventually have to be destroyed.

Other pressures on GYE grizzlies include the potential for oil and gas drilling, industrial logging, and road-building projects in grizzly habitat that have thus far been avoided because of the Endangered Species Act's protection of the grizzly. The problem with swift delisting in the face of habitat threats is that the effects of habitat loss on grizzly mortality might not be seen for a few years after development occurs—when it is too late for the problem to be fixed.[16]

Grizzlies face other threats too. The annual availability of natural foods is a concern. Meat makes up an unusually high proportion of the diet of Yellowstone's grizzlies, partially due to the harsh climate that precludes the growth of large amounts of berries and other natural foods.[17] This paucity of forage posed a problem when the dumps were first closed because the park had been keeping its ungulate population artificially low through culling. The current Interagency Bison Management Plan calls for removal of bison from the park under certain circumstances to reduce the risk that bison might transmit brucellosis to local domestic cattle, possibly meaning fewer winter-killed carcasses for grizzlies to feed upon. Elk also carry the disease, and could be the next target in the brucellosis debate. Yellowstone's cutthroat trout, another staple of the grizzlies' diet, face significant threats from whirling disease and the introduction of predatory lake trout into Yellowstone Lake. Lake trout do not replace cutthroats in the food system for grizzlies because they remain in deep waters rather than moving into rivers and tributaries to spawn.

Whitebark pine, a source of high-fat seeds that are another staple, has already been almost wiped out by blister rust in Glacier National Park, and it is not unlikely that whitebark pine in the GYE will be similarly affected. Army cutworm moths, recently discovered to be the richest food source available to grizzlies in the GYE because of their high protein content (a grizzly foraging on the moths can consume half of its yearly energy needs in thirty days), migrate to high mountain peaks from areas where they are considered agricultural pests, meaning that their numbers could be decreased by the successful use of insecticide hundreds or thousands of miles from the GYE.[18] Finally, Yellowstone's grizzlies are isolated from other populations, which could result in problems of low genetic diversity. Simply stated, the delisting process is likely to be even more controversial and complicated than the listing process, and again will not find all GYE researchers—or residents—on the same side of the table. What the next chapter of this story will bring is unclear.

CONCLUSION:

THE POST-ENLIGHTENMENT BEAR

The close relationship that developed between bears and people in Yellowstone at the turn of the twentieth century took far less time to grow and solidify than it took to undo. After its establishment, it mattered little what kind of narrative the National Park Service put forth about bears—from pet to monster to admonishing fantasy friend. People maintained what they largely believed to be their benevolent status as bear feeders, and the bears continued to please by entertaining. Teaching, warning, amusing, cajoling, and threatening did not work; none of those methods could break the spell cast long ago, enchanting visitors with the notion that in Yellowstone, they could be the true companions of wild bears, with people sharing their bounty and receiving gratitude in return. Within that powerful context, the NPS's antifeeding messages seemed tongue in cheek, rote recitations that, through their omnipresence, actually became part of the narrative of bear–human friendship in the park by contributing to the surreal, even "magical" atmosphere of the roadside carnival. Only when those messages came accompanied by logical, palpable consequences—the consistent removal of actual money from people's wallets as actual punishment for their actions—were visitors jolted out of their decades-old reverie.

Once the spell was broken, the habits of people—and as a result, the habits of bears, opportunistic by nature—changed almost immediately. It is also likely that the changes in cultural attitudes that led to the shift from aesthetic conservation to preservation, along with the park's "updated" mission statement in 1972 and Congress's passage of legislation such as the Endangered Species Act in 1975, indicated that people were ready to give up their marshmallows and move beyond the primitive notion that animals existed to entertain and make people happy. This was a period when more sophisticated, unselfish ideas about the inherent value of nature and wilderness gained acceptance, and human foresight realized the necessity of maintaining biodiversity for the good of humanity itself. When those attitudinal changes were combined with actual law enforcement, bear feeding faded into Yellowstone's past.

Prior to that, though, visitors refused to be taught to stop feeding and, despite innumerable attempts, bears would not "learn" to stop seeking out human food. Repeated relocations and experiments with adverse condition-ing proved ineffectual deterrents. That was the ugly reality behind the "magic": between 1931 and 1975, visitors reported 1,897 bear-related injuries; 1,101 bears were recorded killed due to the "bear problem"; and many others were hurt or maimed, either after being hit by automobiles or in the course of trying to obtain foods—even natural foods such as fish—that people didn't want them to have. It has often been suggested that bears in Yellow-stone were spared from predator control efforts during the park's early years because of the pleasure they gave visitors, but the quality of life to which they were subjected in exchange for being allowed to live gives one pause. A 1920s-era photograph recently acquired by Montana State University's Mer-rill G. Burlingame Special Collections, in which a young male concessions employee is depicted with a black bear, provides a striking example. The bear sits back on its haunches in that familiar, conditioned, docile pose of the Yel-lowstone begging bear, expectantly waiting for the reward that experience with people has taught it to associate with the posture. The man, laughing, stands over the bear, holding a two-by-four high above his head, apparently pretending that he is about to bash the unsuspecting bear's brains in.

Taken in the context of this book, this image does two things. First, it stands as a single, sickening reminder of the casual disrespect and inhumanity with which bears were treated in the park for much of the twentieth century. Roadside feeding was not a carnival, its era not worthy of the yearnful long-ings for "the good old days" described, for instance, in contemporary adver-tising for one Yellowstone-area drive-through bear zoo. Roadside feeding meant degradation, pain, and death; it gave people license to deny the bear's nature as a wild animal and force it instead into a set of human constructs in which its only value lay in its ability to entertain people. Bears that breached those artificial boundaries by attempting to take what they were not offered were deemed criminal and often brought to swift "justice." If antifeeding messages have ever seemed incessant or shrill, it was with good reason.

The photo is also a metaphor for the undeniable fact that despite the ad-vances made over the past few decades in reducing human influence and manipulation in the lives of Yellowstone's bears, their fate remains largely in our hands. It is we who decide how land will be used; how wildlife will be managed; what happens to people who encourage bears to become habitu-ated and dangerous by leaving anthropogenic foods within their reach; and, more importantly, whether we still subscribe to the importance of biodiver-sity and wild things. For several decades, decisions regarding bear manage-ment in Yellowstone National Park, regardless of how hotly contested, have been predicated upon an awareness of that reality and made within the realm of science.

However, as the future of the grizzly is uncertain, so is the future of the scientific narrative. More than a few writers have proposed that the end of the Age of Enlightenment is upon us—that the nation has entered an era in which scientific fact and reason are losing their cachet as the accepted basis for many societal decisions. Even in a country founded on principles of reason, this state of affairs is not really surprising in a world that seems increasingly un*reason*able; our current postmodern condition is one of multiple subjectivities, alternative realities, globalization, hypertechnology, the dissolution of the nation-state, and the concomitant rise of nontraditional types of warfare—all of which result in an equation of unavoidable empirical uncertainty, leading many people to seek alternative structures and systems of explanation where the old ones seem to have failed. In the face of this transition, traditional methods of measuring what's true and real can seem suddenly irrelevant. With no satisfactory system of reasonable explanation to replace it, the future of the scientific narrative—and science itself—in Yellowstone and elsewhere seems less sure. The rise of relativism, in addition to the increasing politicization of science, continually dilutes the historical authority of science to act as a marker for "truth," leaving its overall veracity as a basis for our societal "reality" open to question. At this point, the stakes are ever higher for those concerned with the environment that sustains our existence; conservation itself is rooted in the notion that sustainability can be achieved through scientific study and practice. Ecology is a "science of limits" that evaporate once their scientific underpinnings are undermined.

In this new ideological environment, the problem for the bears of Yellowstone is their own history. In the absence of science, anthropocentric assumptions about bears' habits, motivations, tendencies, lifeways, and needs historically filled the gap and led to horrible situations based solely on human belief about how bears should act. This approach resulted in management rooted in the idea that humans were omnipotently capable of manipulating and controlling bears' actions—regardless of the limits and nature of the animals' nature—and that human pleasure and convenience were paramount over all other considerations. A return to such nonscientific systems—management without ecological limits—would likely be disastrous for both bears and people.

If the evolution of bear (and visitor) management has been one focus of this book, our changing ways of seeing Yellowstone's bears has been the other. As our ways of explaining the world have destabilized, so have our ways of seeing it. Take photography, for instance: once considered a quasi-scientific tool, in the sense that it was indubitably capable of capturing the "truth," technological innovation has forever changed the meaning—the very nature—of this medium. Digital technology makes it possible for us to be depicted in virtual situations we may never have experienced, leaving many people more likely to disbelieve than to believe an even slightly improbable image. The significance of this issue for such an improbable place as Yellowstone, whose very existence was doubted until artists and photographers brought back then-undeniable images of its wonders, is yet to be seen. Additionally, Yellowstone National Park now counts many times more "virtual visitors" via the Internet each year than visitors who actually set foot within its borders. The question remains whether, with the rise of these virtual environments, in which everything we see and experience is filtered through a technological medium, seeing the world with one's own eyes will become more or less important, and whether people's desire to see the natural world for themselves, and have the natural world look back, will increase or simply dissipate. Are we truly "of the wilderness," or are we not?

The story of bears and people in Yellowstone National Park is long and complex and, because it is contemporaneous with the most dynamic century in our nation's history, laden with the influence of intense cultural change that has had meaning for the entire world. As we face an uncertain future, one cannot help but wonder what visitors to Yellowstone will be told about bears in 2020, one hundred years after the odyssey was begun by Jesse James and the tourists he captivated.

Abbreviations: American Heritage Center, University of Wyoming, Laramie (AHC); Montana Historical Society, Helena, Montana (MHS); National Archives, College Park, Maryland (NACP); National Archives, Yellowstone National Park (NAYNP); Record Group (RG); Yellowstone National Park Bear Management Office (YNPBMO); Yellowstone National Park Library (YNPL)

INTRODUCTION

1. Donald Swain, *Wilderness Defender: Horace M. Albright and Conservation* (Chicago: University of Chicago Press, 1970).
2. U.S. Department of the Interior, "Yellowstone National Park, Wyoming," 1922, box K-2, NAYNP.
3. Kerry Gunther and Mark Biel, eds., *Yellowstone National Park Bear Information Book* (Yellowstone National Park, Wyo.: Bear Management Office, Yellowstone National Park, 1994), 40.
4. Paul Schullery, "What Is Natural? Philosophical Analysis and Yellowstone Practice," *Western North American Naturalist* 61(3) (July 2001): 255–256.

CHAPTER 1: ZOOS, FEEDING GROUNDS, AND ROADSIDES

1. Lee Whittlesey, "Yellowstone's Horse-and-Buggy Tour Guides: Interpreting the Grand Old Park, 1872–1920," unpublished manuscript, 67; Aubrey L. Haines, *The Yellowstone Story: A History of Our First National Park,* vol. 2 (Niwot: University Press of Colorado, 1996), 71; Theodore Roosevelt, "Bear Life in the Yellowstone," in *Yellowstone Bear Tales,* Paul Schullery, ed. (Boulder, Colo.: Roberts Rinehart, 1991), 25.
2. Mrs. P. K. Sturgis to Lt. Gen. S. B. M. Young, July 7, 1907, exhibit J, folder 1, item 33, NAYNP.
3. F. J. Haynes to 4th Indorsement, July 24, 1904, exhibit K, folder 1, item 33, NAYNP; Lt. Gen. S. B. M. Young to Major H. C. Benson, Acting Superintendent, Yellowstone National Park, April 23, 1910, folder 2, item 33, NAYNP.
4. E. C. Waters to Capt. George Anderson, November 14, 1894, archive document number 1726, NAYNP; Yellowstone Lake Boat Company to Lt. Gen. S. B. M. Young, September 26, 1907, folder 2, item 33, NAYNP; E. A. Hitchcock to Capt. W. E. Wilder, April 15, 1899, archive document number 3359, NAYNP.
5. Haines, *The Yellowstone Story,* vol. 2, 75; Capt. John Pitcher to E. A. Hitchcock, December 30, 1901, exhibit M, folder 1, item 33, NAYNP; and E. C. Waters to General S. B. M. Young, June 15, 1907, exhibit L; Rodgers to General S. B. M. Young, telegram, June 25, 1907; Jasper S. Gibbs to Lt. Gen. S. B. M. Young, June 12, 1907; Dr. F. W. Vowinckel to Lt. Gen. S. B. M. Young, June 12, 1907, all in exhibit L, folder 1, item 33, NAYNP.
6. Vowinckel to Young, June 12, 1907.
7. E. C. Waters to Major John Pitcher, October 11, 1906, file 6333, item 25, NAYNP; Capt. M. O. Bigelow to Lt. Gen. S. B. M. Young, June 13, 1907, and Jesse E. Wilson to General S. B. M. Young, June 14, 1907, both in exhibit L, folder 1, item 33, NAYNP; Waters to Young, June 15, 1907.

8. Capt. M. O. Bigelow to Lt. Gen. S. B. M. Young, late summer 1907, archive document number 6992, NAYNP.

9. Lt. Gen. S. B. M. Young to E. C. Waters, August 2, 1907, exhibit H, folder 1, item 33, NAYNP.

10. T. Gilbert Pearson to General S. B. M. Young, August 15, 1907, folder 2, and T. S. Palmer to General S. B. M. Young, August 19, 1907, both in folder 2, item 33, NAYNP.

11. W. F. Scott to General S. B. M. Young, August 24, 1907, folder 2, item 33, NAYNP.

12. Lt. Gen. S. B. M. Young to Thomas Ryan, n.d., 1907; Yellowstone Lake Boat Company to Young, September 26, 1907; Lt. Coxe to Superintendent, Yellowstone National Park, September 24, 1907, all in folder 2, item 33, NAYNP; Haines, *The Yellowstone Story*, vol. 2, 76–77.

13. Donald Swain, *Wilderness Defender: Horace M. Albright and Conservation* (Chicago: University of Chicago Press, 1970), 36; Robert M. Utley, "Foreword," in *Creating the National Park Service: The Missing Years,* Horace M. Albright and Marian Albright Schenck, eds. (Norman: University of Oklahoma Press, 1999), xii. Also see Samuel P. Hays, *Conservation and the Gospel of Efficiency: The Progressive Conservation Movement, 1890–1920* (Cambridge, Mass.: Harvard University Press, 1959).

14. See Richard West Sellars, *Preserving Nature in the National Parks: A History* (New Haven, Conn.: Yale University Press, 1997), 188; Hays, *Conservation and the Gospel of Efficiency;* Albright and Schenck, *Creating the National Park Service,* 124–125, 127, 292–293; James A. Pritchard, *Preserving Yellowstone's Natural Conditions: Science and the Perception of Nature* (Lincoln: University of Nebraska Press, 1999); Hal Rothman, *Devil's Bargains: Tourism in the Twentieth-Century American West* (Lawrence: University Press of Kansas, 1998); Swain, *Wilderness Defender;* Robert Shankland, *Steve Mather of the National Parks* (New York: Alfred A. Knopf, 1951); Sellars, *Preserving Nature in the National Parks;* Horace M. Albright and Robert Cahn, *The Birth of the National Park Service: The Founding Years, 1913–1933* (Salt Lake City, Utah: Howe Brothers, 1985); Richard Bartlett, *Yellowstone: A Wilderness Besieged* (Tucson: University of Arizona Press, 1985); Haines, *The Yellowstone Story,* vol. 2.

15. Horace M. Albright to Dr. Barton Warren Evermann, March 20, 1931, file "1—Bear (Yellowstone NP) Jan 1, 1929–Dec 31, 1931," box N-48, NAYNP; Horace M. Albright, "Monthly Report of the Superintendent," June 1924, YNPL.

16. Albright and Schenck, *Creating the National Park Service,* 127.

17. Ibid., 127, 299.

18. Hays, *Conservation and the Gospel of Efficiency.*

19. Pritchard, *Preserving Yellowstone's Natural Conditions,* 34, 42–43, 46, 57, 117.

20. William T. Hornaday, *The Minds and Manners of Wild Animals: A Book of Personal Observations* (New York: Charles Scribner's Sons, 1922); L. Claude Way, "Annual Report of the Superintendent," 1917, Rocky Mountain National Park Library.

21. L. Claude Way, "Annual Report of the Superintendent," 1918, Rocky Mountain National Park Library; Pritchard, *Preserving Yellowstone's Natural Conditions,* 70.

22. E. J. Sawyer, "At the Buffalo Corral," *Yellowstone Nature Notes* 1(2) (June 28, 1924), YNPL; Albright, "Monthly Report," June 1924; E. J. Sawyer, "Weekly Report of the Park Naturalist," Yellowstone National Park, May 16, 1925; E. J. Sawyer, "Weekly Report of the Park Naturalist," May 23, 1925; E. J. Sawyer, "Monthly Report of the Park Naturalist," Yellowstone National Park, April 1926, all in file "144—Reports of Park Naturalist [to Mr. Albright], 1925–1927," box K-11, NAYNP.

23. Horace M. Albright to Sam Woodring, March 9, 1925, NAYNP; Sawyer, "Weekly Report of the Park Naturalist," June 20, 1925, file "144—Reports of Park Naturalist [to Mr. Albright], 1925–1927," box K-11, NAYNP.

24. Dorr Yeager, "Mammoth Pets," *Yellowstone Nature Notes* 5(10) (October 1, 1928), YNPL; E. J. Sawyer, "Weekly Report of the Park Naturalist," March 21, 1925, file "144—Reports of Park Naturalist [to Mr. Albright], 1925–1927," box K-11, NAYNP; E. J. Sawyer, "Weekly Report of Park Naturalist," Yellowstone National Park, June 28, 1925, file "144—Reports of Park Naturalist [to Mr. Albright], 1925–1927," box K-11, NAYNP; E. J. Sawyer, "A Tame Coyote," *Yellowstone Nature Notes* 2(1) (March 1925), YNPL; Sawyer, "Weekly Report," June 20, 1925.

25. Horace M. Albright, "Monthly Report of the Superintendent," June 1925, YNPL; E. J. Sawyer, "Weekly Report of the Park Naturalist," July 4, 1925; and E. J. Sawyer, "Monthly Report of the Park Naturalist," Yellowstone National Park, September 1925, both in file "144—Reports of Park Naturalist [to Mr. Albright], 1925–1927," box K-11, NAYNP.

26. Dorr Yeager, "Juno Entertains," *Yellowstone Nature Notes* 5(5) (1928), YNPL; E. J. Sawyer, "Monthly Report of the Park Naturalist," July 1925; E. J. Sawyer, "Weekly Report of the Park Naturalist," November 18, 1925; and E. J. Sawyer, "Monthly Report of the Park Naturalist, March 1926," all in file "144—Reports of Park Naturalist [to Mr. Albright], 1925–1927," box K-11, NAYNP; Horace M. Albright, "Monthly Report of the Superintendent," July 1925, YNPL.

27. Yeager, "Juno Entertains"; Horace M. Albright and Frank Taylor, *Oh, Ranger! A Book About the National Parks* (Golden, Colo.: Outbooks, 1986), 40.

28. E. J. Sawyer, "Monthly Report of the Park Naturalist," Yellowstone National Park, December 1924, file "144—Reports of Park Naturalist [to Mr. Albright], 1925–1927," box K-11, NAYNP.

29. Dorr Yeager, "Barney," *Yellowstone Nature Notes* (Spring 1931), YNPL; Esse Forrester O'Brien, *Barney* (Austin, Tex.: Steck Company, 1950), 51, 40, 37; Anne Wolfson, *Adventures of Barney Bear in Yellowstone Park* (Albuquerque, N.M.: Babcock & Borough, 1949); O'Brien, *Barney;* Dorr Yeager, *Bob Flame—Ranger* (New York: Sears Publishing Company, 1934).

30. Judith Meyer, *The Spirit of Yellowstone: The Cultural Evolution of a National Park* (Lanham, Md.: Rowman & Littlefield, 1996), 17.

31. Paul Schullery, *The Bears of Yellowstone* (Worland, Wyo.: High Plains Publishing Company, 1992), 93; Earley Vernon Wilcox, "Trip Around Yellowstone Park," *Rocky Mountain Magazine* 3 (January–February 1902): 263–273, file "Yellowstone National Park—Description and Travel, 1900–1920s," vertical files, MHS.

32. Haines, *The Yellowstone Story,* vol. 2, 116–117.

33. Ibid., 117.

34. Mary Bradshaw Richards, *Camping Out in the Yellowstone, 1882* (Salt Lake City: University of Utah Press, 1994), 69.

35. Albright and Taylor, *Oh, Ranger!,* 37.

36. F. Dumont Smith, *Book of a Hundred Bears* (Chicago: Rand, McNally & Company, 1909), 144.

37. Aubrey Haines, "A Guided Tour from Old Faithful to Mammoth Hot Springs," Yellowstone National Park, August 19–21, 2000; Esse Forrester O'Brien, *Clowns of the Forest* (Austin, Tex.: Steck Company, 1948), 96; Phillip Martindale, "Close Contact with Grizzly Bears," 1920s, file "Martindale, Phillip, Close Contact with Grizzly Bears," section Mammals—Ursidae, vertical files, YNPL; Smith, *Book of a Hundred*

Bears; George Baggley, "Memorandum Report and Recommendations on the Present Bear Feeding Grounds to the Superintendent," December 5, 1929, YNPL.

38. Christine Whitacre, "Otter Creek Bear-Feeding Station," National Park Service Intermountain Support Office, July 28, 1998; Edmund Rogers, *Annual Report of the Superintendent for 1938,* 15, YNPL.

39. Horace M. Albright, "General Plan of Administration for the Educational Division," National Park Service, June 4, 1929, NAYNP; Martindale, "Close Contact with Grizzly Bears."

40. Smith, *Book of a Hundred Bears,* 113.

41. Schullery, *The Bears of Yellowstone,* 101.

42. James McBride, "Ranger's Monthly Report," Yellowstone National Park, July 1921, NAYNP. The "yellow cars" were part of the Yellowstone Park Company's fleet of White Motor Company touring cars, which eventually numbered ninety-eight. The cars were used to transport visitors on concessioner-guided tours of the park (Elaine Hale, "What Has Yellow Wheels and Winters in Shrink-Wrap? Buses in Bags!" *The Buffalo Chip: Resource Management Newsletter,* Yellowstone National Park [January–February 2002]: 4); Horace M. Albright, "Monthly Report of the Superintendent," July 1921, YNPL.

43. Horace M. Albright, "Monthly Report of the Superintendent," July 1920, YNPL; Horace M. Albright, "The Great and Near-Great in Yellowstone," *Montana the Magazine of Western History* 22(3) (Summer 1972): 80–89; Horace M. Albright, "Monthly Report of the Superintendent," June 1923, YNPL.

44. Col. L. M. Brett, June 1, 1915, unnamed file, box N-120, NAYNP; Shaw & Powell Camping Company, "Yellowstone Park by Camp," 1913; and First Cavalry Lieutenant Colonel to Amos Shaw, May 27, 1913, both in file "130—Financial Reports—Advertisements of Concessionaires 1913," item 52, NAYNP.

45. Union Pacific Railroad, "Geyserland: Yellowstone National Park," 1926. Collection of author.

46. U.S. Department of the Interior, "Yellowstone National Park, Wyoming," 1922, box K-2, NAYNP.

47. Albright and Taylor, *Oh, Ranger!,* 33.

48. U.S. Department of the Interior, "Motorist's Guide to Yellowstone National Park," 1926, box K-2, NAYNP.

49. Albright and Taylor, *Oh, Ranger!,* 45; O'Brien, *Clowns of the Forest;* Horace M. Albright to Lafayette Hanchett, September 17, 1927, file "715.02, part 1—Yellowstone: Mammals: Bears, July 7, 1925 to July 28, 1930," box 481, entry E7, RG 79, NACP.

50. Albright and Taylor, *Oh, Ranger!,* 33; Albright, "Monthly Report of the Superintendent," July 1923, YNPL.

51. Albright and Taylor, *Oh, Ranger!,* 46; Albright, "Monthly Report of the Superintendent," June 1923, YNPL, 27; *Yellowstone Nature Notes* (August 24, 1924), YNPL.

52. Albright and Taylor, *Oh, Ranger!,* 42–43.

53. Yi-Fu Tuan, *Dominance and Affection: The Making of Pets* (New Haven, Conn.: Yale University Press, 1984), 85.

54. Wendell S. Keate, "Report on Accidents, Injuries and Sickness," Yellowstone National Park, 1925, box A-5, NAYNP; Roger Toll to Horace M. Albright, April 15, 1930, box N-48, NAYNP; Albright, "The Great and Near-Great in Yellowstone"; Horace M. Albright, "New Orders for National Park Bears," *The Backlog: A Bulletin of the Camp Fire Club of America* 22(1) (April 1945): 5–11, file "Albright, Horace M., New Orders

for National Park Bears," section Mammals—Ursidae, vertical files, YNPL, 8; Horace Albright, "The Lady Who Lost Her Dress," in Schullery, *Yellowstone Bear Tales*, 102–103.

CHAPTER 2: ADMITTING YOU HAVE A PROBLEM

1. Horace M. Albright to Joseph Dixon, November 9, 1931, file "1—Bear (Yellowstone NP) Jan 1, 1929–Dec 31, 1931," box N-48, NAYNP.
2. Giles Toll, "Now We Are Entering that Other World: Roger Wolcott Toll and Rocky Mountain National Park," *Colorado Heritage* (Autumn 2004): 21; see James A. Pritchard, *Preserving Yellowstone's Natural Conditions: Science and the Perception of Nature* (Lincoln: University of Nebraska Press, 1999), 86–87.
3. Joseph Dixon, "Report on the Bear Situation in Yellowstone, September 1929," Wildlife Division, National Park Service, 1929, section Mammals—Ursidae, vertical files, YNPL; Pritchard, *Preserving Yellowstone's Natural Conditions*, 107.
4. Dixon, "Report on the Bear Situation."
5. Dorr Yeager, *Yellowstone Nature Notes* (May 1930), YNPL.
6. Phillip Martindale, "A Large Family and Possible Adoption," *Yellowstone Nature Notes* (August 1930), YNPL.
7. National Park Service, "National Park Service Warning—Bears," July 21, 1931, file "1—Bear (Yellowstone NP) Jan 1, 1929–Dec 31, 1931," box N-48, NAYNP; Albright to Dixon, November 9, 1931; Kerry Gunther and Mark Biel, eds., *Yellowstone National Park Bear Information Book* (Yellowstone National Park, Wyo.: Bear Management Office, Yellowstone National Park, 1994), 40.
8. "Bear Incidents Yellowstone National Park, 1931–1932 comparative" (Yellowstone National Park, Wyo., no date), file "Bear Incidents Yellowstone National Park, 1931–1932 comparative," section Mammals—Ursidae, vertical files, YNPL; U.S. Department of the Interior, "Memorandum for the Press," October 6, 1930, file "715.02, part 2—Yellowstone: Mammals: Bears, August 28, 1930 to December 28, 1931," box 481, entry E7, RG 79, NACP; Guy D. Edwards to Horace M. Albright, October 1, 1931, file "1—Bear (Yellowstone NP) Jan 1, 1929–Dec 31, 1931," box N-48, NAYNP.
9. "Bear Incidents Yellowstone National Park, 1931–1932 comparative"; L. H. Rappaport to National Park Service, September 18, 1933, file "2—Bear (Yellowstone NP), Jan 1, 1932–?," box N-48, NAYNP; Myron Wall to Harold Ickes, August 1, 1935, file "715.02, part 4—Yellowstone: Mammals: Bears, August 3, 1933 to November 18, 1940," box 1749, entry E7, RG 79, NACP.
10. Edwards to Albright, October 1, 1931.
11. Roger Toll to Joseph Dixon, February 5, 1932, file "715.02, part 3—Yellowstone: Mammals: Bears, no dates," box 481, entry E7, RG 79, NACP.
12. David Canfield to Roger Toll, January 18, 1932, file "715.02—Bears 1939–1948, 1949–1950," box N-52, NAYNP.
13. George Baggley, "Suggested Plan for Bear Control for Yellowstone National Park," Yellowstone National Park, May 10, 1932, file "715.02, part 3—Yellowstone: Mammals: Bears, no dates," box 481, entry E7, RG 79, NACP, 4.
14. Baggley, "Suggested Plan for Bear Control," 3.
15. Guy D. Edwards to George Baggley, May 24, 1932, file "715.02, part 3—Yellowstone: Mammals: Bears, no dates," box 481, entry E7, RG 79, NACP.
16. Arthur E. Demaray to Dr. H. C. Bryant, May 26, 1932, file "715.02, part 3—Yellowstone: Mammals: Bears, no dates," box 481, entry E7, RG 79, NACP.

17. Horace M. Albright to Superintendent, Yellowstone National Park, June 8, 1932, file "715.02, part 3—Yellowstone: Mammals: Bears, no dates," box 481, entry E7, RG 79, NACP.

18. William Finley to Victor Cahalane, October 9, 1937, file "715.02, part 4—Yellowstone: Mammals: Bears, August 3, 1933 to November 18, 1940," box 1749, entry E7, RG 79, NACP; Victor Cahalane to Mary Meagher, February 22, 1980, file "Bear Management 1980," vertical files, YNPBMO.

19. Joseph Joffe to Director, National Park Service, December 23, 1930; Arthur E. Demaray to Joseph Joffe, January 6, 1931; Arthur E. Demaray to Ralph Benton, January 6, 1931; Arthur E. Demaray to Superintendent, Yellowstone National Park, January 26, 1931; Arthur E. Demaray to W. M. Nichols, January 26, 1931; Arthur E. Demaray to Vernon Goodwin, January 27, 1931; Demaray to Benton, January 6, 1931, all in file "715.02, part 2—Yellowstone: Mammals: Bears, August 28, 1930 to December 28, 1931," box 481, entry E7, RG 79, NACP.

20. Roger Toll to George Wright, September 22, 1932, file "715.02—Bears 1939–1948, 1949–1950," box N-52, NAYNP.

21. George Wright to Roger Toll, September 2, 1932, file "715.02, part 3—Yellowstone: Mammals: Bears, no dates," box 481, entry E7, RG 79, NACP; Adolph Murie to George Wright, November 8, 1935; George Wright to Arthur Demaray, July 18, 1934; Roger Toll to Director, National Park Service, July 27, 1934; and Roger Toll to Arno B. Cammerer, September 19, 1934, all in file "715.02, part 4—Yellowstone: Mammals: Bears, August 3, 1933 to November 18, 1940," box 1749, entry E7, RG 79, NACP.

22. Toll to Cammerer, September 19, 1934.

23. Richard West Sellars, *Preserving Nature in the National Parks: A History* (New Haven, Conn.: Yale University Press, 1997), 95, 99.

24. U.S. Department of the Interior, "Yellowstone National Park," 1936, box K-2, NAYNP.

25. George Wright to Roger Toll, October 22, 1935, file "715.02, part 4—Yellowstone: Mammals: Bears, August 3, 1933 to November 18, 1940," box 1749, entry E7, RG 79, NACP.

26. Toll, "Now We Are Entering that Other World," 29; see Pritchard, *Preserving Yellowstone's Natural Conditions,* 84, 89–97, 105–106.

27. Joseph Dixon to Victor Cahalane, October 26, 1937, file "715.02, part 4—Yellowstone: Mammals: Bears, August 3, 1933 to November 18, 1940," box 1749, entry E7, RG 79, NACP.

28. H. C. Bryant to William Finley, November 4, 1937, file "715.02, part 4—Yellowstone: Mammals: Bears, August 3, 1933 to November 18, 1940," box 1749, entry E7, RG 79, NACP.

29. Edmund Rogers to Director, National Park Service, December 7, 1937, file "715.02, part 4—Yellowstone: Mammals: Bears, August 3, 1933 to November 18, 1940," box 1749, entry E7, RG 79, NACP.

30. Arno B. Cammerer to Superintendent, Yellowstone National Park, March 28, 1938, file "715.02, part 4—Yellowstone: Mammals: Bears, August 3, 1933 to November 18, 1940," box 1749, entry E7, RG 79, NACP.

31. Ibid.

32. Yellowstone National Park, "press release," July 20, 1938, file "715.02—Bears 1939–1948, 1949–1950," box N-52, NAYNP.

33. Pritchard, *Preserving Yellowstone's Natural Conditions,* 142–143.

34. Arno B. Cammerer and Ira W. Gabrielson to Secretary of the Interior, November 24, 1939, file "715.02—Bears 1939–1948, 1949–1950," box N-52, NAYNP.

35. Arthur E. Demaray to Superintendents, Yellowstone and Yosemite National Parks, July 8, 1940, file "715.02, part 4—Yellowstone: Mammals: Bears, August 3, 1933 to November 18, 1940," box 1749, entry E7, RG 79, NACP.

36. Christine Whitacre, "Otter Creek Bear-Feeding Station," National Park Service Intermountain Support Office, July 28, 1998.

37. Newton Drury to Superintendent, Yellowstone National Park, May 27, 1942, file "715.02, part 5—Yellowstone: Mammals: Bears, January 1941 to December 1943," box 1749, entry E7, RG 79, NACP; Paul Schullery, *The Bears of Yellowstone* (Worland, Wyo.: High Plains Publishing Company, 1992), 106.

38. "Bear Disposal," *Livingston Enterprise*, Livingston, Montana, August 17, 1932, file "715.02, part 3—Yellowstone: Mammals: Bears, no dates," box 481, entry E7, RG 79, NACP; Drury to Superintendent, May 27, 1942, file "715.02, part 4—Yellowstone: Mammals: Bears, August 3, 1933 to November 18, 1940," box 1749, entry E7, RG 79, NACP; "Yellowstone National Park Bear Incidents, 1931–1963," YNPL; Acting Superintendent Emmert to Director, National Park Service, December 22, 1939, file "715.02, part 4—Yellowstone: Mammals: Bears, August 3, 1933 to November 18, 1940," box 1749, entry E7, RG 79, NACP.

39. Yellowstone National Park, *Final Environmental Impact Statement: Grizzly Bear Management Program*, October 1982, 44, vertical files, YNPL; Edmund Rogers, "Memorandum for the Director," Yellowstone National Park, August 20, 1942, file "715.02, part 5—Yellowstone: Mammals: Bears, January 1941 to December 1943," box 1749, entry E7, RG 79, NACP.

40. D. H. Bremer, "Individual Bear Injury Report," Yellowstone National Park, August 23, 1942; Newton Drury to Secretary of the Interior, September 15, 1942, both in file "715.02, part 5—Yellowstone: Mammals: Bears, January 1941 to December 1943," box 1749, entry E7, RG 79, NACP.

41. Lawrence Merriam to Ellen A. Hansen, September 10, 1942, file "715.02, part 5—Yellowstone: Mammals: Bears, January 1941 to December 1943," box 1749, entry E7, RG 79, NACP; Paul Schullery, "Historical Perspectives on Yellowstone Bear Management," *Proceedings, Grizzly Bear Symposium,* Casper, Wyo., April 28, 1984, 16.

42. Merriam to Hansen, September 10, 1942; Edmund Rogers, "Superintendent's Annual Report," 1943, 1, YNPL.

43. Lawrence Merriam to Edmund Rogers, September 11, 1942, file "715.02—Bears vol. 1: November 1939 to December 31, 1947," box N-339, NAYNP.

44. Newton Drury to Lawrence Merriam, September 15, 1942, file "715.02, part 5—Yellowstone: Mammals: Bears, January 1941 to December 1943," box 1749, entry E7, RG 79, NACP.

45. Letter to U.S. Department of the Interior, September 14, 1931, file "715.02, part 2—Yellowstone: Mammals: Bears, August 28, 1930 to December 28, 1931," box 481, entry E7, RG 79, NACP; Campers to Roger Toll, July 27, 1932, file "715.02, part 3—Yellowstone: Mammals: Bears, no dates," box 481, entry E7, RG 79, NACP; Joseph Dixon to Roger Toll, August 23, 1931, file "1—Bear (Yellowstone NP) Jan 1, 1929–Dec 31, 1931," box N-48, NAYNP; Arno B. Cammerer to Frank Field, September 19, 1931, file "715.02, part 2—Yellowstone: Mammals: Bears, August 28, 1930 to December 28, 1931," box 481, entry E7, RG 79, NACP; Arno B. Cammerer to William Breniman, August 11, 1937, file "715.02, part 4—Yellowstone: Mammals: Bears, August 3, 1933 to November 18, 1940," box 1749, entry E7, RG 79, NACP; Toll to Joseph Dixon, February 5, 1932; George Wright to Roger Toll, July 19, 1933, file "2—Bear (Yellowstone NP), Jan 1, 1932–?," box N-48, NAYNP; H. C. Bryant to Victor Cahalane, September 4, 1937, file

"715.02, part 4—Yellowstone: Mammals: Bears, August 3, 1933 to November 18, 1940," box 1749, entry E7, RG 79, NACP.

46. National Park Service Branch of Plans and Design, 1939, box 1750, entry E7, RG 79, NACP.

47. Edmund Rogers to Lawrence Merriam, May 15, 1943, file "715.02, part 5—Yellowstone: Mammals: Bears, January 1941 to December 1943," box 1749, entry E7, RG 79, NACP; Carnes, "Comment on Bear Fences," April 19, 1945; and A. W. Burney to Director, National Park Service, June 8, 1945, both in file "715.02, part 6—Yellowstone: Mammals: Bears, January 1944 to June 1949," box 1749, entry E7, RG 79, NACP.

48. Carnes, "Comment on Bear Fences"; Victor Cahalane to Director, National Park Service, June 6, 1945, file "715.02, part 6—Yellowstone: Mammals: Bears, January 1944 to June 1949," box 1749, entry E7, RG 79, NACP.

49. A. W. Burney to Director, June 8, 1945.

50. Edmund Rogers to Regional Director, Region 2, March 5, 1946, file "715.02—Bears 1939–1948, 1949–1950," box N-52, NAYNP.

51. Lawrence Merriam to Edmund Rogers, November 12, 1948, file "715.02—Bears vol. 1: November 1939–December 31, 1947, 1 of 2," box 339, NAYNP; Lawrence Merriam to Newton Drury, May 17, 1946, file "715.02, part 6—Yellowstone: Mammals: Bears, January 1944 to June 1949," box 1749, entry E7, RG 79, NACP; Howard Baker to Director, National Park Service, September 30, 1949, file "715.02—Bears vol. 2: January 1, 1948–," box N-339, NAYNP; Mark Biel, personal communication to author, February 2, 2002.

52. Edmund Rogers, "Memorandum for the Regional Director, Region Two Headquarters," Yellowstone National Park, October 6, 1942, file "715.02—Bears vol. 1: November 1939 to December 31, 1947," box N-339, NAYNP.

53. Ibid.

54. Ibid.; Edmund Rogers to Lawrence Merriam, April 21, 1943, file "715.02—Bears vol. 1: November 1939 to December 31, 1947," box N-339, NAYNP.

55. Lawrence Merriam to Edmund Rogers, April 24, 1943, file "715.02—Bears vol. 1: November 1939 to December 31, 1947," box N-339, NAYNP; Yellowstone National Park, "Motorists Guide," 1940, box K-2, NAYNP; Edmund Rogers to M. S. Benedict, July 2, 1943, file "715.02, part 5—Yellowstone: Mammals: Bears, January 1941 to December 1943," box 1749, entry E7, RG 79, NACP.

56. Sellars, *Preserving Nature in the National Parks,* 91; Paul Schullery and Lee Whittlesey, "Greater Yellowstone Carnivores," in *Carnivores in Ecosystems: The Yellowstone Experience,* A. Peyton Curlee, Tim Clark, Steven C. Minta, and Peter M. Kareiva, eds. (New Haven, Conn.: Yale University Press, 2000), 32.

57. Olaus J. Murie, "Progress Report on the Yellowstone Bear Study," March 15, 1944, file "715.02, part 5—Yellowstone: Mammals: Bears, January 1941 to December 1943," box 1749, entry E7, RG 79, NACP.

58. Horace M. Albright to Dr. Barton Warren Evermann, March 20, 1931, file "1—Bear (Yellowstone NP) Jan 1, 1929–Dec 31, 1931," box N-48, NAYNP; H. C. Bryant to George Wright, October 16, 1931, file "1—Bear (Yellowstone NP) Jan 1, 1929–Dec 31, 1931," box N-48, NAYNP; Merriam to Hansen, September 10, 1942; Newton Drury to Victor Cahalane, March 4, 1944, file "715.02, part 5—Yellowstone: Mammals: Bears, January 1941 to December 1943," box 1749, entry E7, RG 79, NACP; Olaus J. Murie to Newton Drury, March 24, 1944, file N16, "Management of Natural Resources and Areas #1 1982," box N-130, NAYNP.

59. Edward Abbey, *Desert Solitaire: A Season in the Wilderness* (New York: Ballantine Books, 1968), 45–67; Robert Gottlieb, *Forcing the Spring* (Washington, D.C.: Island Press, 1993), 18.

60. Horace M. Albright, "New Orders for National Park Bears," *The Backlog: A Bulletin of the Camp Fire Club of America* 22(1) (April 1945), 11, file "Albright, Horace M., New Orders for National Park Bears," section Mammals—Ursidae, vertical files, YNPL.

61. Horace M. Albright to Newton Drury, April 13, 1944; and Horace M. Albright to Newton Drury, March 21, 1944, both in file "715.02, part 5—Yellowstone: Mammals: Bears, January 1941 to December 1943," box 1749, entry E7, RG 79, NACP; Albright to Drury, March 21, 1944; Newton Drury to Harold L. Ickes, September 15, 1944, file "715.02—Bears 1939–1948, 1949–1950," box N-52, NAYNP.

62. Albright, "New Orders for National Park Bears," 8, 10.

63. Ibid., 6.

64. Ibid., 9.

65. Hillory Tolson to Lawrence Merriam, June 26, 1946, file "715.02, part 6—Yellowstone: Mammals: Bears, January 1944 to June 1949," box 1749, entry E7, RG 79, NACP.

66. Drury to Ickes, September 15, 1944; Lawrence Merriam to W. E. Sisler, November 21, 1945; Newton Drury to Lawrence Merriam, October 4, 1945; and Newton Drury to Secretary of the Interior, October 4, 1945, all in file "715.02—Bears vol. 1: November 1939 to December 31, 1947," box N-339, NAYNP.

67. Lawrence Merriam to Newton Drury, September 26, 1945, file "715.02, part 6—Yellowstone: Mammals: Bears, January 1944 to June 1949," box 1749, entry E7, RG 79, NACP; "Special Report: Canyon Bear Ground Restoration Project," Yellowstone National Park, May 27–31, 1946, file "715.02, part 6—Yellowstone: Mammals: Bears, January 1944 to June 1949," box 1749, entry E7, RG 79, NACP.

68. Newton Drury to Horace M. Albright, November 7, 1945, file "715.02—Bears vol. 1: November 1939 to December 31, 1947," box N-339, NAYNP.

69. Multiple authors, "Excerpts of Comments on the Abolition of 'Bear Show' in Yellowstone National Park," Yellowstone National Park, January 1946; and Newton Drury to A. T. Wilcox, December 19, 1946, both in file "715.02, part 6—Yellowstone: Mammals: Bears, January 1944 to June 1949," box 1749, entry E7, RG 79, NACP; William B. Sanborn, "The Educational Program of Yellowstone National Park," Master's thesis, Claremont Graduate School, 1947, YNPL, 92; Yellowstone National Park Biologist, "Monthly Report of Activities," Yellowstone National Park, September 8, 1948, file "715.02, part 5—Yellowstone: Mammals: Bears, January 1941 to December 1943," box 1749, entry E7, RG 79, NACP; John J. Craighead to Lon Garrison, October 25, 1960, file "N1427—Bear—General 1958–1960," box N-168, NAYNP.

70. Victor Cahalane letter, December 11, 1951, file "715.02—Bears vol. 2: January 1, 1948–," box N-339, NAYNP.

71. Edmund Rogers to Regional Director, Region 2, November 6, 1950, file "715.02—Bears 1939–1948, 1949–1950," box N-52, NAYNP.

72. Fred Johnston to Director, National Park Service, August 10, 1951, file "715.02—Bears vol. 2: January 1, 1948–," box N-339, NAYNP.

73. Victor Cahalane to Chic Young, November 21, 1951, file "715.02—Bears vol. 2: January 1, 1948–," box N-339, NAYNP.

74. Dan Beard to Victor Cahalane, October 4, 1941, file "715.02, part 5—Yellowstone: Mammals: Bears, January 1941 to December 1943," box 1749, entry E7, RG 79, NACP;

Edmund Rogers to Director, National Park Service, July 20, 1940, file "715.02, part 4—Yellowstone: Mammals: Bears, August 3, 1933 to November 18, 1940," box 1749, entry E7, RG 79, NACP.

75. June Lange to Superintendent, Yellowstone National Park, September 30, 1957; Frank E. Sylvester to June Lange, October 11, 1957, both in file "N1427—Bear Management & Control, Damage & Injuries, 1954–61," box N-163, NAYNP.

76. Walter Kittams to Edmund Rogers, August 6, 1948, file "715.02, part 6—Yellowstone: Mammals: Bears, January 1944 to June 1949," box 1749, entry E7, RG 79, NACP; Donald L. Bock, "A Survey of Public Opinion Concerning the Yellowstone Bear Feeding Problem," Colorado A&M School of Forestry, December 4, 1953, YNPL.

77. Bock, "A Survey of Public Opinion."

78. Jack Frost Andrews to Conrad Wirth, August 31, 1956, file "N1427—Bear Management & Control, Damage & Injuries, 1954–61," box N-163, NAYNP.

79. Joseph Bitzer to Hon. Thomas E. Martin, August 21, 1951; Joseph Bizerto Edmund Rogers, August 21, 1951, both in file "715.02—Bears vol. 2: January 1, 1948–," box N-339, NAYNP.

80. Mrs. J. W. Barlow to Superintendent, Yellowstone National Park, August 21, 1956, file "N1427—Bear Management & Control, Damage & Injuries, 1954–61," box N-163, NAYNP.

81. Anonymous source, e-mail to author, January 4, 2001; Berenice Kelley to Lon Garrison, August 6, 1959, file "N1427—Bear Management & Control, Damage & Injuries, 1954–61," box N-163, NAYNP.

82. Johnston to Director, National Park Service, August 10, 1951.

83. Jim Caslick, interview with author, Mammoth Hot Springs, Wyo., February 9, 2001.

84. Caslick, interview with author; George Baggley, June 24, 1931, file "715.02—Bear Cases Yellowstone National Park, May 1 to September 6, 1931," box 481, entry E7, RG 79, NACP.

85. Caslick, interview with author.

86. Glen F. Cole, "Information Paper—Grizzly Bear," November 12, 1969, file "Bear Management 1969," vertical files, YNPBMO; Arthur E. Demaray to Director for Region 2, September 24, 1951, file "715.02—Bears vol. 2: January 1, 1948–," box N-339, NAYNP.

87. James Lloyd to Director, National Park Service, October 10, 1951, file "715.02—Bears vol. 2: January 1, 1948–," box N-339, NAYNP.

88. Demaray to Director for Region 2, September 24, 1951; Lon Garrison to Director, National Park Service, February 19, 1959; Nelson Murdock to Superintendent, Yellowstone National Park, August 17, 1960, all in file "N1427—Bear Management & Control, Damage & Injuries, 1954–61," box N-163, NAYNP. Also see Yellowstone National Park, *Yellowstone's Northern Range: Complexity and Change in a Wildland Ecosystem* (Mammoth Hot Springs, Wyo.: Yellowstone National Park, 1997).

CHAPTER 3: FUNNY BEARS AND TV STARS

1. Bernard de Voto, "Let's Close the National Parks," *Harper's* (October 1953), reprinted by the North American Wildlife Foundation, Acc. 08262, Conrad Wirth Papers 1929–1982, AHC.

2. National Park Service, "Mission 66: Yellowstone National Park," 1956, file "1956," box YPC-91, NAYNP; Richard West Sellars, *Preserving Nature in the National Parks: A History* (New Haven, Conn.: Yale University Press, 1997), 183.

3. Lon Garrison to Director, National Park Service, February 19, 1959, file "N1427—Bear Management & Control, Damage & Injuries, 1954–61," box N-163, NAYNP.

4. Acting Superintendent to Regional Director, November 24, 1959, file "Bears 1959–1961 1961–1963," vertical files, YNPBMO.

5. Ibid.; Howard Baker to Director, National Park Service, no date, 1961; John J. Craighead to Lon Garrison, January 12, 1960, both in file "N1427—Bear—General 1958–1960," box N-168, NAYNP.

6. Frank E. Sylvester to Chief Park Naturalist, October 27, 1959, file "Bears 1959–1961 1961–1963," vertical files, YNPBMO; Merrill Beal to Robert McIntyre, November 2, 1959, vertical files, YNPBMO; Robert N. McIntyre to Acting Chief Park Ranger, Yellowstone National Park, November 3, 1959, vertical files, YNPBMO.

7. Hillory Tolson, "National Park Service Bear Management Program and Guidelines," July 6, 1960, file "2—Bear (Yellowstone NP), Jan 1, 1932–?," box N-48, NAYNP.

8. Lon Garrison to District Managers, Yellowstone National Park, May 31, 1961, vertical files, YNPBMO; Kerry Gunther and Mark Biel, eds., *Yellowstone National Park Bear Information Book* (Yellowstone National Park, Wyo.: Bear Management Office, Yellowstone National Park, 1994), 40; Acting Regional Director, Region Two, to Director, December 2, 1969, file "N1427—Bear Management & Control, Damage & Injuries, 1954–1961," box N-163, NAYNP; Robert N. McIntyre to Richard Frisbee, November 23, 1960, file A9015 "Permits—Collecting Permits 1958–1960," box A-309, NAYNP; Nelson Murdock to Superintendent, Yellowstone National Park, August 17, 1960, file "N1427—Bear Management & Control, Damage & Injuries, 1954–1961," box N-163, NAYNP.

9. Tolson, "NPS Bear Management Program," "Bear Incidents 1931–1963," YNPL. It should be noted that the numbers of injuries and property damage incidents were also higher in this decade than any other, and that all of these numbers corresponded with significant increases in overall visitation.

10. Luis Gastellum to Director for Region 2, April 21, 1961, file "N1427—Wildlife, Mammals, Bear—General, 1958–60," box N-168, NAYNP.

11. Michael Mallory, *Hanna-Barbera Cartoons* (Hong Kong: Hugh Lauter Levin Associates, 1998), 130, 132–133; Umberto Eco, *Travels in Hyperreality* (New York: Harcourt Brace & Company, 1986), 19.

12. Roger Toll to George Wright, June 2, 1933, file "2—Bear (Yellowstone NP), Jan 1, 1932–?," box N-48, NAYNP; George Wright to Roger Toll, June 13, 1933, file "2—Bear (Yellowstone NP), Jan 1, 1932–?," box N-48, NAYNP; Ted Parkinson, "Where Are the Bears?" cassette tape, August 8, 1983, Oral History 83–1, YNPL; George Baggley to unknown, June 24, 1931, file "715.02—Bear Cases Yellowstone National Park, May 1 to September 6, 1931," box 481, entry E7, RG 79, NACP; Jim Caslick, interview with author, Mammoth Hot Springs, Wyo., February 9, 2001; Mallory, *Hanna-Barbera Cartoons,* 136.

13. Lon Garrison to Director for Region 2, April 5, 1961, file "K3831—Posters, Cartoons & Emblems 1957–1962," box K-87, NAYNP.

14. Garrison to Director, February 19, 1959; Howard Chapman to Chief Ranger, March 24, 1961, file "N1427—Bear Management & Control, Damage & Injuries, 1954–61," box N-163, NAYNP; Luis Gastellum to Peter Hanen, April 21, 1961, file "Bears 1959–1961 1961–1963," vertical files, YNPBMO.

15. William B. Sanborn, "The Educational Program of Yellowstone National Park," Master's thesis, Claremont Graduate School, 1947, YNPL, 90.

16. A. Starker Leopold and Durward L. Allen, "Bear Management Review," August 2, 1977, file "Bear Management 1977," vertical files, YNPBMO.

17. http://www.smokeybearstore.com/vault/bambi_bear.asp; U.S. Department of Agriculture (USDA), *The True Story of Smokey Bear,* USA: Western Publishing Company, Inc., 1969.

18. USDA, *The True Story of Smokey Bear.*

19. Letter to Yogi Bear, September 5, 1961, file "Bears 1959–1961 1961–1963," vertical files, YNPBMO.

20. Yogi Bear letter, September 18, 1961, file "Bears 1959–1961 1961–1963," vertical files, YNPBMO.

21. "What Happened to the Bears in Yellowstone?" 1961, file "Bears 1959–1961 1961–1963," vertical files, YNPBMO; Senator Mike Mansfield to Conrad Wirth, November 7, 1961, file "Bears 1959–1961 1961–1963," vertical files, YNPBMO; Lon Garrison to Senator Mike Mansfield, November 1961, file "Bears 1959–1961 1961–1963," vertical files, YNPBMO.

22. Paul Schullery, *The Bears of Yellowstone* (Worland, Wyo.: High Plains Publishing Company, 1992), 139.

23. David de L. Condon to Lon Garrison, December 8, 1958, file "Pre-1959," vertical files, YNPBMO; R. E. Howe to Chief Park Ranger, September 9, 1964, vertical files, YNPBMO; Frank Craighead, Jr., *Track of the Grizzly* (San Francisco: Sierra Club Books, 1982), 7.

CHAPTER 4: SCIENCE VERSUS SCENERY

1. Stewart Udall to Conrad Wirth, March 20, 1961, file "NPS, Mission 66 Road Policies," box 22 B, Acc. 08262, Conrad Wirth Papers, 1929–1982, AHC.

2. Roderick Nash, *Wilderness and the American Mind* (New Haven, Conn.: Yale University Press, 1967), 235, 212–213; Robert Gottlieb, *Forcing the Spring: The Transformation of the American Environmental Movement* (Washington, D.C.: Island Press, 1993), 41–43.

3. Olaus J. Murie, "The Intangible Resources of Wild Country," *Planning and Civic Comment* (January–March 1952), box 46, Acc. 1221, Olaus J. and Margaret E. Murie Papers, AHC; Olaus J. Murie, "Man Looking at Nature," *Discourse: A Review of the Liberal Arts* (Winter 1961–1962): 35–46, box 46, Acc. 1221, Olaus J. and Margaret E. Murie Papers, AHC. For an excellent discussion of the cultural impact of the first view of Earth from space, see William H. Bryant, *Re-visioning Earth: The Image of the Planet in Advanced Consumer Culture,* Master's thesis, University of Wyoming, Laramie, Wyo., 1995.

4. Advisory Board on Wildlife Management, "Wildlife Management in the National Parks," March 4, 1963, in *America's National Park System: The Critical Documents,* Lary Dilsaver, ed. (Lanham, Md.: Rowman & Littlefield, 1994), 237–252.

5. Adolph Murie, "A Plea for Idealism in National Parks: A Critique," January 14, 1964, file "Research 1957–1963: A Murie Commentary—Leopold Speech to Supts," box 4, Acc. 8004-84-08-13, Adolph Murie Papers 1916–1978, AHC.

6. National Park Service, "Road to the Future: Long-Range Objectives and Goals for the National Park Service," 1964, box 17, Acc. 8004, Adolph Murie Papers 1916–1978, AHC, 5; NAS Advisory Committee to the National Park Service on Research, "NAS Advisory Committee on Research in the National Parks: The Robbins Report," August 1, 1963, http://www.cr.nps.gov/history/online_books/robbins/robbins.htm.

7. NAS Advisory Committee, "Research in the National Parks."

8. James A. Pritchard, *Preserving Yellowstone's Natural Conditions: Science and the Perception of Nature* (Lincoln: University of Nebraska Press, 1999), 229.

9. Yellowstone National Park, *Yellowstone's Northern Range: Complexity and Change in a Wildland Ecosystem* (Mammoth Hot Springs, Wyo.: Yellowstone Center for Resources, 1997), 10; Glen F. Cole, "Mission-Oriented Research in Natural Areas of the

National Park Service," May 1969, file "Cole, Glen F., Mission-Oriented Research in Natural Areas of the National Park Service," 1, vertical files, YNPL.

10. R. E. Howe to Chief Park Ranger, September 9, 1964, vertical files, YNPBMO.

11. Frank Craighead, Jr., *Track of the Grizzly* (San Francisco: Sierra Club Books, 1982), 7, 8, 10; John J. Craighead, "Investigator's Annual Report," January 14, 1969, file "Bear Management 1969," vertical files, YNPBMO.

12. Glen F. Cole, "Perspective: Glen F. Cole, Yellowstone National Park Biologist, 1967–1976," *Yellowstone Science* 8(2) (Spring 2000): 13–18.

13. Craighead, *Track of the Grizzly*, 194.

14. Howe to Chief Park Ranger, September 9, 1964; John Good, "Reminiscence from the Firing Line," *Yellowstone Science* 8(2) (Spring 2000): 3–6; John Good to Superintendent, July 6, 1967, file "Bear Management 1967," vertical files, YNPBMO.

15. William Barmore to Superintendent, July 13, 1967, file "Bear Management 1967," vertical files, YNPBMO; Glen F. Cole to Robert Linn, September 12, 1967, file "Bear Management 1967," vertical files, YNPBMO; Robert Linn to Joseph Linduska, May 21, 1968, file "Bear Management 1968," vertical files, YNPBMO.

16. Howe to Chief Park Ranger, September 9, 1964; Glen F. Cole to Jack Anderson, August 3, 1971, file "Bear Management 1971," vertical files, YNPBMO.

17. John J. Craighead and Frank Craighead, Jr., "Management of Bears in Yellowstone National Park," 1967, file "Bear Management 1968," vertical files, 97–98, YNPBMO; Adolph Murie, "Field Notes," July 20, 1968, file "Yellowstone Grizzly/Black Bear, Notes & Reports," box 54, Acc. 8004, Adolph Murie Papers, 1916–1978, AHC.

18. Cole to Linn, September 12, 1967.

19. Craighead and Craighead, "Management of Bears in Yellowstone National Park"; Craighead, *Track of the Grizzly*, 200.

20. Pritchard, *Preserving Yellowstone's Natural Conditions*, 246; Cole to Linn, September 12, 1967; Glen F. Cole to Superintendent, August 11, 1967, file "Bear Management 1967," vertical files, YNPBMO.

21. Dick Coon, "Humans Encroach on Animals' Territory: Wilderness Big Enough for Both," *Great Falls Tribune*, Great Falls, Mont., June 30, 1968; A. Starker Leopold to George Hartzog and John Gottschalk, June 29, 1968, both in file "Bear Management 1968," vertical files, YNPBMO.

22. Stanley Cain, A. Starker Leopold, and Charles Olmsted, "A Bear Management Policy and Program for Yellowstone National Park," Natural Sciences Advisory Committee of the National Park Service, 1969, file "Leopold, A. S., A Bear Management Policy and Program for Yellowstone National Park, 1969," vertical files, YNPL.

23. Glen F. Cole, "Grizzly Bear Management in Yellowstone Park, 1970," November 1970, file "Glen F. Cole, Grizzly Bear Management in Yellowstone Park, 1970," section Mammals—Ursidae, vertical files, YNPL.

24. "Girl Describes Attack by Bear," *Spokane Daily Chronicle*, Spokane, Wash., June 19, 1969, file "Bear Newspaper Clippings, 1969–1970," section Mammals—Ursidae, vertical files, YNPL.

25. "Park Village Operator Says, 'Public Is Nuts,'" *Billings Gazette*, Billings, Mont., June 13, 1969; "Craighead 'Not Surprised' at Grizzly Bear Incident," *Jackson Hole Guide*, Jackson, Wyo., June 12, 1969; "Mauling Won't Alter Practice," *Billings Gazette*, Billings, Mont., June 13, 1969; Richard McCall, "People to Blame for Bear Scare," *Spokane Daily Chronicle*, Spokane, Wash., June 13, 1969; "Tourists Blamed for Bear Attack," *Ogden Standard-Examiner*, Ogden, Utah, June 13, 1969; Bill Winter, "No Trace of Rabies Discovered in Preliminary Tests on Grizzly," *Bozeman Chronicle*, Bozeman,

Mont., June 13, 1969; "Craighead Feels Park at Fault," *Hungry Horse News,* Columbia Falls, Mont., June 13, 1969; Rolf Olson, "Outdoor Itch: Fate of Grizzlies," *Great Falls Tribune,* Great Falls, Mont., July, 1969; "Pits Closed to Keep Bears Out," *Salt Lake Tribune,* Salt Lake City, Utah, June 14, 1969, all in file "Bear Newspaper Clippings, 1969–1970," section Mammals—Ursidae, vertical files, YNPL.

26. Glen F. Cole to Superintendent, June 17, 1969, file "Bear Management 1969," vertical files, YNPBMO; Kerry Gunther and Mark Biel, eds., *Yellowstone National Park Bear Information Book* (Yellowstone National Park, Wyo.: Bear Management Office, Yellowstone National Park, 1994), 39; Paul Schullery, *The Bears of Yellowstone* (Worland, Wyo.: High Plains Publishing Company, 1992), 140; John Craighead to Glen Cole, July 25, 1969, file "Bear Management 1969," vertical files, YNPBMO. These numbers have been highly disputed over the years; many people believe they were far higher. They also do not include grizzlies killed outside the park during this period.

27. Yellowstone National Park, "Bear Management Policy, 1969," file "Bear Management 1969," vertical files, YNPBMO; J. D. Nordgren letter, January 15, 1975, file "Correspondence 1969–1979," vertical files, YNPBMO; "Bears and People Break Bad Habit," *Jackson Hole Guide,* Jackson, Wyo., August 10, 1972, file "1972–1974, Grizzly Management in the Parks," box 4, Acc. 8004, Adolph Murie Papers, 1916–1978, AHC.

28. Nordgren letter, January 15, 1975; Lynn Thompson to Hon. Teno Roncalio, September 30, 1975, file "Correspondence 1969–1979," vertical files, YNPBMO; Glen F. Cole to Superintendent, June 4, 1971; and Glen F. Cole to Superintendent, October 19, 1971, both in file "Bear Management 1971," vertical files, YNPBMO.

29. Ted Scott letter, March 17, 1975, file "Correspondence 1969–1979," vertical files, YNPBMO; Paul Schullery, "Historical Perspectives on Yellowstone Bear Management," *Proceedings, Grizzly Bear Symposium,* Casper, Wyo., April 28, 1984.

30. Jack Anderson, "(g) Camping, section 3," file "Correspondence 1969–1979," vertical files, YNPBMO; Glen F. Cole to Superintendent, July 26, 1972, file "Bear Management 1972," vertical files, YNPBMO.

31. Cole to Superintendent, July 26, 1972.

32. Craighead, *Track of the Grizzly,* 199. Adolph Murie noted that Anderson was also simply opposed to research facilities such as the Craigheads' laboratory being housed within park boundaries—see Murie, "Field Notes"; Glen F. Cole to A. Starker Leopold, January 29, 1969, file "Bear Management 1969," vertical files, YNPBMO.

33. Jack Anderson to Fred Fagergren, February 26, 1969, file "Bear Management 1969," vertical files, YNPBMO; Murie, "Field Notes"; Glen F. Cole to Bob Linn, November 26, 1974, file N-89, box N22, NAYNP.

34. Anderson to Fagergren, February 26, 1969; Jack Anderson to John J. Craighead, April 7, 1969, file "Bear Management 1969," vertical files, YNPBMO; Jack Anderson to John J. Craighead, July 9, 1970, file "Bear Management 1970," vertical files, YNPBMO; Jack Anderson to John J. Craighead, August 13, 1970, file "Bear Management 1970," vertical files, YMPBMO; Jack Anderson to John J. Craighead, July 20, 1971, file "Bear Management 1971," vertical files, YNPBMO; Anderson to Craighead, February 9, 1971; Jack Anderson to John Grandy, February 4, 1972, file "Bear Management 1972," vertical files, YNPBMO; C. K. Townsend to Superintendent, April 16, 1969, file D66, "Signs, Markers, and Memorials, 1969," box K-21, NAYNP.

35. Anderson to Fagergren, February 26, 1969; Anderson to Craighead, April 7, 1969.

36. John Craighead to Jack K. Anderson, April 14, 1969, file "Bear Management 1969," vertical files, YNPBMO.

37. Letter to John McLaughlin, August 16, 1965, vertical files, YNPBMO; John McLaughlin letter, August 30, 1965, vertical files, YNPBMO; S. T. Carlson letter, September 15, 1965, file "Bear Management 1965," vertical files, YNPBMO.

38. John Craighead to Jack Anderson, July 24, 1970, file "Bear Management 1970," vertical files, YNPBMO; Helen Heaton, song lyrics, vertical files, YNPBMO.

39. John Craighead to Dean Solberg, July 7, 1971, file "Bear Management 1971," vertical files, YNPBMO.

40. John Craighead to Jack Anderson, July 13, 1971, file "Bear Management 1971," vertical files, YNPBMO; Anderson to Craighead, July 20, 1971.

41. Craighead, *Track of the Grizzly,* 208; Michael Malloy, "Bear Fight Bares Few Bear Facts," *National Observer,* November 24, 1973, file "Bear Management 1973," vertical files, YNPBMO; NPS Director to Director, Bureau of Sport Fisheries and Wildlife, August 14, 1971, file "Bear Management 1971," vertical files, YNPBMO; University of Colorado Wilderness Study Group to Director, National Park Service, February 3, 1975, file "Bear Management 1975," vertical files, YNPBMO; Alston Chase, *Playing God in Yellowstone: The Destruction of America's First National Park* (New York: Harcourt Brace Jovanovich, 1986); Todd Wilkinson, *Science Under Siege: The Politicians' War on Nature and Truth* (Boulder, Colo.: Johnson Books, 1998), 65–112.

42. "Yellowstone Fighting Grizzly Lawsuit," *Jackson Hole News,* Jackson, Wyo., January 16, 1975, file "Bear Management 1975," vertical files, YNPBMO; Lee Whittlesey, *Death in Yellowstone: Accidents and Foolhardiness in the First National Park* (Boulder, Colo.: Roberts Rinehart, 1995), 197.

43. Paul Schullery, interview with author, Mammoth Hot Springs, Wyo., January 12, 2001; George Wilson, "Yellowstone: Here Come the Tourists," *Washington Post,* Washington, D.C., June 3, 1973, file "Bear Management 1973," vertical files, YNPBMO.

44. National Park Service, "Explore Yellowstone! Ranger Conducted Activities 1969"; National Park Service, "Explore Yellowstone! Ranger Conducted Activities 1971." Both in file "Programs for Interpretive Services, 1953–1958, 1963–1971," box K-20, NAYNP.

45. Jack Anderson to Director, Harper's Ferry Center, June 9, 1971; National Park Service, "Grant Village Listening Chairs (audiostation message script)," Harper's Ferry Center, May 28, 1971, both in file K1817, "Interpretive Activities Interpretive Planning 1971 GF," box K-89, NAYNP.

46. Olaus J. Murie, "Scientific and Esthetic Values of Wilderness," *Proceedings of the Fifth World Forestry Congress,* Seattle, Washington, August 29–September 10, 1960, box 46, Acc. 1221, Olaus J. and Margaret E. Murie Papers, AHC, 5; Rick Krepela to Jack Anderson, May 28, 1971, file K1817, "Interpretive Activities Interpretive Planning 1971 GF," box K-89, NAYNP; Anderson to Director, Harper's Ferry Center, June 9, 1971.

47. The Three Senses Nature Trail was closed after its Braille signs were destroyed by a hammer-wielding vandal sometime in the 1980s. It has never been restored.

48. Letter to George Hartzog, December 7, 1969, file "Bear Management 1969," vertical files, YNPBMO; Harold J. Estey letter, February 19, 1970; Jack Anderson to U.S. Senator Barry Goldwater, July 22, 1971; Jack Anderson letter, August 23, 1971, file "Correspondence 1969–1979," vertical files, YNPBMO; and Jack Anderson letter, August 26, 1971, all in file "Correspondence 1969–1979," vertical files, YNPBMO; Jack Anderson to Representative Dick Shoup, March 14, 1973; and Glen F. Cole to Jack Anderson, March 28, 1973, both in file "Bear Management 1973," vertical files, YNPBMO; "Park Tourists Miss Begging Bears," *Arizona Republic,* Phoenix, Ariz., July 4, 1971, file "Bear

NOTES TO PAGES 100–106 [165]

Management 1971," vertical files, YNPBMO; "Ask the Bear Experts," *Billings Gazette,* Billings, Mont., January 16, 1974, file "Bear Management 1974," vertical files, YNPBMO; National Park Service, "Draft: Where Are All the Bears?" June 27, 1971; and Jack Anderson letter, July 14, 1971, both in file "Correspondence 1969–1979," vertical files, YNPBMO; Anderson to Goldwater, July 22, 1971; Nordgren letter, January 15, 1975; Scott letter, March 17, 1975; John Townsley letter, September 6, 1977, file "Correspondence 1969–1979," vertical files, YNPBMO.

49. Pierre Bourdieu, *Distinction: A Social Critique of the Judgement of Taste* (Cambridge, Mass.: Harvard University Press, 1984), 5.

50. Yellowstone National Park, "Master Plan," National Park Service, 1973, Planning Office, Yellowstone National Park, 2, 19–22.

51. Ibid., 25.

52. Kerry A. Gunther, "Changing Problems in Bear Management Since the Dumps," oral presentation at the Yellowstone Association Institute, Yellowstone National Park, June 16, 2001.

53. George H. Harrison, "They're Killing Yellowstone's Grizzlies," *National Wildlife,* 11(6) (1973): 4–8, 17; Pritchard, *Preserving Yellowstone's Natural Conditions,* 62; "Craighead: No Bears by 1990," *Billings Gazette,* Billings, Mont., January 6, 1974, file "Bear Management 1974," vertical files, YNPBMO; Anderson to Shoup, March 14, 1973; Glen F. Cole to Editors of *BioScience,* January 12, 1970, file "Bear Management 1970," vertical files, YNPBMO; Resources Management Specialist to Chief Ranger, November 12, 1971, file "Correspondence 1969–1979," vertical files, YNPBMO; Craighead to Anderson, July 13, 1971; Anderson to Grandy, February 4, 1972; Jack Anderson to District Rangers et al., August 12, 1974, file "Bear Management 1974," vertical files, YNPBMO; Glen F. Cole, "Management Involving Grizzly Bears and Humans in Yellowstone National Park, 1970–1973," Acc. 04318, Frank C. and John J. Craighead Papers, 1920–1972, AHC.

54. Cole to Editors of *BioScience,* January 12, 1970.

55. Malloy, "Bear Fight Bares Few Bear Facts."

56. Cole to Anderson, August 11, 1967.

57. Glen F. Cole to Superintendent, April 12, 1972, file "Bear Management 1972," vertical files, YNPBMO.

58. Mary Meagher, Douglas B. Houston, and Glen F. Cole to Chief Scientist, National Park Service, March 25, 1974, file "Bear Management 1974," vertical files, YNPBMO.

59. Schullery, *The Bears of Yellowstone,* 144; Pritchard, *Preserving Yellowstone's Natural Conditions,* 247; Cole, "Management Involving Grizzly Bears;" Glen F. Cole to Research files, Yellowstone, September 11, 1974, file "Bear Management 1974," vertical files, YNPBMO.

60. Glen F. Cole to Lynn Greenwalt, November 20, 1974, file "Bear Management 1974," vertical files, YNPBMO.

61. Schullery, *The Bears of Yellowstone,* 145–146; Lewis Regenstein, "Heading for the Last Hibernation," *New York Times,* New York, N.Y., January 24, 1975, file "Bear Management 1975," vertical files, YNPBMO.

62. Interagency Grizzly Bear Study Team, "Annual Report, 1997," http://www.nrmsc. usgs.gov/products/IGBST/1997report.pdf.

63. Richard Knight, "Holding on to Yellowstone's Grizzlies: A Parting Chat with a 24-Year Veteran of Yellowstone's Grizzly Bear Wars," *Yellowstone Science* 6(1) (Winter 1998): 2–9; Pritchard, *Preserving Yellowstone's Natural Conditions,* 252.

CHAPTER 5: THE POLITICS OF PERIL

1. John Townsley to John J. Craighead, November 11, 1975; and John J. Craighead to John Townsley, November 21, 1975, both in file "Bear Management 1975," vertical files, YNPBMO; David Graber to John Good, July 26, 1976, file "Bear Management 1976," vertical files, YNPBMO; Mary Meagher, "Evaluation of Bear Management in Yellowstone National Park, 1977," February 10, 1978, file "Meagher, Mary," vertical files, YNPL.

2. "Possible Questions: Black Bears and Grizzly Bears," Yellowstone National Park, no date, file "Bear Management 1976," vertical files, YNPBMO.

3. Save the Bears of Yellowstone, "Help! Change and Progress Must Have a Limit or at Least an Exemption!"; Save the Bears of Yellowstone, "Save the Bears of Yellowstone"; "West Yellowstone Group Aims to Save the Bears," *Bozeman Hi Country*, Bozeman, Mont., August 25, 1976, all in file "Bear Management 1976," vertical files, YNPBMO.

4. James DeWolf, "Where Are the Bears?" *Billings Gazette*, Billings, Mont., August 13, 1978, file "Bear Management 1978," vertical files, YNPBMO.

5. Film Ventures International, *Grizzly!* promotional material, 1976, file "Bear Management 1976," vertical files, YNPBMO; Bill Schneider, *Where the Grizzly Walks* (Missoula, Mont.: Mountain Press Publishing Company, 1977), 91; Charles Jonkel to Border Grizzly Technical Committee, March 4, 1976, file "Bear Management 1976," vertical files, YNPBMO.

6. A. Starker Leopold and Durward L. Allen, "A Review of Bear Management in the National Park System," August 2, 1977, file "Bear Management 1979," vertical files, YNPBMO.

7. Ibid.

8. National Park Service, press release, Yellowstone National Park, August 16, 1976, file "Bear Management 1976," vertical files, YNPBMO; Bill Brown, "Grizzlies: No Place to Go," transcript, NBC-TV Nightly News, September 7, 1978; file "Bear Management 1978," vertical files, YNPBMO.

9. Letter to Sirs, September 7, 1978, file "Bear Management 1978," vertical files, YNPBMO.

10. Letter to Park Service, 1978, file "Bear Management 1978," vertical files, YNPBMO.

11. Letter to Chief Ranger, Yellowstone National Park, September 8, 1978, file "Bear Management 1978," vertical files, YNPBMO.

12. Letter to John Townsley, September 8, 1978, file "Bear Management 1978," vertical files, YNPBMO.

13. David Richey, "My God, I've Gotten Too Close!" *Outdoor Life*, January 1978, 136.

14. "Grizzlies Holding Steady in Park," *Salt Lake Tribune*, Salt Lake City, Utah, April 9, 1978, file "Bear Management 1978," vertical files, YNPBMO; Richard Knight letter, September 14, 1982, file "Bear Management 1982," vertical files, YNPBMO; Richard Knight, "Holding on to Yellowstone's Grizzlies: A Parting Chat with a 24-Year Veteran of Yellowstone's Grizzly Bear Wars," *Yellowstone Science* 6(1) (Winter 1998): 2–9; "Experts Say Grizzlies More Threatened Than Ever," *Livingston Enterprise*, Livingston, Mont., October 11, 1982, file "Bear Management 1982," vertical files, YNPBMO; Mary Meagher letter, November 30, 1982, file "Bear Management 1982," vertical files, YNPBMO.

15. Alston Chase, "The Last Bears of Yellowstone," *Atlantic Monthly* (February 1983): 63–73.

16. Ibid., 71, 63.
17. Ibid., 66.
18. Cecil Andrus letter, March 25, 1977, file "Bear Management 1977," vertical files, YNPBMO.
19. Letter to President Ronald Reagan, March 4, 1983; letter to Senator John Danforth, March 10, 1983; letter to U.S. Senator John Danforth, March 10, 1983; letter to James Watt, March 19, 1983, all in file "Bear Management 1983," vertical files, YNPBMO.
20. National Park Service, "A Detailed Response from the National Park Service to 'The Grizzly and the Juggernaut' by Alston Chase, *Outside,* January 1986," March 24, 1986, file "Bear Management 1986," vertical files, YNPBMO, 5.
21. R. McGreggor Cawley, *Federal Land, Western Anger* (Lawrence: University Press of Kansas, 1993), 87–88.
22. Ibid., 1, 10, 120, 168.
23. Robert Barbee, "A Bee in Every Bouquet: The Administration of Science in Yellowstone," *Yellowstone Science* 3(1) (Winter 1995): 8–14.
24. James Thompson letter, August 11, 1983; James Thompson letter, May 9, 1983; Robert Barbee to U.S. Senator John Danforth, May 5, 1983; James Thompson letter, June 16, 1983, all in file "Bear Management 1983," vertical files, YNPBMO.
25. Mary Meagher to A. Starker Leopold, February 2, 1983; Nathaniel Reed to Robert Barbee, February 14, 1983; A. Starker Leopold to Mary Meagher, January 13, 1983, all in file "Bear Management 1983," vertical files, YNPBMO; James A. Pritchard, *Preserving Yellowstone's Natural Conditions: Science and the Perception of Nature* (Lincoln: University of Nebraska Press, 1999), 219.
26. Yellowstone National Park, *Final Environmental Impact Statement Grizzly Bear Management Program,* October, 1982, vertical files, YNPL, 12–13; Senator Alan K. Simpson, "Feeding Wildlife," *Wyoming State Tribune,* Cheyenne, Wyo., January 31, 1984, file "Bear Management 1984," vertical files, YNPBMO.
27. Knight, "Holding on to Yellowstone's Grizzlies," 5; Mary Meagher letter, May 31, 1983, file "Bear Management 1983," vertical files, YNPBMO; Ad Hoc Committee to Investigate the Need and Feasibility of the Supplemental Feeding of Yellowstone Grizzly Bears, "Final Report," December 5, 1983, file "Supplemental Feeding 1983," vertical files, YNPBMO.
28. Leopold to Meagher, January 13, 1983; Reed to Barbee, February 14, 1983; Ted Parkinson, "Where Are the Bears?" cassette tape, August 8, 1983, Oral History 83–1, YNPL; Chase, "The Last Bears of Yellowstone."
29. Mary Meagher letter, March 22, 1983, file "Bear Management 1983," vertical files, YNPBMO.
30. Ibid.; Parkinson, "Where Are the Bears?"
31. John Good to Robert Barbee, September 30, 1983, file "Bear Management 1983," vertical files, YNPBMO; Kerry A. Gunther, "Bear Management in Yellowstone National Park, 1960–93," *International Conference on Bear Research and Management* 9(1) (1994): 550; Yellowstone National Park, "Human Use Adjustment Areas—Bear Management Units," 1984, vertical files, YNPBMO.
32. Good to Barbee, September 30, 1983; Yellowstone National Park, "Human Use Adjustment Areas;"; letter to Robert Barbee, June 11, 1983, file "Bear Management 1983," vertical files, YNPBMO.
33. Dan Sholly to Robert Barbee, June 3, 1991, file "Correspondence," vertical files, YNPBMO; Yellowstone National Park, *Final Environmental Impact Statement Grizzly Bear Management Program;* Sue Consolo Murphy and Beth Kaeding, "Fishing

Bridge: 25 Years of Controversy Regarding Grizzly Bear Management in Yellowstone National Park," *Ursus* 10 (1998): 385–393.

34. Clair Johnson, "Gardiner Residents Blast Bear Policies," *Livingston Enterprise*, Livingston, Mont., August 25, 1983, file "Bear Management 1983," vertical files, YNPBMO.

35. Kerry A. Gunther and Hopi E. Hoekstra, "Bear-Inflicted Human Injuries in Yellowstone National Park, 1970–1994," *Ursus* 10 (1998): 377–384.

36. Kerry Gunther and Mark Biel, eds., *Yellowstone National Park Bear Information Book* (Yellowstone National Park, Wyo.: Bear Management Office, Yellowstone National Park, 1994), 39; Lee Whittlesey, *Death in Yellowstone: Accidents and Foolhardiness in the First National Park* (Boulder, Colo.: Roberts Rinehart, 1995), 51–52.

37. Kerry A. Gunther, "Visitor Impact on Grizzly Bear Activity in Pelican Valley, Yellowstone National Park," *International Conference on Bear Research and Management* 8 (1993): 76.

38. Kerry A. Gunther, "Changing Problems in Bear Management Since the Dumps," oral presentation at the Yellowstone Association Institute, Yellowstone National Park, June 16, 2001.

39. Ibid.; Yellowstone Center for Resources, *Yellowstone Center for Resources Annual Report, Fiscal Year 2004*, YCR-2005–03 (Mammoth Hot Springs, Wyo.: National Park Service, 2005), 64.

40. Alston Chase, "The Grizzly and the Juggernaut," *Outside* (January 1986): 29–34, 55–65; National Park Service, "A Detailed Response," 4.

41. National Park Service, "A Detailed Response."

42. Ibid., 4.

43. Paul Schullery, personal communications, April 4, 2005, and May 9, 2002.

44. Paul Schullery, personal communications, April 4, 2005.

45. Ibid.

46. Richard Conniff, *Every Creeping Thing: True Tales of Faintly Repulsive Wildlife* (New York: Henry Holt and Company, 1998), 73; *Yellowstone Science* interview with Steve and Marilynn French, "Getting Past Wow: Grizzly Bear Natural History Goes High-Tech in Yellowstone," *Yellowstone Science*, 3(2) (Spring 1995): 10–12.

47. Schneider, *Where the Grizzly Walks*, 47, 140, 156–173.

48. Paul Schullery, *The Bears of Yellowstone* (Worland, Wyo.: High Plains Publishing Company, 1992), 3.

49. Thomas McNamee, *The Grizzly Bear* (New York: Alfred A. Knopf, 1984), 195.

50. Doug Peacock, *Grizzly Years: In Search of the American Wilderness* (New York: Henry Holt and Company, 1990), 85, 62. Though Peacock (*Grizzly Years*, 179) claimed that he seldom got close to grizzlies intentionally, his experiences seemed a literary precursor, if not an inspiration, for the activities of another man who famously sought personal redemption through close contact with grizzly bears: Timothy Treadwell, whose self-described personal journey back from drug addiction led him to become an "outspoken and visible proponent of a metaphysical bond" between grizzlies and humans. Peacock was opposed, however, to Treadwell's purposeful physical contact with bears and his treatment of them "as friends and family." Films of Treadwell cavorting with grizzlies, and his book about his experiences, *Among Grizzlies: Living with Wild Bears in Alaska* (New York: Ballantine, 1997), made him into a media celebrity, but many believe that the behaviors they chronicled likely contributed to his death, and that of his girlfriend, Amie Huguenard, by bear mauling in Alaska's Katmai National Park on October 5, 2003 (Mike Lapinski, *Death in the Grizzly Maze: The Timothy Treadwell Story* [Helena, Mont.: Falcon, 2005], 11, 13, 50, xiii).

51. Mark S. Boyce, "Review Essay: The Grizzly Bears of Yellowstone," *Yellowstone Science* 5(1) (Winter 1997): 18–20.

52. Dan Sholly letter, August 21, 1989; Dan Sholly letter, September 12, 1989; Dan Sholly letter, October 17, 1989; Robert Barbee to U.S. Representative Ron Marlenee, February 9, 1990; letter to Chief Ranger, March 25, 1990; letter to Robert Barbee, February 10, 1992, all in file "letters," vertical files, YNPBMO; Barbee, "A Bee in Every Bouquet," 13.

53. National Park Service, "Yellowstone" (map), 1984. Denver Public Library, Western History and Genealogy section.

54. National Park Service, "Yellowstone: Official Map and Guide," 1989, collection of author; National Park Service, "Yellowstone" (map).

55. National Park Service, "Yellowstone: Official Map and Guide (1989)"; Margaret Littlejohn, Dana Dolsen, and Gary Machlis, "Visitor Services Project: Yellowstone National Park, Report 25," March 1990, YNPL.

56. For more information, see Todd Wilkinson, *Science Under Siege: The Politicians' War on Nature and Truth* (Boulder, Colo.: Johnson Books, 1998), 65–112.

CHAPTER 6: TODAY'S YELLOWSTONE BEAR

1. Yellowstone Center for Resources, *Yellowstone Center for Resources Annual Report, Fiscal Year 2004,* YCR-2005-03 (Mammoth Hot Springs, Wyo.: National Park Service, 2005), 60.

2. "Drivers Take Toll on Bears," *The Buffalo Chip,* resource management newsletter, Yellowstone National Park (August–September 2004): 11.

3. Mark Biel, personal communication to author, December 3, 2004.

4. Yellowstone Center for Resources, *Yellowstone Center for Resources Annual Report, Fiscal Year 2003,* YCR-AR-2003 (Mammoth Hot Springs, Wyo.: National Park Service, 2004), 52.

5. William Cronon, "The Trouble with Wilderness, or Getting Back to the Wrong Nature," in *Uncommon Ground: Rethinking the Human Place in Nature,* William Cronon, ed. (New York: W. W. Norton & Company, 1996), 69–90.

6. James A. Pritchard, *Preserving Yellowstone's Natural Conditions: Science and the Perception of Nature* (Lincoln: University of Nebraska Press, 1999), 305.

7. Alice Wondrak Biel, "Yellowstone Wildlife Watching: A Survey of Visitor Attitudes and Desires," *Proceedings of Beyond the Arch: Community and Conservation in Greater Yellowstone and East Africa* (Mammoth Hot Springs, Wyo.: Yellowstone Center for Resources, 2004): 328–340.

8. Gail W. Compton, "Visitors and Wildlife: New Information on Attitudes, Risk, and Responsibility," *Yellowstone Science* 2(2) (Winter 1994): 6.

9. Kerry A. Gunther, interview with author, December 12, 2000, Mammoth Hot Springs, Wyo.

10. Ibid.

11. Ibid.

12. Ibid.

13. Kerry A. Gunther and Hopi E. Hoekstra, "Bear-Inflicted Human Injuries in Yellowstone National Park, 1970–1994," *Ursus* (10) 1998: 377–384; Kerry A. Gunther, "Changing Problems in Bear Management Since the Dumps," oral presentation to the Yellowstone Association Institute, Yellowstone National Park, June 16, 2001.

14. Gunther, "Changing Problems in Bear Management," http://www.nps.gov/yell/nature/animals/bear/infopaper/info6.html.

15. Gunther, "Changing Problems in Bear Management."

16. Todd Wilkinson, "Gambling with Grizzlies: Is This the Right Time to Take Yellowstone's Grizzlies off the Endangered Species List?" *Wildlife Conservation* 104 (6) (November–December 2001): 26–35; Gunther, "Changing Problems in Bear Management."

17. Gunther, "Changing Problems in Bear Management"' Wilkinson, "Gambling with Grizzlies."

18. http://www.consgenetics.unr.edu/students/robison/.

MANUSCRIPT COLLECTIONS, RESOURCES FOR DOCUMENTS,
AND REPORTS, AND PHOTOGRAPH SOURCES
American Heritage Center, University of Wyoming, Laramie (AHC)
    Conrad Wirth Collection
    Olaus J. and Margaret E. Murie Collection
    Adolph Murie Collection
    Frank C. and John J. Craighead Collection
Denver Public Library Western History Collection
Montana Historical Society, Helena, Montana (MHS)
National Archives, College Park, Maryland (NACP)
    RG 79 Records of the National Park Service
National Archives, Yellowstone National Park (NAYNP)
    RG 79 Records of the National Park Service
    Photographs
Yellowstone National Park Bear Management Office (YNPBMO)
    Vertical Files
    Photographs
Yellowstone National Park Library (YNPL)

ESSENTIAL SOURCES

Resources for the history of the National Park Service and the development of its management philosophies and policies include Lary Dilsaver, ed., *America's National Park
System: The Critical Documents* (Lanham, Md.: Rowman & Littlefield, 1994); Horace M.
Albright and Robert Cahn, *The Birth of the National Park Service: The Founding Years,
1913–1933* (Salt Lake City, Utah: Howe Brothers, 1985); and Horace M. Albright and Marian Albright Schenck, *Creating the National Park Service: The Missing Years* (Norman:
University of Oklahoma Press, 1999). Richard West Sellars's *Preserving Nature in the National Parks: A History* (New Haven, Conn.: Yale University Press, 1997) provides a com-
prehensive, critical, yet fair look at the history of NPS resource management, and R. Ge-
rald Wright, *Wildlife Research and Management in the National Parks* (Urbana: University
of Illinois Press, 1991) offers insight into the history of NPS wildlife research and management. Biographical information on the NPS's founders can be found in Robert Shankland, *Steve Mather of the National Parks* (New York: Alfred A. Knopf, 1951), and Donald
Swain, *Wilderness Defender: Horace M. Albright and Conservation* (Chicago: University of
Chicago Press, 1970). In *Devil's Bargains: Tourism in the Twentieth-Century American
West* (Lawrence: University Press of Kansas, 1998), Hal Rothman chronicles the history of
NPS boosterism and development in the West.

    Texts informing the history of conservation and environmental philosophy pre-
sented here are Edward Abbey, *Desert Solitaire: A Season in the Wilderness* (New York:
Ballantine Books, 1968); Robert Gottlieb, *Forcing the Spring* (Washington, D.C.: Island
Press, 1993); Samuel. P. Hays, *Conservation and the Gospel of Efficiency: The Progressive
Conservation Movement, 1890–1920* (Cambridge, Mass.: Harvard University Press,
1959); and Roderick Nash, *Wilderness and the American Mind* (New Haven, Conn.: Yale

University Press, 1967). R. McGreggor Cawley's *Federal Land, Western Anger* (Lawrence: University Press of Kansas, 1993) is an excellent account and explanation of the motivations underlying the Sagebrush Rebellion. Alston Chase's *Playing God in Yellowstone: The Destruction of America's First National Park* (New York: Harcourt Brace Jovanovich, 1986) is a provocative counterpoint to NPS philosophy and policy, and problematizes the question of "science" in policy-making. Todd Wilkinson's chapter "A Grizzly Future" in *Science Under Siege: The Politicians' War on Nature and Truth* (Boulder, Colo.: Johnson Books, 1998) provides a separate, still skeptical view of the application of science in that arena.

The quintessential history of Yellowstone National Park is the two-volume *The Yellowstone Story: A History of Our First National Park* (Niwot: University Press of Colorado, 1996), by the late Aubrey L. Haines. Technical information on Yellowstone's bears can be found in Kerry A. Gunther and Mark J. Biel, eds., *Yellowstone National Park Bear Information Book* (Yellowstone National Park, Wyo.: Bear Management Office, Yellowstone National Park, 1994). Frank Craighead, Jr.'s *Track of the Grizzly* (San Francisco: Sierra Club Books, 1982) tells the Craigheads' story from the brothers' perspective. For a look at old-time attitudes toward the bears of Yellowstone, Horace M. Albright and Frank Taylor's *Oh, Ranger! A Book About the National Parks* (Golden, Colo.: Outbooks, 1986) is both informative and outrageous by today's standards. *Yellowstone Bear Tales* (Boulder, Colo.: Roberts Rinehart, 1991), edited by Paul Schullery, is a collection of anecdotal and scientific narratives spanning the period from 1880 to 1950. Of course, Schullery's *The Bears of Yellowstone* (Worland, Wyo.: High Plains Publishing Company, 1992) was one inspiration for this book. Judith Meyer's *The Spirit of Yellowstone: The Cultural Evolution of a National Park* (Lanham, Md.: Rowman & Littlefield, 1996) explains why human values associated with the park should not be discounted in policy-making. James A. Pritchard, in *Preserving Yellowstone's Natural Conditions: Science and the Perception of Nature* (Lincoln: University of Nebraska Press, 1999), has unquestionably provided us with the finest history of the development of natural resource management in Yellowstone.

For more on the concept of "ways of seeing" discussed here, Denis Cosgrove, *Social Formation and the Symbolic Landscape* (Madison: University of Wisconsin Press, 1984) and Trevor Barnes and James Duncan, eds., *Writing Worlds: Discourse, Text, and Metaphor in the Representation of Landscape* (London: Routledge, 1992) are essential texts. James Elkins, *The Object Stares Back* (New York: Harcourt Brace & Company, 1996); John Berger, *About Looking* (New York: Vintage Books, 1980); John Berger, *Ways of Seeing* (London: British Broadcasting Corporation and Penguin Books, 1972); Hal Foster, ed., *Vision and Visuality,* Dia Art Foundation Discussions in Contemporary Culture No. 2 (Seattle: Bay Press, 1988); Susan Sontag's *On Photography* (New York: Delta Books, 1973); and especially John Dorst, *Looking West* (Philadelphia: University of Pennsylvania Press, 1999), all illuminate the mechanics of the "ways of seeing" idea. Dean MacCannell, *The Tourist: A New Theory of the Leisure Class* (New York: Schocken Books, 1976), and John Urry, *The Tourist Gaze: Leisure and Travel in Contemporary Societies* (London: Sage Publications, 1990), contextualize the concept within the realm of tourism, and Timothy Mitchell, *Colonising Egypt* (Berkeley: University of California Press, 1988) explores the modern bounding of space.

Authors central to rethinking our concepts of Nature are too numerous to permit a full account. Texts most central to shaping the ideas presented in this book include Don Mitchell, *The Lie of the Land: Migrant Workers and the California Landscape* (Minneapolis: University of Minnesota Press, 1996); William Cronon, ed., *Uncommon Ground: Rethinking the Human Place in Nature* (New York: W. W. Norton, 1995); Raymond Williams,

The Country and the City (New York: Oxford University Press, 1972); and Neil Smith, *Uneven Development: Nature, Capital, and the Production of Space* (Oxford: Blackwell, 1990). Kenneth Olwig, in "Recovering the Substantive Nature of Landscape," *Annals of the Association of American Geographers* 86(4) (1996): 630–653, has favored us with a reminder that there is a "there there." Writers currently reexamining the relationship between humans and animals include Susan Davis, *Spectacular Nature: Corporate Culture and the Sea World Experience* (Berkeley: University of California Press, 1997); Yi-Fu Tuan, *Dominance and Affection: The Making of Pets* (New Haven, Conn.: Yale University Press, 1984); Jennifer Wolch and Jody Emel, eds., *Animal Geographies: Place, Politics, and Identity in the Nature-Culture Borderlands* (London: Verso, 1998); R. J. Hoage and William A. Deiss, eds. *New Worlds, New Animals: From Menagerie to Zoological Park in the Nineteenth Century* (Baltimore, Md.: Johns Hopkins University Press, 1996); and Jennifer Price, *Flight Maps: Adventures with Nature in Modern America* (New York: Basic Books, 1999).

Hand-feeding, 29, 77 (photo)
    dangers of, 24, 33–34, 37, 59
    See also under Feeding
Hanna–Barbera, 68, 69–70
Hansen, Ellen, 42
Hansen, Martha, 42, 43, 44, 45, 80
Harding, Warren G., 22
Harper's, de Voto in, 63
Hauk, Andrew, 103
Hayden Valley, 92, 95, 98
Haynes, F. J., 8, 23
Heaton, Helen, 100–101
Hold-up bear, 22, 23, 65
Hornaday, William, 14, 15
Horr, Harry, 7
Horror bears, 55, 72, 92, 115–16, 144
Houston, Douglas, 109
Huckleberry Hound Show, The, 68
Huguenard, Amie, 169n50
Human–bear relations, 21, 24–25, 55, 117,
    124, 125–26
    development of, 26, 113, 147
    problems with, 28–29, 61–62
Human behavior, 38, 43, 70, 96, 126, 142,
    148
    wilderness values and, 86
Human use adjustment areas, 124

Ickes, Harold L., 31, 38, 39, 52
Idaho Department of Fish and Game, 111
Imaginary bear, 93
Indian Creek campground, 65
Injuries
    bear-related, 25–30, 32, 36, 37, 39, 42, 43,
      50, 61, 72, 96, 103, 108, 113, 114, 124,
      125–26, 133, 141, 142, 144, 148, 161n9
    drop in bear-related, 41, 65, 68, 70, 94,
      144
Interagency Bison Management Plan, 146
Interagency Grizzly Bear Committee, 122
Interagency Grizzly Bear Study Team
    (IGBST), 111
Interpretive programs, 103, 106
Isle Royale National Park, 98

Jaws (movie), 115
Jax, Daphne, 95
Jesse James (bear), 1, 22, 23, 150
Jones, Buffalo, 14
Jones, "Iron Hand," 69

Jonkel, Charles, 116
Juno (bear), 16, 79 (photo)

Kansas City Country Day School, 120
Katmai National Park, maulings in, 169n50
Kennedy, John F., 86
Kittams, Walter, 57
Knight, Dick, 118, 122

Lake Hotel, 8, 9, 10
    bear shows at, 18, 19
Lamar Valley, 15, 136
Landscapes, human/natural, 21
Lane, Franklin, 11
"Last Bears of Yellowstone, The" (Chase),
    118–19, 127, 129
Leopold, A. Starker, 87, 94
    bear management and, 143
    bear warnings and, 117, 119
    media/messages and, 116
Leopold Report, 87, 88, 89, 90, 91, 92, 122
Life, 87
Lincoln National Forest, 71
Linn, Robert, 92
Listening chairs, 104–5, 115
"Living Land, The" (program), 103–4
Livingston Enterprise, on IGBST, 118
Lloyd, James, 61, 75
Lower Geyser Basin, 105
"Lunch Counter," 19, 79 (photo)

Malloy, Michael, 108–9
Mammoth Hot Springs, 18, 129
    "buffalo show corral" at, 14–15
    feeding bears at, 35, 77 (photo), 79
      (photo), 135
    zoo at, 14–15, 79 (photo)
"Mammoth Pets" (*Yellowstone Nature
    Notes*), 15
Management (NPS), 108, 130
    adaptive, 128
    park, 3, 5, 39, 88
    philosophy shift in, 107
    research and, 92
    resource, 91, 106
    wildlife, 39, 87, 89, 90
    See also Bear management
"Management Involving Grizzly Bears and
    Humans in Yellowstone National
    Park, 1970–1973" (Cole), 108